Statistical and Economic Analysis Using Quantile Regression

利用分位数回归的统计与经济分析（英文版）

霍丽娟 ○ 著

北京理工大学出版社
BEIJING INSTITUTE OF TECHNOLOGY PRESS

版权专有　侵权必究

图书在版编目（CIP）数据

利用分位数回归的统计与经济分析 = Statistical and Economic Analysis Using Quantile Regression：英文 / 霍丽娟著 . —北京：北京理工大学出版社，2019.4

ISBN 978 – 7 – 5682 – 6930 – 8

Ⅰ. ①利… Ⅱ. ①霍… Ⅲ. ①自回归模型 – 应用 – 经济分析 – 研究 – 英文　Ⅳ. ①F224.12

中国版本图书馆 CIP 数据核字（2019）第 069364 号

出版发行 / 北京理工大学出版社有限责任公司	
社　　址 / 北京市海淀区中关村南大街 5 号	
邮　　编 / 100081	
电　　话 / （010）68914775（总编室）	
（010）82562903（教材售后服务热线）	
（010）68948351（其他图书服务热线）	
网　　址 / http：//www.bitpress.com.cn	
经　　销 / 全国各地新华书店	
印　　刷 / 三河市华骏印务包装有限公司	
开　　本 / 710 毫米 × 1000 毫米　1/16	
印　　张 / 15.25	
字　　数 / 212 千字	责任编辑 / 梁铜华
版　　次 / 2019 年 4 月第 1 版	文案编辑 / 梁铜华
2019 年 4 月第 1 次印刷	责任校对 / 周瑞红
定　　价 / 80.00 元	责任印制 / 李志强

图书出现印装质量问题，请拨打售后服务热线，本社负责调换

PREFACE

Due to measuring errors or unexpected phenomena, such as earthquakes, strikes, and financial crises, etc, outliers occur very frequently in real data and may have considerable influences on the classical estimates like the sample mean, sample variance, and mean-based least squares estimation as well. Robust estimates and regressions, which provide a good fit to data while the data contains outliers, have been developed a lot and applied in many fields. Among robust approaches, quantile regression (QR), as an extension of least absolute deviation (LAD) at the median to various quantiles, was proposed firstly by Koenker and Bassett(1978) and has been applied in many academic fields, such as economics and finance. Quantile regression method has a series of advantages. It can get more robust and efficient estimates, and provide a new perspective of allowing researchers to investigate the relationship between economic variables over the entire conditional distribution.

I started to be interested in this field from my doctoral study. At that time, I did preliminary researches on the robust covariance and robust regression, and realized that the quantile regression theory and its application in the fields of economics and finance will be important and valuable. And then, further research was conducted on the quantile regression under the support of Humanities and Social Sciences Fund of the Ministry of Education, grant 17YJC790057 and National Natural Science Foundation of China, grant 71803009. This book, containing some of my research on the robust statistics and quantile regression, first compares several robust covariance measurements and their performances of portfolios. This book also applies the robust regression, quantile regression, to investigate growth convergence in China and 86 non-oil countries, FDI effects on growth, financial risk measurements, and stock market regime-switching issue.

Especially during the financial crisis, the volatility of the economic and financial related data is quite abnormal, which brings challenges to investment decision-making using classical statistics and regression estimates based on the mean. At the same time, in the study of practical problems, researchers and policymakers are usually more concerned with the tail of the overall distribution, such as factors that affect economic growth in less developed and more developed regions. In order to better capture the tail features and obtain more robust estimation results, quantiles and quantile regression have achieved more and more attention. This book has made some explorations and attempts in the quantile regression theory and its application in the economic and financial fields, and I expect more research results coming out in the future. I am very grateful to Tae-Hwan Kim, my Ph.D. advisor, who led me into Econometric study and encouraged me to research on quantile regression. I thank Yunmi Kim, Dongjin Lee, Jinseo Cho, Weiming Li, and Yuchen Jin for their help and efforts in our collaborative work. This book could not have been written without the support of my family. Untold thanks to Jun Kong.

Contents

Chapter 1 Introduction ········· 1
  1.1 Overview ········· 1
  1.2 Quantile Regression and Its Applications ········· 2
  References ········· 5

Chapter 2 Robust Statistics and Robust Regressions ········· 8
  2.1 Introduction to Classical and Robust Approaches to Statistics ········· 8
  2.2 Least Squares Linear Regression ········· 10
  2.3 Robust Regression ········· 12
    2.3.1 Least Absolute Values Regression ········· 12
    2.3.2 M-estimator ········· 13
  2.4 Quantile Regression ········· 13
    2.4.1 Quantile Regression Model ········· 13
    2.4.2 The Finite-sample Distribution of Regression Quantiles ········· 14
    2.4.3 Quantile Regression Asymptotics ········· 16
    2.4.4 Wald Tests ········· 17
    2.4.5 Estimation of Asymptotic Covariance Matrix ········· 18
    2.4.6 Quantile Likelihood Ratio Tests ········· 20
  References ········· 20

Chapter 3 Robust Estimates of Covariance ········· 22
3.1 Conventional Measure of Covariance ········· 22
3.2 Robust Measures of Covariance ········· 25
  3.2.1 Median Absolute Deviation About the Median (MAD) ········· 25
  3.2.2 Gnanadesikan and Kettenring Robust Measures of Covariance ········· 26
  3.2.3 M-estimates ········· 26
  3.2.4 Minimum Volume Ellipsoid Estimate (MVE) ········· 28
  3.2.5 S-estimates ········· 28
  3.2.6 Minimum Covariance Determinant Estimate (MCD) ········· 29
3.3 An Alternative Robust Measure of Covariance ········· 29
3.4 Monte Carlo Simulations ········· 31
3.5 Empirical Application ········· 44
  3.5.1 Empirical Comparison of Robust Estimates ········· 44
  3.5.2 Portfolio Performances of Robust Covariances ········· 47
3.6 Conclusion ········· 55
3.7 Appendix: Derivation of Conventional Covariance with Outlier(s) ········· 56
References ········· 58

Chapter 4 Quantile Regression Serial Correlation Tests ········· 61
4.1 Spurious Autocorrelation in Quantile Models ········· 61
  4.1.1 Standard LM Test for Linear Model with AR(p) Errors ········· 63
  4.1.2 Theoretical Explanation to the Occurance of Spurious Autocorrelation ········· 74
4.2 Correctly-sized Tests ········· 77
  4.2.1 QF test ········· 77
  4.2.2 The QR-LM Test ········· 78

4.3 Monte-Carlo Simulations 80
4.4 An Empirical Example 90
4.5 Conclusion 93
4.6 Appendix 93
References 97

Chapter 5 Growth Empirics Based on IV Panel Quantile Regression
.... 100
5.1 Economic Growth Convergence 100
5.2 Quantile Regression for Panel Data Model with Fixed Effects
.... 105
5.3 Growth Convergence at the Conditional Mean 106
5.4 Growth Convergence at Different Conditional Quantiles
.... 109
5.5 Empirical Results from 86 Non-oil Countries 113
  5.5.1 Data and Samples 113
  5.5.2 Empirical Results 117
  5.5.3 Conclusion 135
5.6 Evidence from China Provincial Panel Data 135
  5.6.1 Literature on China's Regional Economic Development
.... 135
  5.6.2 Model and Data 142
  5.6.3 Empirical Results 142
  5.6.4 Conclusion from China's Empirical Results 151
References 152

Chapter 6 The Impact of FDI on Economic Growth: an Empirical Evidence from IV Panel Quantile Regression
.... 157
6.1 FDI and Economic Growth 158
6.2 IV Quantile Regression Model for Panel Data with Fixed Effects 163

6.3 Data and Empirical Results ……………………………… 165
6.4 Conclusion ……………………………………………… 178
6.5 Appendix ………………………………………………… 179
References …………………………………………………… 179

Chapter 7 Financial Risk Measurement: CoVaR …………… 182

7.1 Financial Risk Transition Mechanism and Source of Risk in China ……………………………………………………… 182
   7.1.1 The Transmission Mechanism of Financial Risk in China ………………………………………………… 183
   7.1.2 Sources of Financial Risk in China ………………… 185
7.2 Risk Measurements: VaR, CoVaR, and ΔCoVaR ………… 190
   7.2.1 Definition of VaR …………………………………… 190
   7.2.2 Calculation of VaR ………………………………… 191
   7.2.3 Definition of CoVaR and ΔCoVaR ………………… 192
   7.2.4 Calculation of CoVaR ……………………………… 194
   7.2.5 CoVaR Model Based on Quantile Regression ……… 195
7.3 Empirical Study on Systemic Financial Risks in China …… 196
   7.3.1 Data Selection ……………………………………… 196
   7.3.2 Data Processing and Descriptive Statistics ………… 197
   7.3.3 Identification of Systemically Important Financial Institutions ………………………………………… 203
7.4 Static Risk Contribution of Financial Sub-industries on Financial System ……………………………………………… 204
   7.4.1 Data Selection ……………………………………… 204
   7.4.2 Data Processing and Descriptive Statistics ………… 205
7.5 Risk Spillover Effects Between Financial Sub-sectors …… 209
   7.5.1 Static Risk Spillover Effects Between Financial Sub-sectors ………………………………………… 209
   7.5.2 Dynamic Risk Spillover Effects Between Financial Sub-industries ……………………………………… 210

7.6　Conclusion ··· 213
References ··· 219
Chapter 8　Markov Regime Switching in Quantile Autoregression Stock Market Return Model ······························· 222
8.1　Introduction to Markov-switching model ················ 222
8.2　Markov-switching Quantile Autoregressive Model for Stock Market Returns ··· 224
8.3　Data Description and Empirical Results ················ 225
8.4　Conclusion ··· 230
References ··· 231

Chapter 1
Introduction

1.1 Overview

Outliers, occurring very frequently in real data, might be caused by measuring error, unexpected phenomena such as earthquakes, strikes, or financial crises like the "9 · 11" attacks in 2001, the global financial crisis in 2008 and so on. Outliers can have a considerable influence on the conventional statistics, like mean, variance, covariance, skewness, kurtosis, etc, and then lead to a misleading understanding of the performance of a variable, relationship between variables, and draw a wrong conclusion based on them. To achieve a more robust statistics while outliers exist has attracted the interests of large numbers of researchers, and vast influential literature on it has been published. See Huber and Ronchetti (2009), Maronna et al. (2006), Rousseeuw and Leroy (1987), etc.

Not only the conventional statistics, but also mean-based least squares estimates are deeply impacted by the occurrence of outliers, since residuals are squared, and therefore we obtain unreliable results. Leroy and Rousseeuw (1987) introduced different kinds of robust regressions, for example, least absolute values regression [L_1 regression, Edgeworth (1887)], M-estimators [Huber (1973)], least median of squares [LMS, Rousseeuw (1984)], least trimmed squares [LTS, Rousseeuw (1983, 1984)], S-estimators [Rousseeuw and Yohai (1984)] and so on. Robust estimates and regressions have been developed a lot and applied in many fields. Among those robust approaches, quantile regression (QR), as an extension of least absolute deviation (LAD) at the median to various quantiles, was proposed firstly by Koenker and Bassett (1978) and has been applied in many academic fields, such as economics and finance, because of its robustness, efficiency and providing a new perspective of allowing researchers to investigate the relationship between economic variables not only at the centre but also over the entire conditional distribution of the dependent variable corresponding to the changes of covariates.

This book investigates the performance of portfolios based on several robust covariances and applies quantile regression to study growth convergence in China and 86 non-oil countries, FDI effects on growth, and financial risk measurements.

1.2 Quantile Regression and Its Applications

In the early stage of the quantile regression literature, the development in both theory and application has taken place mainly in the context of cross-section data. However, the application of quantile regression has subsequently moved into the areas of time-series as well as panel data. Some relevant papers are Koul and Mukherjee (1994), Koul and Saleh (1995), Koenker and Xiao (2004), Xiao (2009), Galvao et al. (2011), Shin et al. (2014), etc, in the time-series domain and Koenker (2004), Geraci and Bottai (2006), Abrevaya and Dahl (2008), Lamarche (2010), Galvao (2011) in the panel data setting.

The two settings of data considered here are time series and panel data, which are widely used in empirical applications. When quantile regression is applied to time-series data models, it is particularly important to check for any sign of autocorrelation because, as correctly pointed out by Koenker (2005), the typical IID (independent and identically distributed errors) condition is usually imposed on the regression error terms in both mean-regression and quantile regression. If the error terms are serially correlated in quantile models, the effect is the same as in any mean models; that is, employing the usual variance-covariance matrix for inference becomes invalid. However, little attention has been paid to the issue of how to test for autocorrelation in quantile regression models. The only significant exception is the work of Furno (2000), where the performance of the conventional Breusch-Godfrey LM test applied to LAD regression models has been studied by Monte Carlo simulations. This book documents the phenomenon of spurious autocorrelation induced by the usual LM test, and then introduces two correct tests (named the F-test and the QR-LM test) for autocorrelation in quantile models, which do not suffer from any size distortion. Monte Carlo simulation demonstrates that the two tests perform fairly well in finite samples, across either different quantiles or different underlying error distributions.

With more observed individuals and longer periods available in empirical research, the more efficient panel data approach has been popularly used. Whether poor countries, or regions, can catch up with rich ones eventually, i.e. whether convergence exists, and if so, how their convergence rates are have been the central topic and main controversy among recent economic growth literature. This book then applies the QRP approach to investigate the center issue that whether economic growth convergence exists in the whole world and inside of China, based on the data of 86 countries and 31 provinces or municipalities in China, respectively. This book also attempts to analyze the impact of Foreign Direct Investment (FDI) on economic growth by using quantile regression. FDI has increased substantially since the 1980s. Countries, especially under-developed countries, compete with each other to attract FDI by reducing tax and granting subsidies. Intense debates on the impact of FDI on domestic economies, especially on the economies of developing host countries, have carried on for several decades and remained a hot topic till now. In order to reduce the omitted variable bias, solve the potential endogeneity of FDI, and allow heterogeneity cross countries, instrumental variable quantile regression for panel data with fixed effects is applied to estimate the impact of FDI on economic growth.

After the outbreak of the global financial crisis in 2008, there has not been huge destruction and panic in China's economic and financial system like in that of Western countries. However, the data since 2008 indicates that potential financial risks may arise in China, such as the liquidity difficulties caused by the maturity mismatch of the banking industry, the moral hazard caused by the financial system and government intervention, the huge non-performing loans, the high level of social leverage, the rapid development of the shadow banking system, and so on. These risks have become a hidden danger of systemic financial risks through the inter-business transactions, balance sheet linkages, asset revaluation effects in the industry, and spillover effects among industries. In chapter 7, a series of quantile regression models will be made to compute individual institute's margin risk contribution to the whole financial market and the tail risk spillover effects between financial subsystems, based on CoVaR. 26 institutes' weekly returns data on the secondary market from January 2008 to March 2019 are chosen from the banking industry, the security industry, the insurance industry, and the real estate industry. The marginal risk contribution of each subsystem to the whole system and the spillover effects between two subsystems are analyzed in this book.

Hamilton (1989) introduced the Markov-switching model in time series anaiysis and found that the growth rate of U.S. GNP switches between positively growing regime and negatively depressing regime. Since this influential paper, regime-switching methods have been successfully and widely applied in macroeconomic and financial fields. Most previous studies used mean-based method or variation, which focused on the issue at the mean of the return only. But, in most cases the performance of the center can not represent the impact at tails of the distribution. Markov-switching quantile autoregression model is recently developed by some researchers, see Liu(2016), Liu and Luger(2017). In the last chapter, Markov-switching quantile autoregression model is applied to analyze the S&P return from Jan. 1980 to Feb. 2018. The empirical findings identify the presence of regimes-switching, and present the estimates of location for different regimes monotonically increasing from left tail to right tail.

References

[1] Abrevaya, Jason, and Christian M Dahl. 2008. The effects of birth inputs on birthweight: evidence from quantile estimation on panel data. *Journal of Business & Economic Statistics*, 26(4): 379 – 397.

[2] Edgeworth F Y. 1887. On Observations relating to several quantities. *Hermathena*, 6(13): 279 – 285.

[3] Furno Marilena. 2000. LM tests in the presence of non-normal error distributions. *Econometric Theory*, 16: 249 – 261.

[4] Galvao Jr, Antonio F. 2011. Quantile regression for dynamic panel data with fixed effects. *Journal of Econometrics*, 164(1): 142 – 157.

[5] Galvao Jr, Antonio F, Gabriel Montes-Rojas, and Jose Olmo. 2011. Threshold quantile autoregressive models. *Journal of Time Series Analysis*, 32(3): 253 – 267.

[6] Geraci, Marco, and Matteo Bottai. 2006. Quantile regression for longitudinal data using the asymmetric Laplace distribution. *Biostatistics*, 8(1): 140 – 154.

[7] Hamilton, James D. A new approach to the economic aralysis of nonstationary time series and business cycle. *Econometrica*, 57: 357 – 384.

[8] Huber, Peter J. 1973. Robust regression: asymptotics, conjectures and Monte Carlo. *The Annals of Statistics*, 1(5): 799 – 821.

[9] Huber, Peter J, and Ronchetti Elvezio M. 2009. Robust statistics. Hoboken: John Wiley & Sons.

[10] Kim, Tae-Hwan, and Halbert White. 2004. On more robust estimation of skewness and kurtosis. *Finance Research Letters*, 1(1): 56 – 73.

[11] Koenker. 2005. Quantile regression. *Econometric Society Monographs*, 38.

[12] Koenker, Roger. 2004. Quantile regression for longitudinal data. *Journal of Multivariate Analysis*, 91(1): 74 – 89.

[13] Koenker, Roger, and Gilbert Bassett Jr. 1978. Regression quantiles. *Econometrica: Journal of the Econometric Society*, 33 – 50.

[14] Koenker, Roger, and Zhijie Xiao. 2004. Unit root quantile autoregression inference. *Journal of the American Statistical Association*, 99(467): 775 – 787.

[15] Koul, Hira L, and Kanchan Mukherjee. 1994. Regression quantiles and related processes under long range dependent errors. *Journal of Multivariate Analysis*, 51(2): 318 – 337.

[16] Koul, Hira L, and AK Md E Saleh. 1995. Autoregression quantiles and related rank-scores processes. *The Annals of Statistics*, 23(2): 670 – 689.

[17] Lamarche, Carlos. 2010. Robust penalized quantile regression estimation for panel data. *Journal of Econometrics*, 157(2): 396 – 408.

[18] Liu, Xiaochun. 2016. MarKov swirtching quantile autoregression. *Statistica Neerlandica*, 70: 356 – 395.

[19] Liu, Xiaochun and Luger, Richard. 2017. Markov-switching quntile autoregression: a gibbs sampling approach. *Studies in Nonlinear Dynamics & Econometrics*.

[20] Markowitz, Harry. 1952. The utility of wealth. *Journal of Political*

Economy, 60(2):151-158.

[21] Maronna, Ricardo A, and Douglas Martin. 2006. Yohai Robust Statistics. *Wiley Series in Probability and Statistics*. John Wiley and Sons, 2:3.

[22] Rousseeuw, Peter, and Victor Yohai. 1984. Robust regression by means of S-estimators. *Robust and Nonlinear Time Series Analysis*. Springer.

[23] Rousseeuw, Peter J. 1983. Regression techniques with high breakdown point. *The Institute of Mathematical Statistics Bulletin*, 12:155.

[24] Repeated Author. 1984. Least median of squares regression. *Journal of the American Statistical Association*, 79(388):871-880.

[25] Rousseeuw, Peter J, and Leroy, Annick M. 1987. Robust Regression and Outlier Detection. Wiley, New York.

[26] Shin, Yongcheol, Byungchul Yu, and Matthew Greenwood-Nimmo. 2014. Modelling asymmetric cointegration and dynamic multipliers in a nonlinear ARDL framework. *Festschrift in Honor of Peter Schmidt. Springer*.

[27] Xiao, Zhijie. 2009. Quantile cointegrating regression. *Journal of Econometrics*, 150(2):248-260.

Chapter 2
Robust Statistics and Robust Regressions

2.1 Introduction to Classical and Robust Approaches to Statistics

Since the 1940s, the statisticians found that even small deviations from the normal distribution could be harmful, and strongly impact the quality of the popular least squares estimator, the classical t-test, F-test, and the results based on them. Hence, the robust statistical procedures were developed as modifications of the classical procedures, which do not fail no matter whether the outliers exist.

Let $x = (x_1, x_2, \cdots, x_n)$ be a set of observed values. The sample mean $\bar{x}$ and sample standard deviation (SD) s are defined by

$$\bar{x} = \frac{1}{n} \sum_{i=1}^{n} x_i, \qquad (2.1)$$

$$s^2 = \frac{1}{n-1} \sum_{i=1}^{n} (x_i - \bar{x})^2. \qquad (2.2)$$

The sample mean is the arithmetic average of the data, and as such one might expect that it provides a good estimate of the center or location of the data. Likewise, one might expect that the sample standard deviation (SD) would provide a good estimate of the dispersion of the data. However, a single outlier can have non-negligible, or even serious adverse impact on these classical estimates. The simplest way to eliminate the impact is removing the outlier from data.

One very old method for estimating the "middle" of the data is to use the sample *median*, which is defined as

$$\text{Med}(x), if \ \#\{x_i > t\} = \#\{x_i < t\}, \quad (2.3)$$

where #A denotes the number of elements of the set A. The corresponding sample median in terms of the *order statistics* ($x_{(1)} < \cdots < x_{(n)}$) can be expressed as:

$$\text{Med}(x) = \begin{cases} x_{(m)}, & \text{if } n \text{ is odd, then } n = 2m\text{-}1 \text{ for some integer} m, \\ \dfrac{x_{(m)} + x_{(m+1)}}{2}, & \text{if } n \text{ is even, then } n = 2m \text{ for some integer} m. \end{cases}$$

(2.4)

The mean and the median are approximately equal if the sample is symmetrically distributed about its center, but not necessarily otherwise. One robust alternative to the SD is the *median absolute deviation about the median* (MAD), defined as

$$\text{MAD}(x) = \text{MAD}(x_1, x_2, \cdots, x_n) = \text{Med}|x - \text{Med}(x)|. \quad (2.5)$$

MAD, firstly, computes the absolute residuals about the sample median, and then gets the median of these absolute residuals. In order to compare MAD with SD, the *normalized* MAD ("MADN") is defined as

$$\text{MADN}(x) = \dfrac{\text{MAD}(x)}{0.674,5}. \quad (2.6)$$

Since the MAD of a standard normal random variable is 0.674,5, that is why the denominator of the above definition is 0.674,5. Obviously, median and MAD are more robust than classical mean and SD, respectively, however, MAD performs poorer than SD without outliers. How to estimate like classical statistics when the data contain no outliers, but without the impact of outliers, is the data-oriented idea of robust estimation.

Among conventional statistics, covariance, as a common measure of the linear dependence of two random variables, has been widely used in many academic fields. One representative field is finance, especially the areas that deal with the construction of portfolios. Since the seminal work of Markowitz (1952), a vast amount of research work has been conducted and many different portfolios have been proposed. The fundamental reason to construct portfolios is to achieve diversification and one can obtain more benefits from diversification when the asset returns included in portfolios are less correlated; that is, the lower the correlation, the greater benefit from diversification. Therefore, it is vital to carefully measure the correlation between asset returns before constructing portfolios and usually the correlation between asset returns is measured by the conventional sample covariance apart from the normalization by standard deviations. Kim and White (2004) demonstrated that the conventional measures of skewness and kurtosis, which are based on the sample average, are very sensitive to outliers. Hence, it is a quite plausible conjecture that the conventional measure of covariance can be also sensitive to outliers because it is also computed as a sample average.

Two intuitively appealing and easily computable robust measures of covariance are introduced and compared with the conventional one by Monte Carlo simulation in this book. The performance of two well-known portfolios, the minimum-variance portfolio and the optimal risky portfolio, are also compared with some existing robust covariance estimators in the existing statistics literature, which are constructed by several robust covariances using some return data obtained from Professor Kenneth R French's website.

2.2 Least Squares Linear Regression

The classical linear model assumes a relation of the type:

$$y_i = x_{i1}\beta_1 + x_{i2}\beta_2 + \cdots + x_{ik}\beta_k + e_i \quad \text{for} \quad i = 1,\cdots,n, \quad (2.7)$$

where n is the sample size, and k is the number of unknown coefficients. The variables $x_{i1},\cdots,x_{ik}$ are explanatory variables or independent variables, whereas the variable y_i is the response variable or dependent variable. In classical theory, the *error term* e_i is assumed to be normally distributed with mean zero and unknown standard deviation

σ. In order to discover the impacts of independent variables on dependent variable, one then tries to estimate the vector of unknown parameters

$$\boldsymbol{\beta} = \begin{pmatrix} \beta_1 \\ \beta_2 \\ \vdots \\ \beta_k \end{pmatrix}. \quad (2.8)$$

Apply a regression estimator to independent and dependent variables, then

$$\hat{\boldsymbol{\beta}} = \begin{pmatrix} \hat{\beta}_1 \\ \hat{\beta}_2 \\ \vdots \\ \hat{\beta}_k \end{pmatrix}. \quad (2.9)$$

where the estimates $\hat{\beta}_j$ are regression coefficients. Multiplying the explanatory variables with these $\hat{\beta}_j$ we can get

$$\hat{y}_i = x_{i1} \hat{\beta}_1 + \cdots + x_{ik} \hat{\beta}_k, \quad (2.10)$$

where $\hat{y}_i$ is the *predicted* or *fitted value* of y_i. The *residual* r_i of the ith observation is the difference between what is actually observed and what is estimated:

$$r_i = y_i - \hat{y}_i. \quad (2.11)$$

The most popular regression estimator, $\hat{\boldsymbol{\beta}}$, can be achieved from

$$\min_{\hat{\beta}} \sum_{i=1}^{n} r_i^2. \quad (2.12)$$

This is the well-known *least squares* (LS) method, which can be computed easily and yield a beautiful mathematical theory, under Gaussian assumptions of error distribution. LS has become a standard mechanism for the generation of statistical techniques.

2.3 Robust Regression

However, some researchers have realized that the data usually do not completely satisfy the classical assumptions. Since the residuals squared in eq. (2.12), even a single outlier often has dramatic effects on the quality of the statistical analysis.

Either in x or in y, regression outliers pose a serious threat to standard least squares analysis. Basically, *regression diagnostics*, which removes or corrects the outliers by pinpointing influential points, and *robust regression* are two ways to handle the regression outliers problem. However, it is often difficult and complex to diagnose outliers for the former way.

Robust regression can devise estimators that are not so strongly affected by outliers. Perhaps the major difficulty with robustizing the least squares approach is that both the dependent and independent variables may be corrupted by gross errors. Robust regression is not a way that simply ignores the outliers, but identifies the outliers based on the residuals from a robust regression.

2.3.1 Least Absolute Values Regression

Since the residuals, r_i in eq. (2.11) are squared, the outliers have a large influence on LS estimators. Edgeworth (1887) first proposed a robust regression estimator, *least absolute values* regression estimator, which is determined by:

$$\min_{\hat{\beta}} \sum_{i=1}^{n} |r_i|. \tag{2.13}$$

This is also called L_1 regression, whereas the least squares reqression is L_2 regression. Compared with least squares, the L_1 regression is more robust with respect to outliers and protects us against outlying y_i.

2.3.2 M-estimator

Huber(1967) considered replacing the squared residuals, r_i^2, by another function of residuals to propose M-estimators, which yields

$$\min_{\hat{\beta}} \sum_{i=1}^{n} \rho(r_i), \qquad (2.14)$$

where ρ is a symmetric properly chosen function. Differentiating this expression with respect to the regression coefficients $\hat{\beta}_j$ yields

$$\sum_{i=1}^{n} \psi(r_i)\boldsymbol{x}_i = \boldsymbol{0}, \qquad (2.15)$$

where $\psi(\cdot) = (\partial/\partial\boldsymbol{\beta})\rho(\cdot)$, $\boldsymbol{x}_i$ is the row vector of explanatory variables of the ith individual, $\boldsymbol{x}_i = (x_{i1}, x_{i2}, \cdots, x_{ik})$, and $\boldsymbol{0} = (0,0,\cdots,0)$. The corresponding standardized expression of eq. (2.15) by the residuals by means of some estimates of σ can be shown as

$$\sum_{i=1}^{n} \psi(r_i/\hat{\sigma})\boldsymbol{x}_i = \boldsymbol{0} \qquad (2.16)$$

After M-estimators, some other robust estimators have been proposed, such as GM-estimators, L-estimators, R-estimators, least median of squares(LMS), S-estimators, and so on, more details can be found in Huber (1996), Rousseeuw and Leroy (2005), and Maronna et al. (2018), etc.

2.4 Quantile Regression

2.4.1 Quantile Regression Model

Koenker and Bassett (1978) used the analogs of sample quantiles for linear regression to propose an L-estimators, quantile regression at τ quantiles:

$$\min_{\hat{\beta}} \sum_{i=1}^{n} \rho_\tau(r_i), \qquad (2.17)$$

where $\rho_\tau(\epsilon) = \epsilon(\tau - I(\epsilon))$ is the loss function for quantile regression shown as Figure 2.1, and

$$I(\epsilon) = \begin{cases} 0, \epsilon \geq 0 \\ 1, \epsilon \leq 0. \end{cases} \qquad (2.18)$$

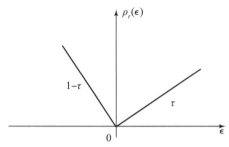

Figure 2.1: Loss function of quantile regression, $\rho_\tau(\epsilon)$

For the compact expression of the linear model

$$y_i = x'_i \boldsymbol{\beta}_\tau + u_i. \qquad (2.19)$$

The solution of $\hat{\boldsymbol{\beta}}_\tau$ at τ-quantile is:

$$\sum_{i=1}^{n} \rho_\tau(y_i - x'_i \hat{\boldsymbol{\beta}}_\tau) = \min, \qquad (2.20)$$

where x_i are fixed and τ-quantile of u_i is zero, and then $\hat{\boldsymbol{\beta}}_\tau$ is an estimate of $\boldsymbol{\beta}_\tau$. Least absolute values estimator is a special case of quantile regression, specifically, the solution to eq. (2.17) at quantile $\tau = 0.5$ is the L_1 estimator. Quantile regression is very useful with heteroskedastic data. If u_i are identically distributed, then $\boldsymbol{\beta}_\tau$ for different τ differ only in the intercept, and hence quantile regression does not give much useful information. However, if u_i have different variabilities, then $\boldsymbol{\beta}_\tau$ will also have different slopes, which identify meaningful information for researchers. There is a very large literature on regression quantiles, see Koenker(2005) for references.

2.4.2 The Finite-sample Distribution of Regression Quantiles

Suppose $Y_1, Y_2, \cdots, Y_n$ are IID (independent and identically distributed) random variables with common distribution function F, with continuous density function f in a neighborhood of $\xi_\tau = F^{-1}(\tau)$, where $f(\xi_\tau)$ is positive. The objective function of the τth sample quantile,

$$\hat{\xi}_\tau = \inf_\xi \{\xi \in \mathbb{R} | \sum_{i=1}^{n} \rho_\tau(Y_i - \xi) = \min!\}. \qquad (2.21)$$

The objective function $\sum_{i=1}^{n} \rho_\tau(Y_i - \xi)$ is convex, since it is the sum of convex functions. Consequently, its gradient

$$g_n(\xi) = n^{-1} \sum_{i=1}^{n} (I(Y_i < \xi) - \tau) \qquad (2.22)$$

is monotonically increasing in ξ. By monotonicity, $\hat{\xi}_\tau$ is greater than ξ if and only if $g_n(\hat{\xi}_\tau) < 0$, and so

$$P\{\sqrt{n}(\hat{\xi}_\tau - \xi_\tau) > \delta\} = P\{g_n(\xi_\tau + \delta/\sqrt{n}) < 0\} \qquad (2.23)$$

$$= P\{n^{-1} \sum_{i=1}^{n} (I(Y_i < \xi_\tau + \delta/\sqrt{n}) - \tau) < 0\}. \qquad (2.24)$$

The summands take the values $(1-\tau)$ and $-\tau$ with probabilities $F(\xi_\tau + \delta/\sqrt{n})$ and $1 - F(\xi_\tau + \delta/\sqrt{n})$, respectively. The expectation of $g_n(\xi_\tau + \delta/\sqrt{n})$ is

$$E\, g_n(\xi_\tau + \delta/\sqrt{n}) = (1-\tau) F(\xi_\tau + \delta/\sqrt{n}) - \tau(1 - F(\xi_\tau + \delta/\sqrt{n}))$$

$$= (F(\xi_\tau + \delta/\sqrt{n}) - \tau)$$

$$= \frac{F(\xi_\tau + \delta/\sqrt{n}) - F(\xi_\tau)}{\delta/\sqrt{n}} \cdot \delta/\sqrt{n}$$

$$\to f(\xi_\tau) \delta/\sqrt{n}, \qquad (2.25)$$

and the variance of $g_n(\xi_\tau + \delta/\sqrt{n})$ is

$$V(g_n(\xi_\tau + \delta/\sqrt{n})) = (1-\tau)^2 F(\xi_\tau + \delta/\sqrt{n}) +$$
$$(-\tau)^2 (1 - F(\xi_\tau + \delta/\sqrt{n})) -$$
$$(F(\xi_\tau + \delta/\sqrt{n}) - \tau)^2$$

$$= F(\xi_\tau + \delta/\sqrt{n})(1 - F(\xi_\tau + \delta/\sqrt{n}))/n$$

$$\to \tau(1-\tau)/n. \qquad (2.26)$$

So, rewriting eq. (2.24) further as

$$P\{\sqrt{n}(\hat{\xi}_\tau - \xi_\tau) > \delta\} = P\{g_n(\xi_\tau + \delta/\sqrt{n}) < 0\}$$

$$= P\left\{\frac{g_n(\xi_\tau + \delta/\sqrt{n}) - f(\xi_\tau)\delta/\sqrt{n}}{\sqrt{\tau(1-\tau)/n}} < -\frac{f(\xi_\tau)\delta/\sqrt{n}}{\sqrt{\tau(1-\tau)/n}}\right\}$$

$$= P\left\{\frac{g_n(\xi_\tau + \delta/\sqrt{n}) - f(\xi_\tau)\delta/\sqrt{n}}{\sqrt{\tau(1-\tau)/n}} < -\omega^{-1}\delta\right\}$$

$$\to 1 - \Phi(\omega^{-1}\delta), \qquad (2.27)$$

where ω is set to satisfy

$$\omega^2 = \frac{\tau(1-\tau)}{f^2(\xi_\tau)}.$$

Therefore, one can conclude that

$$\sqrt{n}(\hat{\xi}_\tau - \xi_\tau) \sim N(0, \omega^2). \tag{2.28}$$

Set $\hat{\zeta}_n = (\hat{\xi}_{\tau_1}, \hat{\xi}_{\tau_2}, \cdots, \hat{\xi}_{\tau_m})$ with $\zeta_n = (\xi_{\tau_1}, \xi_{\tau_2}, \cdots, \xi_{\tau_m})$, then the joint distribution of several quantiles can be expressed as

$$\sqrt{n}(\hat{\zeta}_\tau - \zeta_\tau) \sim N(0, \Omega), \tag{2.29}$$

where $\Omega = (\omega_{ij})_{m \times m}$, and

$$(\omega_{ij}) = (\tau_i \wedge \tau_j - \tau_i \tau_j)/(f(F^{-1}(\tau_i))f(F^{-1}(\tau_j))). \tag{2.30}$$

2.4.3 Quantile Regression Asymptotics

Considering the classical linear regression model with IID errors $\{u_i\}$,

$$y_i = x_i^T \beta + u_i. \tag{2.31}$$

Suppose that $\{u_i\}$ have a common distribution function F with associated density f, with $f(F^{-1}(\tau_i)) > 0$ for $i = 1, \cdots, m$, and $n^{-1} \sum x_i x_i \equiv Q_n$ converges to a positive definite matrix Q_0. So the joint quantile regression process for mp-variate quantile estimator $\hat{\zeta}_n = (\hat{\beta}_n(\tau_1)^T, \cdots, \hat{\beta}_n(\tau_m)^T)^T$ takes the form

$$\sqrt{n}(\hat{\zeta} - \zeta) = (\sqrt{n}(\hat{\beta}_n(\tau_j) - \beta(\tau_j)))_{j=1}^m \sim N(0, \Omega \otimes Q_0^{-1}). \tag{2.32}$$

The classical IID error assumption gives an ideal and simple limiting distribution of the quantile regression estimators. However, in many cases, it is not reasonable to assume IID error for the model. In non-IID error settings like the conditional location-scale model, the asymptotic theory of estimators is more complicated. Followed by Huber (1967) sandwich form, the limiting distribution of $\sqrt{n}(\hat{\beta}(\tau) - \beta(\tau))$ in the case of non-IID error:

$$\sqrt{n}(\hat{\beta}(\tau) - \beta(\tau)) \sim N(0, \tau(1-\tau)H_n^{-1}J_n H_n^{-1}), \tag{2.33}$$

where

$$J_n(\tau) = \frac{1}{n}\sum_{i=1}^{n} x_i x_i^T, \text{ and} \quad (2.34)$$

$$H_n(\tau) = \lim_{n \to \infty} \frac{1}{n}\sum_{i=1}^{n} x_i x_i^T f_i(\xi_i(\tau)). \quad (2.35)$$

where the term $f_i(\xi_i(\tau))$ denotes the conditional density of the response variable, y_i, at the τth quantile. In the IID case, f_i are identical, which is a special case of the sandwich form.

While expanding to vectors of quantile regression results, the asymptotic covariance matrix for $\hat{\boldsymbol{\beta}}(\tau) = (\hat{\boldsymbol{\beta}}(\tau_1), \cdots, \hat{\boldsymbol{\beta}}(\tau_m))$ follows that

$$\sqrt{n}(\hat{\boldsymbol{\beta}}(\tau) - \boldsymbol{\beta}_\tau) \sim N(0, \boldsymbol{\Omega}), \quad (2.36)$$

where $\boldsymbol{\Omega}_{mp \times mp} = (\omega_{ij})_{m \times m}$, and the blocks of the asymptotic covariance matrix, ω_{ij}, is

$$\text{Acov}(\sqrt{n}(\hat{\boldsymbol{\beta}}(\tau_i)) - \boldsymbol{\beta}(\tau_i), \sqrt{n}(\hat{\boldsymbol{\beta}}(\tau_j)) - \boldsymbol{\beta}(\tau_j))$$
$$= [\tau_i \wedge \tau_j - \tau_i \tau_j] H_n(\tau_i)^{-1} J_n H_n(\tau_j)^{-1}, i,j = 1, \cdots, m. \quad (2.37)$$

2.4.4 Wald Tests

Koenker and Bassett (1982a) proposed a test for location shift of two-sample, that is a test of equality between the interquantile ranges of the two samples. Consider the two-sample model

$$Y_i = \alpha_1 + \alpha_2 x_i + u_i, \quad (2.38)$$

where

$$x_i = \begin{cases} 0, \text{ for } n_1 \text{ observations in the first sample;} \\ 1, \text{ for } n_2 \text{ observations in the second sample.} \end{cases}$$

The estimate of the slope parameter α_2 at the τth quantile is the difference between two samples, so the location shift test across quantiles τ_1 and τ_2 turns to a test of the hypothesis

$$\alpha_2(\tau_2) - \alpha_1(\tau_1) = 0. \quad (2.39)$$

Based on eq. (2.32), the asymptotic variance of $\hat{\alpha}_2(\tau_2) - \hat{\alpha}_1(\tau_1)$ can be shown as

$$\sigma^2(\tau_1,\tau_2) = \left[\frac{\tau_1(1-\tau_1)}{f^2(\xi_1)} - 2\frac{\tau_1(1-\tau_2)}{f(\xi_1)f(\xi_2)} + \frac{\tau_2(1-\tau_2)}{f^2(\xi_2)}\right]\left[\frac{n}{mn_2 - n_2^2}\right], \quad (2.40)$$

where $\xi_2 = F^{-1}(\tau_i)$. Let
$$T_n = (\hat{\alpha}_2(\tau_2) - \hat{\alpha}_2(\tau_1))/\hat{\sigma}(\tau_1,\tau_2), \quad (2.41)$$
be the asymptotic normal distributed statistic for the test of the null hypothesis (2.39).

Koenker and Bassett (1982b) proposed a general linear hypothesis on the vector $\zeta = (\beta(\tau_1)^T, \cdots, \beta(\tau_m)^T)^T$ of the form
$$H_0 : R\zeta = r \quad (2.42)$$
under H_0, the test statistic
$$T_n = n(R\hat{\zeta} - r)^T[RV^{-1}R^T]^{-1}(R\hat{\zeta} - r) \sim \chi_q^2, \quad (2.43)$$
where $(V_n)_{mp \times mp}$ matrix with ijth block
$$V_n(\tau_i,\tau_j) = [\tau_i \wedge \tau_j - \tau_i \tau_j] H_n(\tau_i)^{-1} J_n H_n(\tau_j)^{-1}, i,j = 1, \cdots, m, \quad (2.44)$$
where q denotes the rank of the matrix R.

2.4.5 Estimation of Asymptotic Covariance Matrix

Since the asymptotic precision of quantile estimates and the quantile regression estimates depend on the reciprocal of "sparsity function," proposed by Tukey (1965), which is also called quantile-density function proposed by Parzen (1979):
$$s(\tau) = [f(F^{-1}(\tau))]^{-1}. \quad (2.45)$$
Differentiate the identity $F(F^{-1}(t)) = t$ with respect to t, one can get
$$f(F^{-1}(t)) \frac{d}{dt}[F^{-1}(t)] = 1 \quad (2.46)$$
$$\Rightarrow \frac{d}{dt}[F^{-1}(t)] = [f(F^{-1}(t))]^{-1} \quad (2.47)$$
$$\Rightarrow \frac{d}{dt}[F^{-1}(t)] = s(t). \quad (2.48)$$
So, the sparsity function s is the derivative of the quantile function F^{-1}, and can be estimated by using a simple difference quotient of the

empirical quantile function:
$$\hat{s}_n(t) = [\hat{F}_n^{-1}(t+h_n) - \hat{F}_n^{-1}(t-h_n)]/2h_n, \qquad (2.49)$$
where $\hat{F}^{-1}$ is an estimate of F^{-1}, and the bandwidth $h_n \to 0 (n \to \infty)$

As for the choice of h_n, Bofinger (1975), based on standard density estimation, used the following bandwidth sequence that minimizes mean squared error:
$$h_n = n^{1/5} [4.5 s^2(\tau)/(s''(\tau))^2]^{1/5}. \qquad (2.50)$$
Since $s(\tau)/s''(\tau)$ is not very sensitive to F, after Gaussian distribution is substituted, the bandwidth is
$$h_n = n^{-1/5} \left[\frac{4.5 \varphi^4 \Phi^{-1}(t)}{(2\Phi^{-1}(t)^2 + 1)^2} \right]. \qquad (2.51)$$
As for F_n^{-1}, it can be simply achieved by the residuals from quantile regression fit:
$$\hat{u}_i = y_i - x_i^T \hat{\beta}(\tau), \quad i = 1, \cdots, n. \qquad (2.52)$$
So, the empirical quantile function is
$$F_n^{-1}(t) = \hat{u}_{(i)}, \quad t \in [(i-1)/n, i/n]. \qquad (2.53)$$
Usually this residual-based approach is preferable when sample size is large. However, when sample size is small or moderate, $F_n^{-1}(\tau)$ can be shown as
$$F_n^{-1}(\tau) = (n^{-1} \sum x_i)^T \hat{\beta}_n(\tau). \qquad (2.54)$$
(i) For the IID error model shown as model eq. (2.31), the limiting distribution is
$$\sqrt{n}(\hat{\beta}_n(\tau) - \beta(\tau)) \sim N(0, \omega^2(\tau) D_0^{-1}), \qquad (2.55)$$
where $\omega^2(\tau) - \tau(1-\tau)/[f^2(F^{-1}(\tau))]$, and $D_n = \lim n^{-1} \sum x_i x_i^T$.

(ii) For the non-IID error model, Powell suggested a simple way to estimate H_n in eq. (2.35), which used the following kernel form
$$\hat{H}_n(\tau) = (nh_n)^{-1} \sum K(\hat{u}_i(\tau)/h_n) x_i x_i^T, \qquad (2.56)$$
where $\hat{u}_i(\tau) = y_i - x_i^T \hat{\beta}(\tau)$ and h_n is a bandwidth parameter satisfying $h_n \to 0$ and $\sqrt{n} h_n \to \infty$.

2.4.6 Quantile Likelihood Ratio Tests

Extend a test of linear hypothesis for median regression by Koenker and Bassett(1982b)

$$H_0: R\beta = r \tag{2.57}$$

in the IID error model eq. (2.31).

Define $\hat{\sigma}(\tau) = n^{-1}\hat{V}(\tau)$, $\tilde{\sigma}(\tau) = n^{-1}\tilde{V}(\tau)$, where

$$\hat{V}(\tau) = \min_{\{b \in \mathbb{R}^p\}} \sum \rho_r(y_i - x_i^T b), \tag{2.58}$$

$$\tilde{V}(\tau) = \min_{\{b \in \mathbb{R}^p \mid Rb = r\}} \sum \rho_r(y_i - x_i^T b). \tag{2.59}$$

For the τ quantile, two test statistics are shown as

$$L_n(\tau) = \frac{2}{\tau(1-\tau)s(\tau)}[\tilde{V}_n(\tau) - \hat{V}_n(\tau)] \sim \chi_q^2, \tag{2.60}$$

$$\Lambda_n(\tau) = \frac{2n\hat{\sigma}(\tau)}{\tau(1-\tau)s(\tau)}\ln(\tilde{\sigma}(\tau)/\hat{\sigma}(\tau)) \sim \chi_q^2, \tag{2.61}$$

By far, theories and empirical applications of quantile regression have been developed a lot. More details can be found in Koenker(2005) and relative literature.

References

[1] Bofinger, Eve. 1975. Optimal condensation of distributions and optimal spacing of order statistics. *Journal of the American Statistical Association*,70(349):151-154.

[2] Edgeworth, Francis Y. 1887. On observations relating to several quantities. *Hermathena*,6(13):279-285.

[3] Huber,Peter J. 1967. The behavior of maximum likelihood estimates under nonstandard conditions. Proceedings of the Fifth Berkeley Symposium on Mathematical Statistics and Probability.

[4] Huber,Peter J. 1996. Robust statistical procedures. *Siam*,68.

[5] Koenker. 2005. Quantile regression. *Econometric Society monographs*,

38.
[6] Koenker, Roger, and Gilbert Bassett. 1982b. Tests of linear hypotheses and l" 1 estimation. *Econometrica: Journal of the Econometric Society*,50:1577 −1583.
[7] Koenker, Roger, and Gilbert Bassett Jr. 1978. Regression quantiles. *Econometrica: Journal of the Econometric Society*,46:33 −50.
[8] Koenker, Roger, and Gilbert Bassett. 1982a. Robust tests for heteroscedasticity based on regression quantiles. *Econometrica*,50: 43 −61.
[9] Maronna,Ricardo A,R Douglas Martin,Victor J Yohai,and Matías Salibián-Barrera. 2018. Robust statistics: theory and methods (with R). Wiley.
[10] Parzen, Emanuel. 1979. Nonparametric statistical data modeling. *Journal of the American Statistical Association*, 74 (365): 105 −121.
[11] Rousseeuw,Peter J,and Annick M Leroy. 2005. Robust regression and outlier detection. vol. 589. John Wiley & Sons.
[12] Tukey, John W. 1965. Which part of the sample contains the information? Proceedings of the National Academy of Sciences of the United States of America,53(1):127.

Chapter 3
Robust Estimates of Covariance

In this chapter, the performances of several alternative robust measures of covariance are investigated and compared with the conventional one. For this, closely following the main idea in Kim and While (2004), Bonato (2011), Ergun(2011) and White et al. (2010) in that robust measures of covariance introduced here are based on quantiles instead of averages. After the conventional and robust measures of covariance by Monte Carlo simulations are compared, the measures to the construction of two commonly-used portfolios are applied: the minimum-variance portfolio and the optimal risky portfolio using US stocks. The instability of portfolio optimization has been noticed [e.g. Jobson and Korkei (1980, 1981), Michaud (1989)]. An out-of-sample experiment performed in the empirical section indicates that a potentially large investment gain can be realized when the proposed robust measures are used in place of the conventional measure of covariance.

3.1 Conventional Measure of Covariance

Considering two stochastic processes $\{x_t\}_{t=1,\cdots,T}$ and $\{y_t\}_{t=1,\cdots,T}$ where x_t are assumed to be IID (independent and identically distributed) with a CDF (cumulative distribution function) F_x and y_t are also assumed to be IID with a CDF F_y. The conventional measure of covariance (denoted by C) is given by:

Chapter 3 Robust Estimates of Covariance

$$C := E[(x_t - \mu_x)(y_t - \mu_y)],$$

where $\mu_x := E(x_t)$, $\mu_y := E(y_t)$, and the expectation E is taken with respect to the joint CDF of x_t and y_t. The conventional measure C is of course a population parameter and it must be estimated. Its usual estimation is achieved by replacing the population expectation E with its corresponding sample mean:

$$\hat{C} = \frac{1}{T}\sum_{t=1}^{T}[(x_t - \hat{\mu}_x)(y_t - \hat{\mu}_y)],$$

where $\hat{\mu}_x = \frac{1}{T}\sum_{t=1}^{T}x_t$ and $\hat{\mu}_y = \frac{1}{T}\sum_{t=1}^{T}y_t$.

The above sample covariance $\hat{C}$ is based on a sample average and therefore if there are outliers in either x_t or y_t, it might be influenced by them. In order to exhibit the influence of an outlier on the conventional measure of covariance, assuming that, without loss of generality, the single outlier occurs at time $[\tau T]$ with $\tau \in (0,1)$ only in x_t and its size is m_x; i.e. $x_{[\tau T]}$ will be replaced with $x_{[\tau T]} + m_x$ to inject the outlier into the sample. [1] With this single outlier, the sample covariance becomes

$$\hat{C} = \hat{C}_0 + \frac{m_x}{T}(y_{[\tau T]} - \hat{\mu}_y), \qquad (3.1)$$

where $\hat{C}_0$ is the sample covariance computed without the single outlier. The size of distortion (i.e. $\hat{C} - \hat{C}_0 = \frac{m_x}{T}(y_{[\tau T]} - \hat{\mu}_y)$) depends on three factors: (i) the size of the outlier (m_x), (ii) the sample size (T) and (iii) the deviation of $y_{[\tau T]}$ from its sample mean $\hat{\mu}_y$. The first two factors are obvious, but the third one is somewhat surprising. When there is an outlier in x_t at time $[\tau T]$, what is happening in y_t at the same time is also important.

Next, consider the case in which x_t has an outlier (m_x) at time $[\tau T]$ and

---

[1] Note that the function $[a]$ is the usual integer function taking the integer part of the real number a.

y_t has also an outlier (m_y) at time $[sT]$ with $s \in (0,1)$. The sample covariance in this case is shown as follows:

$$\hat{C} = \hat{C}_0 + \frac{m_y}{T}(x_{[sT]} - \hat{\mu}_x) + \frac{m_x}{T}(y_{[\tau T]} - \hat{\mu}_y) - \frac{m_x m_y}{T^2} + \frac{m_x m_y}{T}1_{[[\tau T] = [sT]]}, \quad (3.2)$$

where $\hat{C}_0$ is again the sample covariance computed when there is no outlier in both x_t and y_t. All the derivations for the two results in eq. (3.1) and eq. (3.2) are provided in Appendix.

The four components of the distortion (i.e. $\hat{C} - \hat{C}_0$) in the conventional sample covariance caused by outliers are shown in eq. (3.2). The two terms $\frac{m_y}{T}(x_{[sT]} - \hat{\mu}_x)$ and $\frac{m_x}{T}(y_{[\tau T]} - \hat{\mu}_y)$ exactly correspond to the previous case with one outlier only in x_t. The third term $\frac{m_x m_y}{T^2}$ is new, but its impact is likely to be small since it is the order of $O(T^{-2})$ unless the interaction term of the two outliers (m_x, m_y) is huge. The final term $\frac{m_x m_y}{T}1_{[[\tau T] = [sT]]}$ is the most interesting because (i) its influence can be large since its order is only $O(T^{-1})$ and (ii) it exists only when the two outliers occur at the same time (i.e. $[\tau T] = [sT]$). One can easily conjecture from the analytical expression of the distortion that the conventional measure of covariance based on the sample averages will be sensitive to outliers, and the impact of outliers on the conventional measure will be the largest when the outliers occur at the same time in both variables.

Finally, it should be noted that the distortion in the conventional measure of covariance is a finite sample phenomenon and all the terms in eq. (3.2) causing the distortion will eventually vanish as the sample size increases to infinity as will be shown in Monte Carlo simulations below.

3.2 Robust Measures of Covariance

The classical statistics are excessively sensitive to outliers. Outliers may have a serious adverse influence, and even a single sufficient large outlier, the impact could be unbounded. To overcome the non-robustness of the classical statistical measures, statisticians have put a great deal of effort, and the non-robustness of the classical measure of covariance caught their attention too. Huber(1964) proposed M-estimate to get affine equivariant robust location parameter and scale parameter and Huber (2009) was considered as a classic groundbreaking book on robust statistics. Gnanadesikan and Kettenring(1972) defined a robust covariance and correlation coefficient between two random variables by their robust variances. The disadvantages emerge while applying it into p-vector. The complexity and troublesome of possible non-positive covariance matrix are explained in section 8.2 of Huber(2009). Rousseeuw(1983, 1984) proposed another affine equivariant estimate with high breakdown point, Minimum Volume Ellipsoidestimate (MVE). More efficient S-estimates were proposed by Rousseeuw (1984), based on the least median of squares estimator. A trimmed scale for covariance estimate, i.e. Minimum Covariance Determinant estimate (MCD), was introduced by Rousseeuw (1984). All these contributions to robust statistics give us a more rational view while we analyze data with a part of outliers.

3.2.1 Median Absolute Deviation About the Median(MAD)

It is known that median absolute deviation about the median(MAD) as a robust estimate of standard deviation is not influenced by a small part of atypical data. Huber(2009) concluded it is the single most useful ancillary estimate of scale estimator on account of its easy computation and broad use.

$$\text{MAD}(x) = \text{Med}\{\mid x - \text{Med}(x) \mid\}, \quad (3.3)$$

where $\text{Med}(x)$ is the median of x. Since MAD of a standard normal random variable is 0.675, normalized MAD (MADN) is defined to compare with standard deviation as:

$$\text{MADN}(x) = \frac{\text{MAD}(x)}{0.675}. \qquad (3.4)$$

The MAD is not influenced very much by the presence of one or several large outliers, so it is a good robust alternative to the sample SD. While the data set contains no outliers, median or MAD usually performs poorly than classical $\bar{x}$ or s. The motivation of robust statistics is trying to behave like the classical ones when there are no outliers, but insensitive to outliers otherwise.

3.2.2 Gnanadesikan and Kettenring Robust Measures of Covariance

Gnanadesikan and Kettenring (1972) proposed a robust covariance of two random variables x and y by their robust variances as:

$$\text{Cov}_{gk}(x,y) = \frac{1}{4ab}[S(ax+by)^2 - S(ax-by)^2], \qquad (3.5)$$

where $S(x)$ is a robust scale estimate of x, $a = \frac{1}{S(x)}$, and $b = \frac{1}{S(y)}$. And a more preferable robust covariance can be written as:

$$\text{Cov}_{gk}(x,y) = \frac{S(ax+by)^2 - S(ax-by)^2}{S(ax+by)^2 + S(ax-by)^2} S(x)S(y). \qquad (3.6)$$

This robust measure is obviously free of distribution. However, Huber (2009) points out the complexity and trouble caused by possible non-positive definite covariance matrix while applied to a p-vector $x = (x_1, x_2, \cdots, x_p)$.

3.2.3 M-estimates

In multivariate analysis, covariance matrix is an important measure on the relationship among variables. For a more detailed description of these measures please refer to Maronna, Martin and Yohai (2006).

But here in this chapter we only consider a bivariate situation, so that the covariance will be easy to compare between these two variables $z = (x, y)'$ as a bivariate observation from a distribution F. Classical measures of location and covariance matrix are

$$E(z) = \mu = (\mu_1, \mu_2)' = (E(x), E(y))', \qquad (3.7)$$

$$\text{Var}(z) = \Sigma = E((z - \mu)(z - \mu)'). \qquad (3.8)$$

The density function of F takes the following form $f(z, \mu, \Sigma) = \frac{1}{\Sigma} h(d(z, \mu, \Sigma))$, where $d(z, \mu, \Sigma) = (z - \mu)' \Sigma^{-1} (z - \mu)'$ is the squared Mahalanobis distance between the vectors z and μ. While $h(s) = c \cdot \exp(-s/2)$ with $c = (2\pi)^{-p/2}$, f is multivariate normal density function; while $h(s) = \dfrac{c}{(s + v)^{(p+v)/2}}$, c is a constant, and f is p-variate Student distribution with v degree of freedom ($p = 2$ here); and while $v = 1$, f is multivariate Cauchy density. Sampling from above density function, one get an IID sample $\{z_t\}_{t=1,\cdots,T}$. The likelihood function is:

$$L(\mu, \Sigma) = \frac{1}{|\Sigma|^{T/2}} \prod_{t=1}^{T} h(d(z_t, \mu, \Sigma)). \qquad (3.9)$$

Maximizing $L(\mu, \Sigma)$ is equivalent to

$$\min_{\mu, \Sigma}: -2\ln L(\mu, \sigma) = T\ln|\hat{\Sigma}| + \sum_{t=1}^{T} \rho(d_i), \qquad (3.10)$$

where $\rho(s) = -2\ln h(s)$ and $d_t = d(z_t, \mu, \Sigma)$. Differentiating with respect to μ and Σ one can get:

$$\sum_{t=1}^{T} W(d_t)(z_t - \mu) = 0 \qquad (3.11)$$

$$\frac{1}{T} \sum_{t=1}^{T} W(d_t)(z_t - \mu)(z_t - \mu)' = \Sigma, \qquad (3.12)$$

where $W(\cdot)$ is the derivative of $\rho(\cdot)$, i.e. $W(d) = \rho'(d)$, and $W(\cdot)$ in eq. (3.11) and eq. (3.12) are not necessary to be equal. The solutions of above equations ($\hat{\mu}, \hat{\Sigma}$) are called M-estimates ("M" for "maximum likelihood – type") as in Huber (2009), which was first proposed in Huber (1964).

3.2.4 Minimum Volume Ellipsoid Estimate(MVE)

Rousseeuw (1984) proposed an affine equivariant estimation with maximal breakdown point, i.e. MVE, by getting the center of the minimal volume ellipsoid covering (at least) $[T/2 + 1]$ points. See Rousseeuw and Leroy(1987).

The Mahalanobis distance $d = d(z, \mu, \Sigma)$ of z is the vector with elements $d(z_t, \mu, \Sigma)$, $t = 1, 2, \cdots, T$. Our objection is to minimize the distance and in order to avoid the smallest eigenvalue of estimate of the covariance matrix, $\hat{\Sigma}$, to be close to zero, the constraint $|\hat{\Sigma}| = 1$. Maronna, Martin and Yohai(2006) defines the simplest way to express the MVE as

$$\min_{\mu, \Sigma} \mathrm{Med}(d(z, \mu, \Sigma)). \qquad (3.13)$$

$\hat{\Sigma}$ satisfies the above expression and $|\hat{\Sigma}| = 1$ is the MVE estimate of the covariance matrix. This is equivalent to the problem that among all ellipsoids $\{z: d(z, \mu, \Sigma) \leqslant 1\}$ containing more than half points, the MVE is the one giving the minimum value of $|\Sigma|$. While Davies (1992) pointed out the inefficiency of MVE estimate. But it is usually used as initial estimate for M-estimation and S-estimation.

3.2.5 S-estimates

Rousseeuw and Yohai (1984) proposed S-estimates as a robust M-estimate of covariance by minimizing the scale of residual in linear regression. Further, Davies(1987) defined S-estimates of covariance as an M-scale estimate satisfying

$$\frac{1}{T} \sum_{t=1}^{T} \rho\left(\frac{d_t}{\hat{\sigma}}\right) = \delta, \qquad (3.14)$$

where ρ is a smooth bounded function that is symmetric around 0, $\rho(0) = 1$, and decreases monotonically to 0 as $x \to \infty$ and $\hat{\sigma} = \sigma(d(z, \hat{\mu}, \hat{\Sigma}))$. If ρ is differentiable, the solution of $\hat{\sigma}$ must satisfy estimating equations of the form eq. (3.11) and eq. (3.12). See Maronna, Martin and Yohai (2006).

$$\sum_{t=1}^{T} W(\frac{d_t}{\hat{\sigma}})(z_t - \mu) = 0, \qquad (3.15)$$

$$\frac{1}{T}\sum_{t=1}^{T} W(\frac{d_t}{\hat{\sigma}})(z_t - \mu)(z_t - \mu)' = c\hat{\Sigma}, \qquad (3.16)$$

where $W(d) = \rho'(d)$, $\sigma = \sigma(d_1, d_2, \cdots, d_T)$ and c is a scalar such that $|\hat{\Sigma}| = 1$.

3.2.6 Minimum Covariance Determinant Estimate (MCD)

MCD estimates were proposed in Rousseeuw (1984), which used a trimmed scale for $\hat{\sigma}$ but not M-scale estimate as a robust measure of covariance. As the introduction of this in Maronna, Martin and Yohai (2006), let $d_{(1)} \leq d_{(2)} \cdots \leq d_{(T)}$ be the ordered values of the squared distances $d_t = d(z, \mu, \Sigma)$ and define the trimmed scale of the squared distances as $\hat{\sigma} = \sum \lim_{t=1}^{h} d_{(t)}$ for $1 \leq h < T$. An estimate $(\hat{\mu}, \hat{\Sigma})$ that minimizes the $\hat{\sigma} = d(z, \mu, \Sigma)$ under the condition of $|\hat{\Sigma}| = 1$ is called a Minimum Covariance Determinant (MCD) estimate. A fast MCD (FAST-MCD) algorithm was introduced by Rousseeuw and Driessen (1999) to solve the computation time-consuming problem of MCD.

3.3 An Alternative Robust Measure of Covariance

The key idea in Kim and White (2004), Bonato (2011), Ergun (2011) and White et al. (2010) is that the conventional measures of skewness and kurtosis are sensitive to outliers because they are based on sample averages and they robustify the conventional measures by basing them on quantiles because quantiles do not change much unless the number of outliers is substantially large. Follow the idea and propose to replace the population expectation E with a particular quantile *Median* which will be denoted by M. It has been well known in the statistics literature that the expected value (E) or the median (M) of a random variable can equally measure the centre of the distribution of the random variable and the median is more robust than the expected value in the presence of outliers under the assumption of symmetry. Therefore, one robust measure of covariance (denoted by C_{R1}) introduced here is

$$C_{R1} = M[(x_t - \mu_x)(y_t - \mu_y)],$$

where the median M is taken with respect to the joint CDF of x_t and y_t. The natural estimator for C_{R1} will be the corresponding sample median

$$\hat{C}_{R1} = \hat{M}[(x_t - \hat{\mu}_x)(y_t - \hat{\mu}_y)], \qquad (3.17)$$

where $\hat{M}$ is the sample median.

From the expression of the median interaction deviation about the mean in eq. (3.17), it is noted that the centring terms $\hat{\mu}_x$ and $\hat{\mu}_y$ are also based on sample averages so that these terms might be sensitive to outliers. Therefore, one can also consider replacing them with the corresponding medians as well to propose the following:

$$C_{R2} = M[(x_t - \kappa_x)(y_t - \kappa_y)],$$

where κ_x and κ_y are the population medians of x_t and y_t, i.e., $\kappa_x = M(x_t)$, $\kappa_y = M(y_t)$. ① The natural estimator for C_{R2} is

$$\hat{C}_{R2} = \hat{M}[(x_t - \hat{\kappa}_x)(y_t - \hat{\kappa}_y)],$$

where $\hat{\kappa}_x$ and $\hat{\kappa}_y$ are the sample medians of x_t and y_t. Here refer to this measure as the "comediance" between x_t and y_t. ②

---

① Let $z_t = (x_t - \mu_x)(y_t - \mu_y)$. Clearly, C and C_{R1} are the mean and median of z_t. Hence, the usual warnings about the mean and median parameters should apply to C and C_{R1}; that is, (i) there is a trade-off between efficiency and robustness, (ii) they are equal only when z_t is symmetrically distributed. If the interest is the "center" of z_t, then the two are just alternative and competing measures. On the other hand, if the objective is to measure C, the users should be aware of the usual warnings mentioned above.

② It can be proved that $M[(x_t - \kappa_x)(y_t - \kappa_y)] = 0$ is equivalent to $E[\text{sign}\{(x_t - \kappa_x)(y_t - \kappa_y)\}] = 0.5$ where $\text{sign}\{z_t\}$ is defined as $\text{sign}\{z_t\} = 1$ if $z_t \geq 0$ and $\text{sign}\{z_t\} = 0$ if $z_t < 0$. Therefore, the null hypothesis that $C_R = 0$ can be tested using the non-parametric sign and rank testing procedures in Pratt and Gibbons (1981) and Campbell and Dufour (1997).

In the presence of outliers, the proposed two measures (C_{R1}, C_{R2}) are likely to be more robust than the conventional measure (C), and the comediance (C_{R2}) would be more robust to outliers than C_{R1} by construction. Moreover, they are conceptually simple to understand and implement in applied research.

The conventional measure of covariance depends heavily on some moment conditions for the underlying distributions of x_t and y_t. For example, the conventional measure does not exist if the distribution of the product $(x_t - \mu_x)(y_t - \mu_y)$ does not have the first moment (as in the Cauchy distribution). However, the proposed robust measure comediance is not susceptible to such moment conditions. In fact, the comediance between x_t and y_t requires no moment condition and is well-defined for any underlying distributions of x_t and y_t.

Although C_{R1} and C_{R2} are robust to outliers by construction, their finite sample performances are unknown and can be demonstrated by simulations. Such simulations are carried out in the next section, and for comparison, some existing robust covariance measures in the literature included, such as (i) the Campbell covariance estimator (donoted by Campbell) in Campbell (1980), (ii) the sign and rank covariance estimators(denoted by Sign and Rank) in Visuri et al. (2000) and Ollila et al. (2002), and (iii) the minimum covariance determinant estimator (denoted by MCD) in Rousseeuw et al. (2004). [1]

3.4　Monte Carlo Simulations

In this section, Monte Carlo simulations are conducted to investigate the behavior of the conventional measure (C) and the robust measures (C_{R1}

---

[1]　A MATLAB code to implement the minimum covariance determinant estimator is freely available from a MATLAB library called "LIBRA" provided by the Katholieke Universiteit Leuven and the University of Antwep.

and C_{R2}) of covariance in the presence of outliers. Monte Carlo simulations in this section closely follow the design of Kim and White (2004) and Bonato(2010). The standard normal distribution $N(0,1)$ and student t-distribution with DF(degree of freedom) 5 and 1 [T-5, T-1] are chosen to represent thin, moderately heavy and extremely heavy tailed symmetric distributions, respectively. For an asymmetric distribution, using the lognormal distribution with $\mu = 1, \sigma = 0.4$ (centered at zero by subtracting the mean value) denoted by LN(1,0.4). It is known that T-1, also called Cauchy distribution, has no first or higher moments. The inclusion of T-1 has been motivated by recent work. For example, Bonato (2011) tested and concluded that some time-series data are compatible as coming from a distribution with infinite moments and Ergun(2011) has also provided some empirical evidence that the first few moments of S & P500 does not seem to exist at some time periods.

Two processes $\{x_t\}_{t=1,\cdots,T}$ and $\{y_t\}_{t=1,\cdots,T}$ are generated independently from the above four distributions with sample sizes $T = 50, 100, 300, 500$ and calculate the conventional and robust measures of covariance. The experiment is repeated 1,000 times generating 1,000 samples of both the conventional and robust measures. Since these two processes $\{x_t\}_{t=1,\cdots,T}$ and $\{y_t\}_{t=1,\cdots,T}$ are drawn independently, the true value of covariance is zero obviously. If there is no outlier, one should expect both measures to be well centred at the true value of zero.

The results for the conventional measure of covariance are displayed in Figures 3.1 – 3.4. Each figure is constructed by 4 windows representing 4 distributions and each window shows 4 boxplots for 4 different sample sizes. The vertical axis in each figure indicates sample sizes. Each boxplot represents the lower (25%), median (50%), and upper (75%) quartiles. The size of both whiskers extending from the box is set to be the same as the size of each box (i.e. the inter-quartile range). The numbers lying at the end of each whisker show that how many observations are beyond the end of the whiskers.

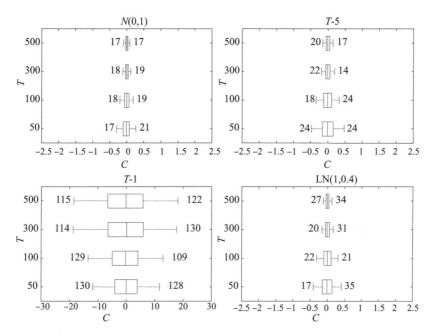

Figure 3.1 Sampling distributions of C (Box-plots): no outlier case

Figure 3.1 describes the performance of C when there is no outlier in the dataset. It can be seen that the conventional measure under three distributions $[N(0,1), T\text{-}5, LN(1,0.4)]$ performs well and seems to converge to the true value, zero, reasonably quickly. But for $T\text{-}1$, the sample covariance does not converge. On the contrary, it seems to diverge since the sampling distribution becomes wider as the sample size increases. Therefore, the majority of the time, the values of the conventional measure are far from the true value of zero so that one can falsely conclude that the two series are correlated. This type of spurious correlation is not caused by outliers, but caused by blindly applying the conventional measure to observations coming from very heavy tailed distributions. Figure 3.2 shows the case where there is a single outlier in x_t only. Following Kim and White(2004), one can use 48.62 times of the 25th percentile of sample $\{x_t\}_{t=1,\cdots,T}$ as an outlier and this value of outlier replaced the observation $x_{[0.3*T]}$ in each sample.① As can be seen in Figure 3.2, the influence is noticeable since each box and whisker becomes wider for all three symmetric distributions [$N(0,1)$, T-5, $LN(1,0.4)$].

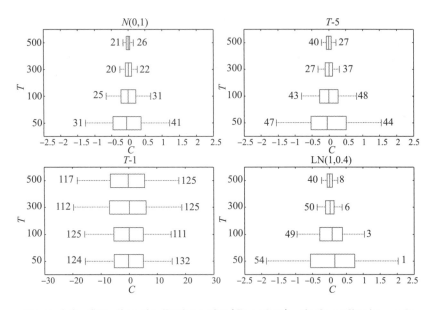

Figure 3.2 Sampling distributions of C (Box-plots) : single outlier in x_t only

The case where there are outliers in both x_t and y_t at different times is also considered. An outlier for y_t is generated exactly in the same way as for x_t ; i. e. the value of the outlier for y_t is 48.62 times of the 25th percentile of sample $\{y_t\}_{t=1,\cdots,T}$ and the observation $y_{[0.6*T]}$ is replaced by the outlier so that the two outliers occur at different times. The simulation results are shown in Figure 3.3. The impact of outliers occurring at different times on the conventional measure is fairly large for the three distributions [$N(0,1)$, T-5, $LN(1,0.4)$]. The sampling distribution of C becomes greatly wider, which implies that the likelihood of falsely

---

① See Kim & White(2004) for detailed explanations about the size of outliers.

accepting correlation between x_t and y_t has increased. This is the second type of spurious correlation and is caused by outliers, compared to the first type of spurious correlation caused by heavy-tailed distributions.

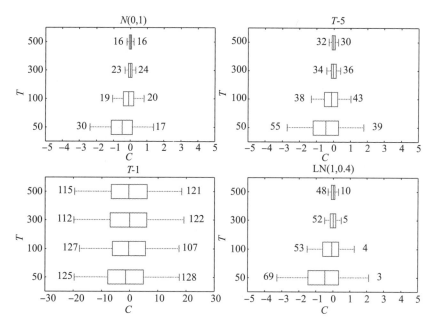

Figure 3.3 Sampling distributions of C (Box-plots):
outliers in x_t and y_t at different times

The final case for outliers occurring at the same time is displayed in Figure 3.4 which clearly visualizes the impact on the conventional measure. The discovered distortion is spectacular in this case. For example, let us consider the lognormal case for which the impact seems to be the largest. The center of box-plots is approximately 34 and 18 for $T = 50, 100$ respectively which is far from the true value of zero. It is moving towards zero as T increases; it changes to about 7 and 4 for $T = 300, 500$, indicating that the impact diminishes as the sample size increases. However, even at very large sample such as $T = 500$, the entire sampling distribution of the conventional measure is much above the true value of zero, which means that researchers falsely accept spurious correlation 100% of the time.

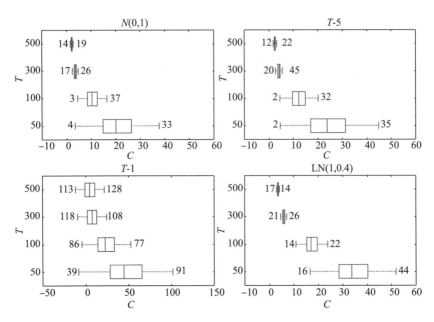

Figure 3. 4 Sampling distributions of C (Box-plots) :
outliers in x_t and y_t at the same time

Next, the behaviors of the proposed robust covariance measures C_{R1}, C_{R2} are considered when they are applied to the same environments as above. Figures 3. 5 – 3. 8 display the behaviors of the first robust measure (C_{R1}) of covariance. For the thin and moderately heavy tailed distributions [$N(0, 1)$, T-5, $LN(1, 0.4)$], the robust measure C_{R1} performs well and is not influenced by outliers except when the sample size is very small such as $T = 50$. However, as soon as the sample size reaches 100, the impact almost completely disappears, regardless of how the outliers occur. The small sample distortion at $T = 50$ can be explained by the fact that C_{R1} is based on the means of x_t and y_t (μ_x, μ_y) and the estimates of these means are greatly influenced by outliers, particularly in small samples. In addition, C_{R1} does not seem to be completely immune to extremely heavy tailed distribution such as T-1. The sampling distribution of C_{R1} is still wide, even though the severity of the problem has been substantially reduced when compared to C. This problem is also caused by the same reason as above in that the means of x_t and y_t are not well-defined for T-1, and therefore their estimates are not stable.

Considering the performance of C_{R1}, one might conjecture that the second robust measure C_{R2} based on the medians of x_t and y_t may not possess any of the two problems of C_{R1} (i. e. small sample sensitivity and wide sampling distribution for heavy tailed distributions). The results for C_{R2} are displayed in Figures 3. 9 - 3. 12. As conjectured, the sampling distribution of C_{R2} is quite well concentrated around the true value of zero regardless of (i) tail-thickness of underlying distributions and (ii) the types of outliers. In other words, under any conditions considered in the simulation experiments, there is no chance at all to be misled by any type of spurious correlation when the second robust measure C_{R2} is used.

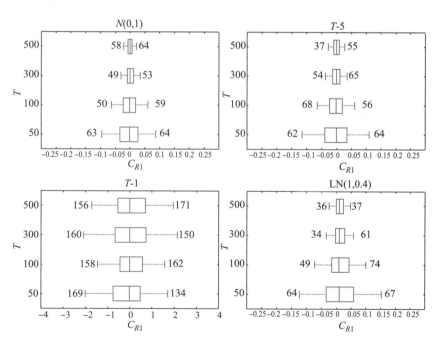

Figure 3. 5 Sampling distributions of C_{R1} (Box-plots) : no outlier case

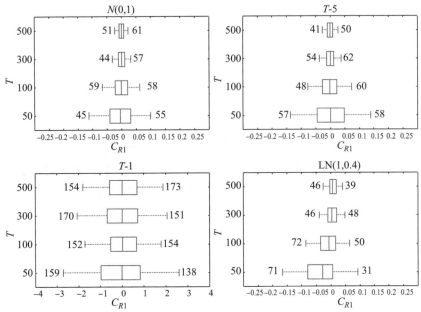

Figure 3.6 Sampling distributions of C_{R1} (Box-plots) : single outlier in x_t only

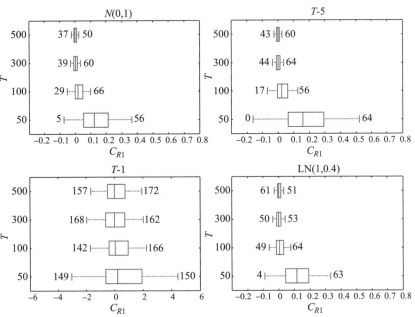

Figure 3.7 Sampling distributions of C_{R1} (Box-plots) :
outliers in x_t and y_t at different times

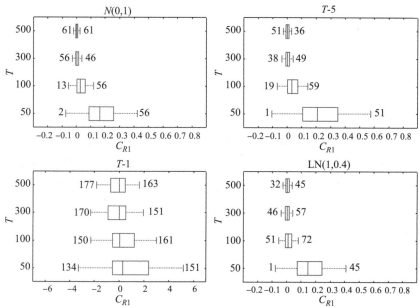

Figure 3.8 Sampling distributions of C_{R1} (Box-plots):
outliers in x_t and y_t at the same time

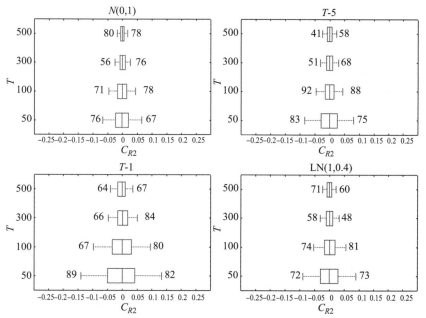

Figure 3.9 Sampling distributions of C_{R2} (Box-plots): no outlier case

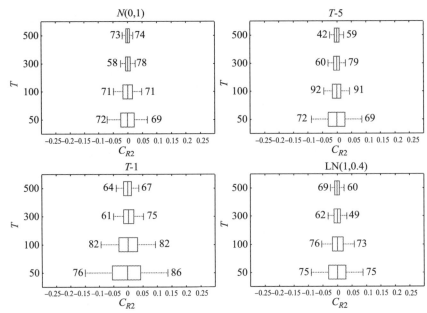

Figure 3.10 Sampling distributions of C_{R2} (Box-plots): single outlier in x_t only

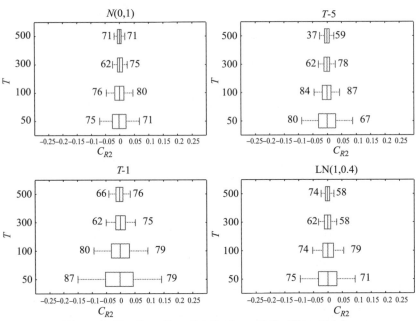

Figure 3.11 Sampling distributions of C_{R2} (Box-plots):

outliers in x_t and y_t at different times

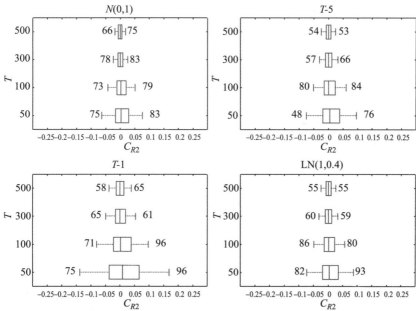

Figure 3.12 Sampling distributions of C_{R2} (Box-plots) :
outliers in x_t and y_t at the same time

Since other robust measures would be robust to outliers and exhibit similar box-plots while there are no outliers, single outlier in x_t, and one outlier in x_t and one outlier in y_t at different times, only the results while outliers happened at the same time for the other four robust measures are shown in Figures 3.13 – 3.16, respectively, for Campbell, Sign, Rank, and MCD. Overall, these robust measures also show good performance in that they are not affected by outliers and are fairly robust to fat-tailed distributions, although there are some minor degrees of variation across different measures. The Campbell estimator in Figure 3.13 is slightly sensitive to fat-tailed distributions; its sampling distribution for T-1 becomes much wider than that for the other three distributions [$N(0,1)$, T-5, LN(1, 0.4)]. By comparing Figures 3.12 and 3.13, it can be argued that the sampling distribution of the comediance estimator is more heavily concentrated around the true value, zero. The *Sign* and *Rank* estimators in Figures 3.14 and 3.15 display a small bias when the sample size is small such as $T = 50,100$ although the bias quickly disappears as the sample size increases. The last one, MCD, as shown in Figure 3.16, is also somewhat sensitive to fat-tailed distributions.

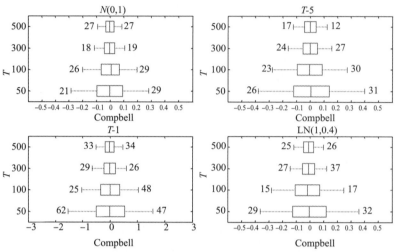

Figure 3.13 Sampling distributions of Compbell (Box-plots) : outliers in x_t and y_t at the same time

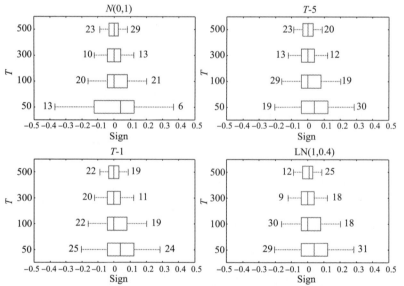

Figure 3.14 Sampling distributions of Sign (Box-plots) : outliers in x_t and y_t at the same time

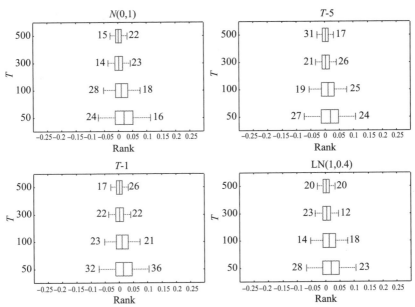

Figure 3.15 Sampling distributions of Rank (Box-plots):
outliers in x_t and y_t at the same time

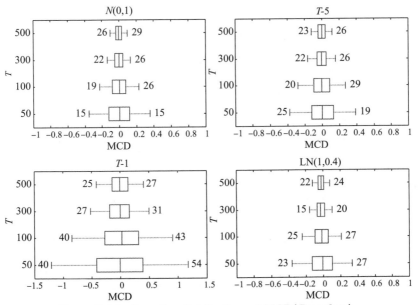

Figure 3.16 Sampling distributions of MCD (Box-plots):
outliers in x_t and y_t at the same time

3.5 Empirical Application

3.5.1 Empirical Comparison of Robust Estimates

In this section, classical and robust above measures of covariance are computed by using the weekly return of Dow Jones Industrial Average in the US and other 5 main weekly return of indices in different countries, which are FTSE 100 in the UK, DAX in German, CAC40 in France, TSX in Canada, and Nikkei in Japan. 521 observations of every index are generated by the time span from Jan. 3rd, 2000 to Dec. 28th, 2009 and the unit is percent return. Table 3.1 shows the classical and robust measures of covariance between the US and the other 5 countries.

Table 3.1 Classical and robust measures of covariance between the US and other 5 countries

Countries	$Cov_{classical}$	C_{R2}	Cov_{gk}	M-est	MVE	MCD	S-est
US & UK	5.501,0	1.245,4	3.278,1	3.488,3	3.666,6	3.662,4	3.428,7
US & France	6.530,0	1.695,5	4.340,3	4.625,8	4.922,6	4.870,9	4.692,2
US & Canada	4.953,3	0.799,6	2.564,6	2.305,6	2.433,7	2.574,4	2.566,9
US & Japan	4.330,1	0.987,1	2.848,8	2.429,7	3.384,2	3.209,4	2.914,0
US & German	7.342,1	1.814,7	4.783,5	4.576,9	4.801,2	5.296,1	4.893,5

From the table above, it is obvious that, no matter what kind of measures of covariance they are, the positive covariance shows that the weekly stock market returns in 5 countries have the same trend to the one in the US. Actually, classical sample covariance is indeed magnified by outliers, compared to other robust measures.

In the first decade of this century, US suffered from several influential events. Subprime crisis impacts U.S. stock market most deeply. The reason and countermeasure are not considered in this chapter, but the linear relationship between stock market in the US and those in these 5 countries cares. The weekly return of Dow Jones Industrial Average decreased sharply by 18.2% during the week of Oct. 6th, 2008, since the US stock market underwent the worst decline since the 1987 stock market crash as well. In the same week stock returns in the other 5 countries went through the hardest time during the ten years. In Japan, the weekly return of Nikkei 225 dropped 24.3%, which is the most serious decline during that week among these 6 countries including the US. And in Canada, although the weekly return of TSX suffered from the most serious crash during these ten years, the drop of 16.1% is the smallest compared with the other 5 countries. The weekly returns of CAC 40 in France, DAX in German and FTSE 100 in UK underwent the biggest drop of 22.2%, 21.6%, and 21.0%, respectively during the ten years. Just after two weeks, the stock markets experienced hugest raise of weekly return in these countries except France and Canada. And during the week of Sep. 11th, 2001, weekly return of Dow Jones suffered from a drop of 14.2%, and the weekly return of the other 5 countries dropped deeply in the same week as well.

As mentioned previously, whether the outliers happened at the same time matters while the classical sample covariance is computed. And the fact that the return of the other 5 countries keeps the same trend to U.S. stock market while seriously influential events happened makes the sample covariance doubtful. In table 3.2 one can calculate the classical and robust measures of covariance after deleting the biggest outlier of weekly return of Dow Jones Industrial Average and the data of the other 5 countries at the same time, which happened in the week of Oct. 6th, 2008. In table 3.3, the biggest five absolute value of weekly return of Dow Jones Industrial Average and the corresponding data in the other 5 countries at the same week are deleted.

Table 3.2 Classical and robust measures of covariance between US and other 5 countries

(Deleting the biggest outlier of all 6 countries, which happened in the week of Oct. 6th, 2008)

Countries	Cov$_{classical}$	C_{R2}	Cov$_{gk}$	M-est	MVE	MCD	S-est
US & UK	4.773,3	1.215,7	3.274,5	3.375,6	3.735,9	3.647,3	3.414,7
US & France	5.765,8	1.667,2	4.309,1	4.619,0	4.848,8	4.860,6	4.673,0
US & Canada	4.394,9	0.775,4	2.552,0	2.309,9	2.518,3	2.598,4	2.552,9
US & Japan	3.486,7	0.960,1	2.831,2	2.413,6	3.357,2	3.195,4	2.900,5
US & German	6.596,9	1.827,0	4.800,7	4.581,3	5.303,1	5.324,2	4.873,5

Table 3.3 Classical and robust measures of covariance between US and other 5 countries

(Deleting the biggest 5 outliers of Dow Jones return and the other 5 countries' returns of the same weeks)

Countries	Cov$_{classical}$	C_{R2}	Cov$_{gk}$	M-est	MVE	MCD	S-est
US & UK	5.118,5	1.163,2	3.217,4	3.356,6	3.691,3	3.602,0	3.373,0
US & France	6.015,7	1.636,1	4.300,1	4.595,8	4.784,7	4.811,4	4.615,9
US & Canada	4.592,6	0.740,4	2.526,2	2.295,6	2.439,0	2.569,7	2.511,2
US & Japan	3.974,9	0.897,1	2.855,1	2.384,1	2.944,1	3.204,5	2.860,1
US & German	6.743,6	1.802,7	4.759,8	4.557,7	4.996,8	5.289,7	4.814,0

It can be seen from table 3.2, the classical covariances between US and the other 5 countries get smaller obviously, compared with table 3.1. But the other robust measures of covariance don't change much at all. After deleting the biggest 5 absolute values of return of Dow Jones and the data of the other 5 countries at the same weeks, the sample covariances change to raise a little. In fact, except the biggest and second biggest absolute values of Dow Jones return are negative, the other 3 outliers are positive. After deleting these 5 biggest outliers, the classical sample covariance might be bigger than deleting only one biggest outlier. The performances of sample covariances display the sensitivity to the outliers. However, our C_{R2} is very robust compared to classical covariance. The other measures of covariance perform robustly as well.

3.5.2 Portfolio Performances of Robust Covariances

Employing the proposed measures C_{R1}, C_{R2} as well as four other robust estimators, one can construct two optimal portfolios, namely the minimum-variance portfolio and the optimal risky portfolio. Constructing these portfolios typically requires the use of many stocks, but to highlight the use of the proposed measure as well as other robust measures, here employ a simple set-up. For this, only two stocks are used to estimate the covariance between the two stocks using both conventional covariance and a robust measure, which generate two portfolios. The two portfolios are identical except for their covariance estimates. By evaluating the performance of these two portfolios, the value added by robust measures can be shown.

Given that there are so many pairs of stock to choose, two fairly broad-based portfolios are used instead: a small cap (high book-to-market) portfolio and a large cap (low book-to-market) portfolio from Professor Kenneth R. French's website.[1] The sample period is from January 5, 2001 to May 6, 2011 (540 weekly observations). There are twelve weekly portfolios (6 value-weighted and 6 equally-weighted portfolios grouped by small/large cap and low/middle/high book-to-market). Ten portfolios among these experienced the largest decline in their returns during the week of October 6, 2008, when the subprime mortgage crisis hit the U.S. economy. Choose the small cap/high book-to-market portfolio (denoted by SH) because it has the largest drop[2] in terms of the relative size (i.e. the actual extreme value divided by the 25 th percentile

---

[1] The link to the website is http://mba.tuck.dartmouth.edu/pages/faculty/ken.french/index.html.

[2] The value of the largest drop was -16.9% during the subprime mortgage crisis and the 25th percentile of the sample is -0.86%. Therefore, the relative size of the largest outlier is 19.7.

of the sample). The obvious counterpart to be combined for diversification is the large cap/low book-to-market portfolio(denoted by BL), which also shows the largest drop during the same week of October 6,2008. Given that the two portfolios experienced the largest drop at the same time, one may conjecture based on our simulation results that the conventional measure is very likely to be influenced by the declines, and thus that its use as an input in portfolio optimization can weaken the performance of the resulting portfolio.

Table 3.4 shows the results for the whole sample period. For the two portfolios (the minimum-variance portfolio and the optimal risky portfolio), one can calculate their returns (sample mean), risks (sample standard deviations), and Sharpe ratios based on different covariance measures. Table 3.4 also provides the computed portfolio weights assigned to SH and BL. For both minimum variance portfolio and optimal risky portfolio, the Sharpe ratio decreases, substantially in some cases, when robust measures are used, except for the Campbell covariance, whose performance is nearly identical to that of the conventional measure.

Table 3.4 Portfolio performance based on the whole sample

(January 5,2001 – May 6,2011)					
Minimum-variance Portfolio	Return	Risk	Sharpe ratio	Weight (SH)	Weight (BL)
Conventional Cov(C)	0.363,0	2.728,7	0.133,0	0.868,2	0.131,8
C_{R1}	0.303,3	2.778,4	0.109,2	0.588,4	0.411,6
Comediance(C_{R2})	0.303,6	2.778,0	0.109,3	0.589,6	0.410,4
Campbell covariance	0.370,9	2.729,4	0.135,9	0.905,4	0.094,6
Sign covariance	0.300,4	2.783,3	0.107,9	0.574,7	0.425,3
Rank covariance	0.277,0	2.830,5	0.097,8	0.464,7	0.535,3
MCD	0.310,2	2.767,7	0.112,1	0.620,8	0.379,2

Continued

Optimal risky portfolio	Return	Risk	Sharpe ratio	Weight (SH)	Weight (BL)
(January 5,2001 – May 6,2011)					
Conventional Cov(C)	0.669,0	3.806,4	0.175,8	2.303,7	-1.303,7
C_{R1}	0.364,8	2.728,7	0.133,7	0.876,8	0.123,2
Comediance(C_{R2})	0.366,3	2.728,8	0.134,2	0.883,9	0.116,1
Campbell covariance	0.621,4	3.530,9	0.176,0	2.080,7	-1.080,7
Sign covariance	0.346,2	2.732,8	0.126,7	0.789,6	0.210,4
Rank covariance	0.180,8	3.157,3	0.057,3	0.013,5	0.986,5
MCD	0.406,9	2.754,6	0.147,7	1.074,5	-0.074,5

The results in table 3.4 provide a good summary of the *past* performance of the two portfolios in that optimally computed portfolio weights are assigned to past returns. Therefore, the results are neither practical nor informative with respect to the potential *future* performance of the two portfolios. In this regard, out-of-sample portfolios are constructed by using a fixed rolling window method. The size of the estimation window is set to 200 observations, which is close to a four-year sample period. The optimal weights (denoted by $w_{1,201}$ and $w_{2,201}$) for SH and BL respectively can be calculated by using the first 200 observations. The weights ($w_{1,201}$ and $w_{2,201}$) are the portfolio holding for the next one week (i.e., week 201), for which the realized returns for SH and BL are given by $r_{1,201}$ and $r_{2,201}$. Therefore, the realized return (denoted by R_{201}) by holding the portfolio for that week is $R_{201} = w_{1,201}r_{1,201} + w_{2,201}r_{2,201}$.

Then using the return observations from week 2 to week 201, one can calculate the portfolio weights $w_{1,202}$ and $w_{2,202}$, which holds for week 202. The realized return is given by $R_{202} = w_{1,202}r_{1,202} + w_{2,202}r_{2,202}$. In this way, keep moving the estimation window one by one toward the end of the sample period. Once this procedure is completed, a series of realized portfolio returns ($R_{201}, R_{202}, \cdots, R_{540}$) are generated. The portfolio's return and risk can be computed as the sample mean and standard deviation of these 340 out-of-sample portfolio returns.

Table 3.5 shows the out-of-sample results. The use of all robust measures increases the return on the minimum variance portfolio while reducing its risk, except for the Campbell covariance. As a result, the Sharpe ratio increases by a range of 2.5% – 12.3%. The largest gain (12.3%) is achieved by the Campbell covariance. The improvement is even more pronounced for the optimal risky portfolio, for which the Sharpe ratio increases by nearly 35% – 38%. Particularly, the proposed comediance measure generates the largest improvement. These results indicate that the use of the proposed measures instead of the conventional measure can enhance portfolio performance in the presence of outliers.

Table 3.5 Portfolio performance based on rolling samples

(January 5,2001 – May 6,2011)						
Measures	Minimum-variance portfolio			Optimal risky portfolio		
	Return	Risk	Sharpe ratio	Return	Risk	Sharpe ratio
Conventional Cov(C)	0.246,7	3.011,4	0.081,9	0.370,2	5.387,1	0.068,7
C_{R1}	0.250,4	2.965,8	0.084,4	0.260,3	2.999,9	0.086,8
Comediance(C_{R2})	0.250,5	2.965,3	0.084,5	0.285,0	3.005,6	0.094,8
Campbell covariance	0.279,9	3.041,5	0.092,0	0.260,3	4.483,2	0.058,1
Sign covariance	0.249,3	2.969,9	0.084,0	0.279,1	3.000,3	0.093,0
Rank covariance	0.249,3	2.970,6	0.083,9	0.278,4	3.001,0	0.092,8
MCD	0.253,4	2.954,4	0.085,8	0.287,7	3.040,7	0.094,6

In the above out-of-sample exercise, one can compute not only portfolio weights for each estimation window, but also all these covariance measures. Figure 3.17 shows the time-series plots of the seven covariance measures. It is clear that the conventional measure increases sharply during and after the week of the subprime mortgage crisis, whereas all the robust measures are stable. Among the robust measures, the Campbell covariance shows the largest variation, followed by the MCD and then by our two robust measures, whereas the sign and rank covariances are fairly close to zero.

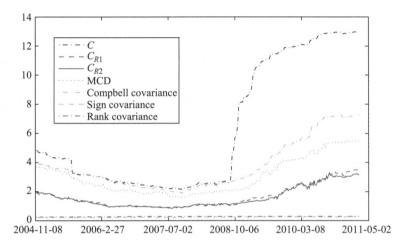

Figure 3.17 Time-series plots of covariance measures

Figure 3.17 indicates that the largest decline caused by the subprime mortgage crisis is approximately in the middle of the out-of-sample period. Given that the gains in table 3.5 generated by the use of robust measures may be achieved after this crisis, it is interesting to repeat the out-of-sample experiment for the pre-crisis and post-crisis periods (i.e. before and after the week of October 6, 2008) to determine separately the potential costs and benefits of using robust measures. The results are shown in table 3.6. In line with our expectations, all of the robust measures result in a better minimum variance portfolio than the conventional measure during the post-crisis period, but they are slightly worse during the pre-crisis period. On the other hand, the results for the optimal risky portfolio are somewhat surprising. All of the robust measures generate larger Sharpe ratios than the conventional measure during the post-crisis period, as expected. However, the margin of improvement is even larger during the pre-crisis period. One would note that the Sharpe ratio generated by the conventional measure during the pre-crisis period is negative (− 0.0436), mainly due to two large negative returns. [1] It is well known in the finance literature (e.g. Michaud, 1989; Best and Grauer, 1991; Letterman, 2003; Kolusheva, 2008) that the optimal risky portfolio can be unstable in terms of out-of-sample performance. For a fair comparison, the same results without these two observations are shown in table 3.7. It is observed in the table that the performance of the optimal risky portfolio is quite comparable across all covariance measures during the pre-crisis period (i.e. showing either not much of a loss or even a gain achieved for robust measures relative to the conventional measure), whereas all of the robust measures perform better during the post-crisis period.

Table 3.6 Portfolio performance based on rolling samples:
pre-crisis period vs post-crisis period

Measures	Minimum-variance portfolio			Optimal risky portfolio		
	Return	Risk	Sharpe ratio	Return	Risk	Sharpe ratio
Conventional Cov(C)						
Pre-crisis	0.068,4	1.757,6	0.038,9	−0.122,3	2.807,1	−0.043,6
Post-crisis	0.647,8	3.992,8	0.162,2	1.252,3	7.647,7	0.163,8
C_{R1}						
Pre-crisis	0.063,4	1.837,7	0.034,5	0.077,4	1.721,3	0.044,9
Post-crisis	0.664,0	3.850,2	0.172,5	0.731,1	4.010,8	0.182,3
Comediance(C_{R2})						
Pre-crisis	0.063,6	1.836,8	0.034,6	0.078,3	1.717,2	0.045,6
Post-crisis	0.663,8	3.849,7	0.172,4	0.728,9	4.005,2	0.182,0
Campbell covariance						
Pre-crisis	0.069,9	1.754,4	0.039,8	−0.126,1	2.990,6	−0.042,2
Post-crisis	0.729,5	4.044,9	0.180,4	0.979,1	5.878,8	0.166,6

---

[1] Two large negative returns are observed based on the Campbell covariance, but none for the rest of robust covariance measures.

Continued

Measures	Minimum-variance portfolio			Optimal risky portfolio		
	Return	Risk	Sharpe ratio	Return	Risk	Sharpe ratio
Sign covariance						
Pre-crisis	0.061,3	1.848,8	0.033,1	0.074,0	1.755,6	0.042,1
Post-crisis	0.664,4	3.850,0	0.172,6	0.720,2	3.970,3	0.181,4
Rank covariance						
Pre-crisis	0.061,2	1.850,6	0.033,1	0.073,7	1.763,4	0.041,8
Post-crisis	0.664,5	3.850,1	0.172,6	0.719,0	3.966,4	0.181,3
MCD						
Pre-crisis	0.068,7	1.808,2	0.038,1	0.071,0	1.715,1	0.041,4
Post-crisis	0.663,1	3.849,1	0.172,3	0.746,8	4.070,6	0.183,5

Table 3.7　Portfolio performance based on rolling samples without two large negative returns: pre-crisis period vs post-crisis period

Measures	Minimum-variance portfolio			Optimal risky portfolio		
	Return	Risk	Sharpe ratio	Return	Risk	Sharpe ratio
Conventional Cov(C)						
Pre-crisis	0.035,6	1.734,8	0.020,5	0.072,3	2.008,5	0.036,0
Post-crisis	0.647,8	3.992,8	0.162,2	1.252,3	7.647,7	0.163,8
C_{R1}						
Pre-crisis	0.040,4	1.830,5	0.022,1	0.066,7	1.720,3	0.038,8
Post-crisis	0.664,0	3.850,2	0.172,5	0.731,1	4.010,8	0.182,3
Comediance(C_{R2})						
Pre-crisis	0.040,5	1.829,6	0.022,1	0.068,2	1.716,2	0.039,7
Post-crisis	0.663,8	3.849,7	0.172,4	0.728,9	4.005,2	0.182,0
Campbell covariance						
Pre-crisis	0.037,0	1.731,1	0.021,4	0.089,0	2.065,5	0.043,1
Post-crisis	0.729,5	4.044,9	0.180,4	0.979,1	5.878,8	0.166,6

Continued

Measures	Minimum-variance portfolio			Optimal risky portfolio		
	Return	Risk	Sharpe ratio	Return	Risk	Sharpe ratio
Sign covariance						
Pre-crisis	0.039,1	1.842,6	0.021,2	0.058,7	1.753,4	0.033,5
Post-crisis	0.664,4	3.850,0	0.172,6	0.720,2	3.970,3	0.181,4
Rank covariance						
Pre-crisis	0.039,1	1.844,5	0.021,2	0.057,8	1.760,9	0.032,8
Post-crisis	0.664,5	3.850,1	0.172,6	0.718,9	3.966,4	0.181,3
MCD						
Pre-crisis	0.043,4	1.797,8	0.024,1	0.078,6	1.704,6	0.046,1
Post-crisis	0.663,1	3.849,1	0.172,3	0.746,8	4.070,6	0.183,5

One may question the significance of the 38% increase in the Sharpe ratio based on the proposed measure as shown in table 3.5. The Sharpe ratio in table 3.5 has been computed using weekly returns. The annualized Sharpe ratio can be approximated by multiplying the weekly figure by $\sqrt{52}$. Thus, the annualized Sharpe ratios are approximately 0.495 for the conventional measure (C) and 0.626, 0.684 for the proposed measures C_{R1}, C_{R2}, respectively. The usual interpretation of these annual numbers is that they are equivalent to the "annual return per unit of risk," which is not very intuitive. For this reason, practitioners in the finance industry tend to use an alternative measure called the M^2-measure, which is defined as

$$M^2 = \sigma_b S - \mu_b,$$

where S is the Sharpe ratio, μ_b is the return on some benchmark portfolio and σ_b is the risk of the benchmark.[1] The market portfolio is typically used as the benchmark portfolio. Hence, the M^2-measure is interpreted as

---

[1] The M^2-measure was proposed by Modigliani F and Modigliani L(1997). For a detailed discussion, see Bodie, Kane and Marcus(2009, p. 855).

the excess return on a portfolio over the benchmark when the portfolio's risk is identical to that of the benchmark.

Over the sample period, the sample mean and standard deviation of annual returns on the S & P500 index are 2.14% and 19.09%, respectively. Thus, the annualized M^2-measures are 7.32% and 10.91% for the conventional measure and the proposed measure, respectively. In other words, if the level of risk is set to 19.09%, then the optimal risky portfolio based on the conventional measure performs better than the market by 7.32%, whereas that based on the proposed measures performs better than the market by 9.81% from C_{R1} and 10.91% from C_{R2}. The annual difference is nearly 2.49% by C_{R1} and 3.59% by C_{R2}. Substituting the proposed measures for the conventional measure entails virtually no additional cost; thus, the resulting monetary gains can be substantial.

3.6 Conclusion

Through both an analytical derivation and Monte Carlo simulations, the results have demonstrated that outliers can have considerable influence on the conventional measure of covariance. It was also shown that outliers are most likely to influence the conventional measure when they occur at the same time in two variables. An implication is that the calculated conventional measure can be large even when the true covariance is zero, reflecting the phenomenon of a spurious correlation. Simulations demonstrate that the proposed measures show good performance in finite samples and that its performance is comparable to existing robust covariance measures such as the Campbell, Sign, Rank, and MCD covariance measures. The proposed measures are more intuitively appealing and more easily computable than other robust measures. Hence, the proposed measure can be complementary to the conventional covariance measure. The empirical application of the proposed measure as well as the other robust measures to portfolio optimization indicates the potential for a large investment gain by substituting robust measures for the conventional one. It should be noted that the out-of-sample exercise is just one example that shows the usefulness of the proposed measure. It is feasible for use in many other areas requiring covariance estimation.

3.7 Appendix: Derivation of Conventional Covariance with Outlier(s)

Suppose that there are two stochastic processes $\{x_t\}_{t=1,\cdots,T}$ and $\{y_t\}_{t=1,\cdots,T}$. The sample covariance based on these observations is given by

$$\hat{C}_0 = \frac{1}{T} \sum_{t=1}^{T} [(x_t - \hat{\mu}_x)(y_t - \hat{\mu}_y)],$$

where $\hat{\mu}_x = \frac{1}{T} \sum_{t=1}^{T} x_t$, $\hat{\mu}_y = \frac{1}{T} \sum_{t=1}^{T} y_t$.

First, let's see the result for the case in which there is an outlier only in x_t at time $[\tau T]$ such that the observation $x_{[\tau T]}$ is replaced by $x_{[\tau T]} + m_x$. With this change, the new sample mean for x_t is $\hat{\mu}_x + \frac{m_x}{T}$ and the new sample covariance (denoted by $\hat{C}$) accounting for these outliers is given by

$$\hat{C} = \frac{1}{T} \sum_{t=1(t \neq \tau T])}^{T} [(x_t - \hat{\mu}_x)(y_t - \hat{\mu}_y)] - \quad (3.18)$$

$$\frac{1}{T} \sum_{t=1(t \neq \tau T])}^{T} \frac{m_x}{T}(y_t - \hat{\mu}_y) + \quad (3.19)$$

$$\frac{1}{T}(x_{[\tau T]} + m_x - \hat{\mu}_x - \frac{m_x}{T})(y_{[\tau T]} - \hat{\mu}_y). \quad (3.20)$$

Note that the third term in eq. (3.20) is decomposed into three terms as follows

$$\frac{1}{T}(x_{[\tau T]} - \hat{\mu}_x)(y_{[\tau T]} - \hat{\mu}_y) - \frac{1}{T}\frac{m_x}{T}(y_{[\tau T]} - \hat{\mu}_y) + \frac{m_x}{T}(y_{[\tau T]} - \hat{\mu}_y).$$

$$(3.21)$$

Chapter 3 Robust Estimates of Covariance 57

It is clear that the first term in eq. (3.21) is combined with eq. (3.18) to produce $\hat{C}_0$ and that the second term in eq. (3.21) is combined with eq. (3.19) to produce zero. Therefore, the desired result is

$$\hat{C} = \hat{C}_0 + \frac{m_x}{T}(y_{[\tau T]} - \hat{\mu}_y).$$

We now assume that there are outliers (m_x and m_y) in both x_t and y_t at time $[\tau T]$ for x_t and $[sT]$ for y_t. That is, the observation $x_{[\tau T]}$ is replaced by $x_{[\tau T]} + m_x$ and likewise $y_{[sT]}$ by $y_{[sT]} + m_y$. The new sample mean for y_t is similarly given by $\hat{\mu}_y + \frac{m_y}{T}$. The new sample covariance (denoted by $\tilde{C}$) accounting for these outliers is given by

$$\tilde{C} = \frac{1}{T}\sum_{t=1(t\neq \tau T],[sT])}^{T}[(x_t - \hat{\mu}_x)(y_t - \hat{\mu}_y)] - \frac{1}{T}\sum_{t=1(t\neq \tau T],[sT])}^{T}\frac{m_y}{T}(x_t - \hat{\mu}_x) -$$

$$\frac{1}{T}\sum_{t=1(t\neq \tau T],[sT])}^{T}\frac{m_x}{T}(y_t - \hat{\mu}_y) + \frac{1}{T}\sum_{t=1(t\neq \tau T],[sT])}^{T}\frac{m_x m_y}{T^2} +$$

$$\frac{1}{T}(x_{[\tau T]} + m_x - \hat{\mu}_x - \frac{m_x}{T})(y_{[\tau T]} + m_y 1_{[[\tau T]=[sT]]} - \hat{\mu}_y - \frac{m_y}{T}) +$$

$$1_{[[\tau T]\neq [sT]]}\frac{1}{T}(x_{[sT]} - \hat{\mu}_x - \frac{m_x}{T})(y_{[sT]} + m_y - \hat{\mu}_y - \frac{m_y}{T})$$

$$= \frac{1}{T}\sum_{t=1(t\neq \tau T],[sT])}^{T}[(x_t - \hat{\mu}_x)(y_t - \hat{\mu}_y)] - \frac{1}{T}\sum_{t=1(t\neq \tau T],[sT])}^{T}\frac{m_y}{T}(x_t - \hat{\mu}_x) - \frac{1}{T}\sum_{t=1(t\neq \tau T],[sT])}^{T}\frac{m_x}{T}(y_t - \hat{\mu}_y) + \frac{1}{T}\sum_{t=1(t\neq \tau T],[sT])}^{T}\frac{m_x m_y}{T^2} +$$

$$\frac{1}{T}(x_{[\tau T]} - \hat{\mu}_x)(y_{[\tau T]} - \hat{\mu}_y) - \frac{1}{T}\frac{m_y}{T}(x_{[\tau T]} - \hat{\mu}_x) - \frac{1}{T}\frac{m_x}{T}(y_{[\tau T]} - \hat{\mu}_y) + \frac{1}{T} \cdot$$

$$\frac{m_x m_y}{T^2} + \frac{m_y 1_{[[\tau T]=[sT]]}}{T}(x_{[\tau T]} - \hat{\mu}_x) + \frac{m_x}{T}(y_{[\tau T]} - \hat{\mu}_y) +$$

$$\frac{m_x m_y 1_{[[\tau T]=[sT]]}}{T} - \frac{m_x m_y}{T^2} - \frac{m_x m_y 1_{[[\tau T]=[sT]]}}{T^2} + 1_{[[\tau T]\neq [sT]]}\frac{1}{T}(x_{[sT]} -$$

$$\hat{\mu}_x)(y_{[sT]} - \hat{\mu}_y) - 1_{[[\tau T]\neq [sT]]}\frac{1}{T}\frac{m_y}{T}(x_{[sT]} - \hat{\mu}_x) - 1_{[[\tau T]\neq [sT]]}\frac{1}{T}\frac{m_x}{T} \cdot$$

$$(y_{[sT]} - \hat{\mu}_y) + 1_{[[\tau T]\neq [sT]]}\frac{1}{T}\frac{m_x m_y}{T^2} + 1_{[[\tau T]\neq [sT]]}\frac{m_y}{T}(x_{[sT]} - \hat{\mu}_x) -$$

$$1_{[[\tau T] \neq sT]]} \frac{m_x m_y}{T^2}$$

$$= \hat{C}_0 + \frac{m_y}{T}(x_{[sT]} - \hat{\mu}_x) + \frac{m_x}{T}(y_{[\tau T]} - \hat{\mu}_y) + \frac{m_x m_y}{T} 1_{[[\tau T] = [sT]]} - \frac{m_x m_y}{T^2}.$$

References

[1] Best M. J. , Grauer R. R. 1991. On the sensitivity of mean-variance efficient portfolios to changes in asset means: some analytical and computational results. *The Review of Financial Studies*, 4:315 − 342.

[2] Bodie Z. , Kane A. , Marcus A. J. 2009. Investment(8th ed). New York: Irwin/McGraw-Hill.

[3] Bonato M. 2011 Robust estimation of skewness and kurtosis in distributions with infinite higher moments. *Finance Research Letters*, 8:77 −87.

[4] Campbell N. A. 1980. Robust procedures in multivariate analysis I: robust covariance estimation. *Applied Statistics*, 29:231 −237.

[5] Campbell B. , Dufour J. M. 1997. Exact nonparametric tests of orthogonality and random walk in the presence of a drift parameter. *International Economic Review*, 38:151 −173.

[6] Davies P. L. 1987. Asymptotic behaviour of S-estimates of multivariate location parameters and dispersion matrices. *The Annals of Statistics*, 15(3):1269 −1292.

[7] Ergun A. T. 2011. Skewness and kurtosis persistence: conventional vs. robust measures. Discussion Paper.

[8] Gnanadesikan, R. and Kettenring, J. R. 1972. Robust estimates, residuals, and outlier detection with multiresponse data. *Biometrics*, 28:81 −124.

[9] Huber P. J. 1964. Robust estimation of a location parameter. *Ann. Math. Statist.*, 35:73 −101.

[10] Huber P. J. 2009. Robust Statistics (2nd ed.). Hoboken, NJ: John Wiley & Sons Inc.

[11] Jobson J. D., Korkie B. 1981. Putting Markowitz theory to work. *Journal of Portfolio Management*, 7:70 – 74.

[12] Jobson J. D., Korkie B., Ratti V. 1979. Improved estimation for Markowitz efficient portfolios using James-Stein type estimators. In Proceedings of the American Statistical Association, Business and Economics Statistics Section, 41:279 – 284.

[13] Kane A., Kim T. – H., White H., 2011. Active portfolio management: the power of the Treynor – Black model. *Progress in Financial Markets Research*.

[14] Kim T. – H., White H. 2004. On more robust estimation of skewness and kurtosis. *Finance Research Letters*, 1:56 – 73.

[15] Kolusheva D. 2008. Out-of-sample performance of asset allocation strategies. Discussion Paper.

[16] Litterman R. 2003. Modern investment management: an equilibrium approach. New York: Wiley.

[17] Maronna R. A., Martin R. D. and Yohai V. J. 2006. Robust statistics. Theory and Method, Wiley, New York.

[18] Michaud R. O. 1989. The Markowitz optimization enigma: is "optimized" optimal? *Financial Analysts Journal*, 45:31 – 42.

[19] Modigliani F., Modigliani L. 1997. Risk adjusted performance. *Journal of Portfolio Management*:45 – 54.

[20] Ollila E., Oja H., Hettmansperger T. P. 2002. Estimates of regression coefficients based on the sign covariance matrix. *Journal of the Royal Statistical Society*, B, 64:447 – 466.

[21] Pratt J., Gibbons J. D. 1981. Concepts of nonparametric theory. New York: Springer-Verlag.

[22] Rousseeuw P. J. 1983. Multivariate estimation with high breaakdown point, paper presented at Fourth Pannonian Symposium on Mathematical Statistics and Probability, Bad Tatzmannsdorf,

Austria, September 4 – 9, 1983. Abstract in IMS Bull. 1983, 12: 234. appeared in 1985, Mathematical Statistics and Applications, Vol. B, edited by W. Grossmann, G. Pflug, I. Vincze, and W. Wertz, Reidel, Dordrecht, The Netherlands:283 – 297.

[23] Rousseeuw P. J. 1984. Least median of squares regression. *Journal of the American Statistical Association*, 79:871 – 880.

[24] Rousseeuw P. J., Aelst S. V., Driessen K. V., Agullo J. 2004. Robust multivariate regression. *Technometrics*, 46:293 – 305.

[25] Rousseeuw P. J. and Driessen K. V. 1999. A fast algorithm for the minimum covariance determinant estimator. *Technometrics*. 41 (3):212 – 223.

[26] Rousseeuw P. J. and Leroy A. M. 1987. Robust regression and outlier detection. Wiley, NewYork.

[27] Rousseeuw P. J. and Yohai V. 1984. Robust regression by means of S-estimators, robust and nonlinear time series. J. Franke, W. Härdle and R. D. Martin (eds.), Lectures Notes in Statistics 26:256 – 272, New York: Springer.

[28] Visuri S., Koivunen V., Oja H. 2000. Sign and rank covariance matrices. *Journal of Statistical Planning and Inference*, 91:557 – 575.

[29] White H., Kim T. – H., Manganelli S. 2010. Modeling autoregressive conditional skewness and kurtosis with multi-quantile CAViaR. In*Volatility and Time Series Econometrics*: *Essays in Honour of Robert F. Engle*, Oxford University Press.

Chapter 4
Quantile Regression Serial Correlation Tests

In this chapter, it is demonstrated by Monte Carlo simulations that an application of usual Breusch-Godfrey LM test to residuals from the baseline quantile regression can result in potentially large size distortions, especially at either low or high quantiles. This chapter then introduces two correct tests (named the F-test and the QR-LM test) for autocorrelation in quantile models, which do not suffer from any size distortion. Monte Carlo simulation demonstrates that the two tests perform fairly well in finite samples, across either different quantiles or different underlying error distributions.

4.1 Spurious Autocorrelation in Quantile Models

Quantile regression models have been increasingly used in many applied areas in economics due to their flexibility to allow researchers to investigate the relationship between economic variables not only at the centre but also over the entire conditional distribution of the dependent variable. In the early stage of the quantile regression literature, the main development in both theory and application has taken place mainly in the context of cross-section data. However, the application of quantile regression has subsequently moved into the areas of time-series as well as panel data. Some relevant papers are Koul and Mukherjee (1994), Koul and Saleh (1995), Koenker and Xiao (2004), Galvao (2009), Xiao

(2009), Galvao et al. (2011), Galvao et al. (2009), Greenwood-Nimmo et al. (2011), Cho et al. (2015) in the time-series domain and Koenker (2004), Geraci and Bottai(2007), Abrevaya and Dahl(2008), Lamarche (2010), Galvao(2011) in the panel data setting.

As Koenker (2005) pointed, the typical IID (independent and identically distributed) condition is usually imposed on the regression error terms in both mean-regression and quantile regression. When quantile regression is applied to time-series data models, it is particularly important to check for any sign of autocorrelation because the typical IID If the error terms are serially correlated in quantile models, the effect is the same as in any mean models; that is, employing the usual variance-covariance matrix for inference becomes invalid and the estimates based on the usual variance-covariance matrix become inefficient.

In the quantile regression literature, there have been some efforts to investigate the asymptotic properties and the least absolute deviations (LAD) estimator, which is a special case of quantile regression, and to derive the correct asymptotic variance-covariance matrix of the LAD estimator in the presence of autocorrelation. For example, see Davis and Dunsmuir(1997) and Weiss(1990,1991). Weiss(1990) investigates how to test for AR(1) serial correlation in LAD regression models, while Furno (2000) studies a testing procedure for random coefficient autocorrelated (RCA) errors based on LAD residuals. However, little attention has been paid to the issue of how to test for autocorrelation in quantile regression models. The only significant exception is the work of Furno (2000) where the performance of the conventional Breusch-Godfrey LM test applied to LAD regression models has been studied by Monte Carlo simulations.

Knowing the presence or absence of autocorrelation can be important in conditional quantile models not only for valid inferences as mentioned above, but also for achieving more efficient estimation because efficient quantile estimation is not generally obtained under serially correlated error terms as shown in Komunjer and Vuoung (2010). If any evidence of autocorrelation is found, then one can make the quantile model under consideration dynamic and then apply the estimation strategy proposed in Komunjer and Vuoung (2010) to achieve efficient quantile estimation.

In the absence of any theoretical prescription, one might attempt as a rule of thumb to apply the usual LM test to the residuals from the baseline quantile regression. In this chapter, it is demonstrated that such an application of the LM test can result in potentially large size distortions, especially in either low or high quantiles. For example, when the error distribution is the standard normal, the empirical rejection rates for the null hypothesis of no autocorrelation are around 30% for both 0.05 and 0.95 quantiles when the nominal size is 5%. Given that quantile models are usually regarded as a supplementary tool for OLS-type mean regression and therefore are mainly used to investigate either low and high quantiles, such severe size distortions can be a serious problem. After documenting the phenomenon of spurious autocorrelation induced by the usual LM test, a correctly-sized test for autocorrelation in quantile regression models is needed, which does not suffer from size distortion.

4.1.1 Standard LM Test for Linear Model with AR(p) Errors

Starting with the linear model with AR(p) errors for LAD estimation:

$$y_t = x_t' \boldsymbol{\beta}_\theta + \epsilon_{\theta t}, \qquad (4.1)$$

$$\epsilon_{\theta t} = \rho_1 \epsilon_{\theta t-1} + \rho_2 \epsilon_{\theta t-1} + \cdots + \rho_p \epsilon_{\theta t-p} + v_{\theta t}, \qquad (4.2)$$

where x_t is a $k \times 1$ vector of explanatory variables whose first column is one, t denotes the number of observations, $\theta \in (0,1)$ is a pre-specified quantile level, and $\boldsymbol{\beta}_\theta$ is the vector of unknown quantile parameter to be estimated. Weiss (1990) studies the LAD case with $\theta = 1/2$ and $p = 1$. Assume that $v_{\theta t}$ are independently distributed and there is no endogenous variable in x_t. More regularity conditions on the error terms will be specified in detail later.

The primary null hypothesis designed to be tested throughout the paper is given by

$$H_0: \rho_1 = \rho_2 = \cdots \rho_p = 0. \qquad (4.3)$$

Since autocorrelation is a common phenomenon for time series data, it might be possible that some ρ_i are not zero. In the presence of autocorrelated errors, quantile estimates become less efficient, and more importantly any inference based on the conventional variance-covariance matrix becomes invalid, as shown in Weiss(1990) for the case of LAD regression. Therefore, the importance of checking for autocorrelation in quantile models is the same as in OLS-type mean regression models. Nevertheless, no formal investigation into this important issue has been carried out so far. In the absence of any theoretical prescription that can be used in quantile regression, one might attempt, as a rule of thumb, to apply the usual LM test to the residuals of a baseline quantile regression. It can be shown that this rule-of-thumb approach can result in potentially significant size distortions(i.e. spurious autocorrelation).

We first demonstrate the phenomenon of spurious autocorrelation caused by the naive application of the LM test. The standard LM test is based on the quantile residuals($e_{\theta t}$) obtained from the following quantile regression

$$y_t = x'_t \hat{\boldsymbol{\beta}}_\theta + e_{\theta t},$$

where $\hat{\boldsymbol{\beta}}_\theta$ is the quantile regression estimator. Once the quantile residuals $e_{\theta t}$ are obtained, the auxiliary regression of $e_{\theta t}$ on x_t and $e_{\theta t-1}, e_{\theta t-2}, \cdots, e_{\theta t-p}$ by OLS is carried out as follows

$$e_{\theta t} = x'_t \hat{\boldsymbol{\gamma}} + \hat{\rho}_1 e_{\theta t-1} + \hat{\rho}_2 e_{\theta t-2} + \cdots + \hat{\rho}_p e_{\theta t-p} + \hat{v}_{\theta t}, \qquad (4.4)$$

where $\hat{v}_{\theta t}$ are the residuals from the auxiliary regression in eq. (4.4). As in the original Breusch-Godfrey LM test for conditional mean models, all the explanatory variables x_t are included in auxiliary regression eq. (4.4) to allow for a possible dynamic model in which a lagged dependent variable y_{t-1} is included in x_t. The LM statistic denoted as LM_T is given by $T \times R^2$, where R^2 is the R-square from the auxiliary regression in eq. (4.4), and the LM statistic is compared with an appropriate critical value from the chi-squared distribution with p degrees of freedom(DF).

Suppose that the error terms in eq. (4.1) are not serially correlated, i. e. Cov($\epsilon_{\theta t}, \epsilon_{\theta s}$) = 0 for $t \neq s$. Then, any rejection of the null of no autocorrelation larger than a pre-specified significance level indicates the phenomenon of spurious regression. To illustrate the performance of the LM test explained above, the data generation process(DGP) and simulation set-up are shown as follows. Assume a linear model and include only one scalar exogenous variable(w_t) in the model so that the DGP is given by

$$y_t = \beta_{0\theta} + \beta_{1\theta} w_t + \epsilon_{\theta t}, \quad (4.5)$$

where w_t are independently generated from the standard normal distribution. To focus on the size property of the LM test, the error terms $\epsilon_{\theta t}$ are also independently generated from a distribution. Three different distributions are considered to generate the error terms, which are the standard normal distribution $N(0,1)$, and student t-distribution with five degrees of freedom $t(5)$ to represent thin and moderately heavy tailed symmetric distributions, respectively, and lastly the lognormal distribution with $\mu = 1, \sigma = 0.4$ (centered at zero by subtracting the mean value) denoted by LN(1,0.4) to represent an asymmetric distribution.

Once w_t and $\epsilon_{\theta t}$ are generated as described above, the dependent variable y_t is generated through eq. (4.5) with $\beta_{0\theta} = 1$ and $\beta_{1\theta} = 1$ and with various sample sizes $T = 50; 300; 500; 1,000; 3,000; 5,000$. For the initial simulations, $p = 2$ is set for the auxiliary regression in eq. (4.4) although the effect of varying the value of p is studied later. The rejection probability(i. e. the empirical size) of the LM test is calculated through 1,000 replications, and the nominal size is fixed at 5% in all simulations. Table 4.1 shows the empirical sizes of the LM test for various quantile indexes $\theta = 0.05, 0.1, 0.25, 0.5, 0.75, 0.9, 0.95$. One can also include the empirical sizes of the LM test based on LS regression for the purpose of comparison. Table 4.1 consists of three panels, each of which corresponds to one of the three error distributions[$N(0,1), t(5)$, $t(1)$ and LN(1,0.4)]. In each panel, sample sizes are in rows, while each column represents a different quantile index (θ).

We first consider the $N(0,1)$ case displayed in the top panel in table 4.1. When the LM test is carried out for LS regression, the empirical sizes are fairly close to the nominal size 5%, regardless of the sample size, which is expected and well-known. However, when the LM test is implemented for quantile models, very different results can be observed. To begin with, when based on median (or LAD) regression with $\theta = 0.5$, the rejection frequencies, although slightly over-sized, are relatively close to the nominal size. However, as the quantile index θ moves toward either low or high quantiles, the size distortion increases symmetrically around $\theta = 0.5$. For example, the rejection probability is about 20% for $\theta = 0.1, 0.9$, but it increases even further to around 30% for $\theta = 0.05, 0.95$. It is interesting to note that size distortions do not seem to decrease or to vanish as the sample size increases, even up to $T = 5,000$.[①] The second panel of table 4.1 shows the rejection frequencies of the LM test when the error term is generated by the moderately fat-tailed distribution $t(5)$. The results are quite similar to the $N(0,1)$ case, except that size distortions become more pronounced at extreme quantiles like $\theta = 0.05, 0.95$ where the empirical sizes are in the range of 35% to 45%.

---

① In OLS-LM test [i.e. the base model in eq. (4.5) being estimated by OLS], the effect of including w_t in the auxiliary regression is negligible under the conditions as specified in the current simulation set-up: (i) w_t is exogenous and (ii) no lag of y_t is included as an explanatory variable. However, when the base model is estimated by quantile regression, it induces non-negligible size distortions either at low or high quantiles as shown in table 4.1. Hence, one might wonder what makes such a difference. As we will show in the next section, the usual F-test does not suffer from any size distortion. In quantile regression, the residuals $e_{\theta t}$ are not orthogonal to w_t, which in turn prevents the LM statistic LM_T from being asymptotically equivalent to the usual F-statistic. Therefore, we conjecture that such non-equivalence between the LM statistic and the F statistic might cause the non-negligible effect of including w_t in the auxiliary regression.

The case that the error term is generated from the extremely fat-tailed $t(1)$ distribution is shown in the third panel of table 4.1. Different from the previous two cases, most rejection frequencies are much smaller and depend on the sample size. When $T = 50$, the empirical sizes are either close to or above the 5% nominal size, but they start to decrease as the sample size increases. The decreasing trend continues even after $T = 5,000$ so that the separate case with $T = 10,000$ is added. In such a large sample, the LM test is severely under-sized, especially for LS regression; the rejection probability is just 1.2%. The decreasing trend of empirical sizes also applies to quantile models as well although it is less pronounced than LS regression. The finding is consistent with Weiss (1990), where the possible inconsistency of the LM test was pointed out when the error term in auxiliary regression does not satisfy the first moment condition.

The bottom panel of table 4.1 shows the results when the error term is generated from the asymmetric lognormal distribution $LN(1,0.4)$. The results are in sharp contrast to all of the previous cases in that the empirical sizes are no longer symmetric around the median $\theta = 0.5$. The rejection probability increases moderately as θ moves to lower quantiles (e.g. it is about 14% when $\theta = 0.05$; an increase of 6% from the median value), whereas it increases sharply as θ moves toward the high end of the distribution (e.g. the rejection probability is about 50% when $\theta = 0.95$; an increase of 42% from the median value).

Table 4.1 Rejection frequencies (%) of conventional LM Test ($p = 2, \rho = 0$)

T	OLS	$\theta = 0.05$	$\theta = 0.1$	$\theta = 0.25$	$\theta = 0.5$	$\theta = 0.75$	$\theta = 0.9$	$\theta = 0.95$
				$N(0,1)$				
50	5.7	29.5	19.6	10.2	7.7	10.8	20.5	29.9
300	5.1	34.1	19.0	9.9	7.0	8.5	18.9	31.1
500	5.2	36.4	23.2	10.9	7.4	10.3	21.6	33.6

Continued

T	OLS	$\theta=0.05$	$\theta=0.1$	$\theta=0.25$	$\theta=0.5$	$\theta=0.75$	$\theta=0.9$	$\theta=0.95$
$N(0,1)$								
1,000	4.5	33.2	19.2	9.9	6.3	9.4	19.3	33.1
3,000	4.6	31.2	21.8	8.1	6.7	8.7	18.7	31.1
5,000	5.6	30.2	20.5	10.0	8.3	10.1	21.3	32.6
$t(5)$								
50	4.2	35.8	21.7	7.6	6.1	7.3	20.1	37.6
300	4.3	37.9	21.9	7.9	6.3	8.2	21.6	38.4
500	5.0	40.7	23.1	9.2	7.2	9.8	21.8	44.6
1,000	5.3	38.7	20.4	8.7	7.7	10.3	21.5	39.4
3,000	5.4	41.1	22.6	9.3	7.4	9.0	22.0	42.3
5,000	5.2	40.8	23.4	9.7	6.9	10.3	22.3	43.3
$t(1)$								
50	4.0	36.1	11.4	4.9	5.3	5.2	13.0	34.8
300	3.1	16.5	6.4	5.5	5.6	5.6	6.1	15.2
500	3.4	12.1	5.3	5.0	5.4	5.5	5.6	13.4
1,000	3.3	9.7	6.2	5.8	5.5	6.0	6.0	10.0
3,000	1.8	4.7	3.1	3.3	3.5	3.4	3.6	5.3
5,000	1.9	6.0	4.1	4.3	4.2	4.5	4.1	4.8
50	1.2	4.0	2.8	3.0	3.2	3.2	3.2	3.9
$LN(1,0.4)$								
50	5.0	14.9	12.4	8.4	7.3	10.4	31.8	49.6
300	4.5	14.3	11.0	7.9	7.2	9.9	32.3	51.3
500	4.8	15.6	12.3	8.7	7.3	12.4	36.7	53.7
1,000	4.9	15.5	11.8	8.6	7.2	11.2	33.9	55.8
3,000	4.8	13.3	11.4	9.3	7.9	10.6	34.0	53.8
5,000	5.4	12.5	11.8	9.0	8.2	12.4	36.5	52.0

All of the previous results on the rejection probability of the LM test presented in table 4.1 is again graphically displayed in figures 4.1 − 4.4, each of which corresponds to each of the four error distributions. The figures visually confirm the previous discussion.

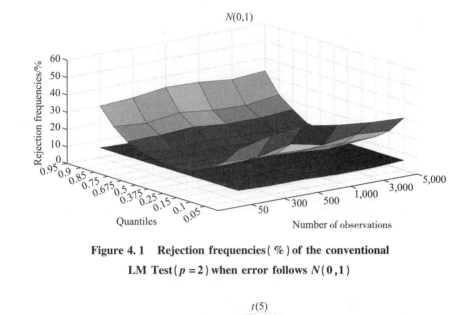

Figure 4.1 Rejection frequencies(%) of the conventional LM Test($p = 2$) when error follows $N(0,1)$

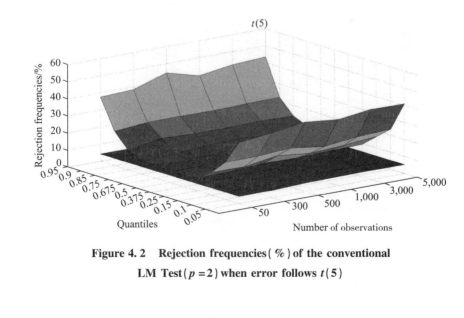

Figure 4.2 Rejection frequencies(%) of the conventional LM Test($p = 2$) when error follows $t(5)$

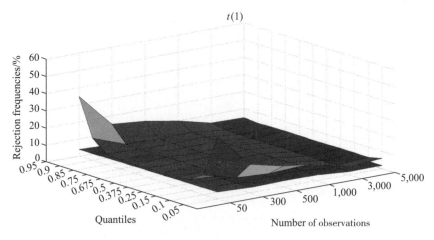

Figure 4.3 Rejection frequencies(%) of the conventional LM Test($p=2$) when error follows $t(1)$

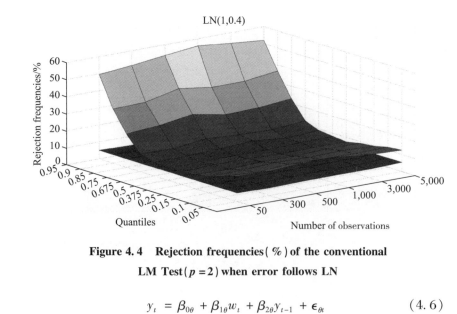

Figure 4.4 Rejection frequencies(%) of the conventional LM Test($p=2$) when error follows LN

$$y_t = \beta_{0\theta} + \beta_{1\theta}w_t + \beta_{2\theta}y_{t-1} + \epsilon_{\theta t} \quad (4.6)$$

where $\beta_{2\theta} = 0.7$ instead of the static model in eq. (4.5). The empirical sizes of the usual LM test when data are generated by eq. (4.6) are reported in table 4.2. It can be only observed in the table that size distortions in all cases are much greater in the dynamic model than in the previous static model.

Table 4.2 Rejection frequencies (%) of conventional LM test ($p=2$)

T	OLS	$\theta=$ 0.05	$\theta=$ 0.1	$\theta=$ 0.25	$\theta=$ 0.5	$\theta=$ 0.75	$\theta=$ 0.9	$\theta=$ 0.95
$N(0,1)$								
50	5.6	53.5	36.8	15.6	10.3	16.5	34.7	55.0
300	5.1	58.4	38.8	15.9	11.4	16.6	37.4	57.6
500	4.5	58.1	37.1	16.3	9.6	16.6	37.1	55.8
1,000	5.4	57.5	36.0	17.8	10.3	17.6	36.6	57.5
3,000	5.0	57.5	36.6	16.7	11.6	15.7	38.2	55.1
5,000	5.5	56.5	39.3	15.1	10.9	16.9	38.7	56.8
$t(5)$								
50	4.8	62.5	41.5	14.4	9.8	14.0	38.3	63.5
300	5.0	67.8	39.4	13.5	11.5	14.0	40.0	66.1
500	4.3	68.6	40.0	13.0	9.2	13.6	41.3	69.3
1,000	4.8	69.4	41.9	15.0	10.3	14.0	41.9	70.7
3,000	4.4	67.6	40.6	14.4	9.4	13.3	41.0	68.2
5,000	4.8	68.5	41.0	14.0	8.9	12.4	42.3	69.7
$t(1)$								
50	4.4	48.5	20.8	8.7	9.3	8.7	20.4	47.9
300	4.0	25.9	11.0	9.2	10.1	9.5	10.4	25.4
500	3.3	18.9	8.1	8.2	8.2	8.4	8.6	21.1
1,000	3.3	12.6	7.3	6.9	7.2	7.4	7.5	12.8
3,000	2.6	7.7	5.6	6.0	5.8	6.2	6.0	8.0
5,000	2.5	6.0	5.9	5.8	5.8	5.9	5.5	6.4
10,000	2.1	5.7	4.4	4.2	4.3	4.2	4.5	5.4
$LN(1,0.4)$								
50	4.7	28.3	20.8	14.4	9.7	19.7	55.4	78.4

Continued

T	OLS	$\theta=0.05$	$\theta=0.1$	$\theta=0.25$	$\theta=0.5$	$\theta=0.75$	$\theta=0.9$	$\theta=0.95$
				LN(1,0.4)				
300	4.5	28.1	21.4	14.5	11.1	18.8	58.8	81.7
500	3.9	27.8	20.4	12.9	8.7	18.4	59.1	80.5
1,000	5.6	27.4	21.4	14.5	11.5	21.8	60.5	80.9
3,000	5.2	24.9	19.0	13.5	11.4	19.7	57.7	79.0
5,000	5.0	26.2	19.6	14.6	10.9	20.8	57.0	81.0

Thus far, the number of lags used in the auxiliary regression is fixed at two ($p=2$) in all simulations. One might be curious on the effect of using different values for p. Take the results with $\theta=0.9$ from table 4.1 as the baseline case and attempt to use other values of p; specifically $p=1,2,4$, and 12, which is typically used in applications depending on the frequency (monthly, quarterly, or yearly) of data. The results are reported in table 4.3.

Table 4.3 Rejection frequencies (%) of the conventional LM test (size)

T	OLS				Quantile regression ($\theta=0.9$)			
	$p=1$	$p=2$	$p=4$	$p=12$	$p=1$	$p=2$	$p=4$	$p=12$
				N(0,1)				
50	5.4	5.7	5.3	1.5	28.5	20.5	14.0	2.2
300	5.5	5.1	4.8	3.9	24.8	18.9	15.7	8.6
500	4.8	5.2	5.8	4.6	28.2	21.6	16.4	9.6
1,000	5.2	4.5	3.9	4.9	24.7	19.3	14.6	11.4
3,000	4.5	4.6	4.2	4.3	24.9	18.7	14.4	9.1
5,000	4.7	5.6	6.3	3.9	27.4	21.3	17.0	10.1
				t(5)				
50	4.5	4.2	3.3	0.7	28.1	20.1	11.9	2.4

Chapter 4 Quantile Regression Serial Correlation Tests

Continued

T	OLS				Quantile regression($\theta=0.9$)			
	$p=1$	$p=2$	$p=4$	$p=12$	$p=1$	$p=2$	$p=4$	$p=12$
				$t(5)$				
300	4.8	4.3	4.3	3.5	29.5	21.6	16.2	8.4
500	6.1	5.0	5.3	4.9	28.6	21.8	17.5	10.7
1,000	5.3	5.3	4.7	4.5	27.7	21.5	15.0	11.4
3,000	3.7	5.4	4.7	3.9	27.7	21.9	16.9	11.2
5,000	4.4	5.2	3.7	4.4	29.0	22.3	16.2	12.0
				$t(1)$				
50	2.8	4.0	4.3	4.9	16.0	13.0	10.2	3.9
300	2.4	3.1	4.9	7.6	8.7	6.1	6.0	7.6
500	1.9	3.4	3.4	6.0	7.8	5.6	4.4	5.9
1,000	2.5	3.3	4.6	8.5	7.9	6.0	5.6	9.0
3,000	1.5	1.8	3.2	5.3	6.4	3.6	4.1	5.6
5,000	1.2	1.9	2.2	3.8	5.7	4.1	2.5	3.9
10,000	1.1	1.3	1.7	4.4	6.2	3.3	2.0	4.5
				$LN(1,0.4)$				
50	4.8	5.0	4.8	1.1	41.3	31.8	22.5	4.3
300	4.7	4.5	5.1	2.4	40.1	32.3	25.7	16.2
500	4.6	4.8	4.3	4.4	43.2	36.7	27.9	18.8
1,000	4.9	4.9	4.9	4.9	43.1	33.9	26.6	18.3
3,000	5.0	4.8	4.7	4.2	40.1	34.0	27.0	17.6
5,000	4.0	5.4	5.3	4.2	40.4	36.5	30.0	18.6

It is well known that using different values of p does not have any effect on the size property of the LM test when it is based on LS regression. This is confirmed in the first four columns in table 4.3. The rejection probability does not vary with p for LS regression. The only exception occurs when $p = 12$ and $T = 50$. For example, the empirical size is 1.5% for the $N(0,1)$ case with $p = 12$ and $T = 50$. This must be due to the small number of degrees of freedom in the auxiliary regression for the LM test because there are too many parameters to be estimated relative to the sample size.

The invariance property of the LM test with respect to the value of p, however, breaks down for quantile regression as clearly shown in columns 5 – 8 in table 4.3. A common pattern over all the three error distributions is that the rejection probability tends to decrease as p increases. For example, the rejection probability with $T = 500$ in the case of the $t(5)$ error distribution is given by 28.6%, 21,8%, 17.5% and 10.7% for $p = 1,2,4$, and 12, respectively. Therefore, the size distortion problem in the LM test used in quantile regression models can be lessened by employing a large value of p. However, not only will it not completely eliminate the problem, but it is also likely to cause a reduction in power of the LM test.

4.1.2 Theoretical Explanation to the Occurance of Spurious Autocorrelation

The main reason is that the asymptotic distribution of the LM statistic, LM_T is not the usual chi-squared distribution with p degrees of freedom. In deriving the correct asymptotic distribution of LM_T, two cases are considered: (i) the quantile error $\epsilon_{\theta t}$ is heteroscedastic in the sense that $E[\epsilon_{\theta t} \mid x_t] = x'_t \gamma_0$ under the null hypothesis for some value of γ_0, and (ii) $\epsilon_{\theta t}$ is homoscedastic in the sense that $E[\epsilon_{\theta t} \mid x_t]$ is constant. Obviously, the latter is a special case of the former. To formerly derive the correct asymptotic distribution of LM_T, first impose the following standard assumptions. In all assumptions, lemmas, theorems and calculations below, the primary null hypothesis in eq. (4.3) will be imposed, even when it is not explicitly stated. Thus, the assumptions imposed on $\epsilon_{\theta t}$ below are the same as for $v_{\theta t}$ under the null hypothesis.

Assumption 1

(i) Given $\theta \in (0,1)$, the true quantile parameter β_θ is an interior point in the parameter space Θ.

(ii) The quantile error $\epsilon_{\theta t}$ is independent of x_{t-i} for $i > 0$ and satisfies the quantile version of the orthogonality condition $E(\psi_\theta(\epsilon_{\theta t}) \mid x_t) = 0$ almost surely for every t where $\psi_\theta(u) = \theta - 1_{[u \leq 0]}$.

(iii) The distribution function of $\epsilon_{\theta t}$ conditional on x_t has a continuous density $f_{\epsilon_{\theta t}}(\cdot)$ that satisfies $0 < f_{\epsilon_{\theta t}}(0) < \infty$ for all $t = 1, \cdots, T$.

(iv) The sequence $\{(x_t, \epsilon_{\theta t})\}$ is mixed with either φ of size $-r/2(r-1)$, $r \geq 2$ or α of size $-r/(r-2)$, $r > 2$.

(v) Let $z_t = (x'_t, \tilde{\epsilon}'_{\theta t})'$ where $\tilde{\epsilon}'_{\theta t} = (\epsilon_{\theta t-1}, \cdots, \epsilon_{\theta t-p})'$. Then, $E|z_{ti}|^{2(r+\delta)} < \Delta < \infty$ for some $\delta > 0$, and for all $i = 1, \cdots, k+p$ and t.

(vi) $E[|z_{ti}\epsilon_{\theta t}|^r] < \infty$ for every t.

(vii) $E[\frac{1}{T}\sum_{t=1}^{T} z_t z'_t]$ is positive, definite uniformly in T.

When deriving the asymptotic distribution of the LM statistic, one will need to deal with the probability limit of two sample moments M_{Tz} and Q_T, which are respectively defined as:

$$M_{Tz} = \frac{1}{T}\sum z_t z'_t = \begin{pmatrix} \frac{1}{T}\sum x_t x'_t & \frac{1}{T}\sum x_t \tilde{\epsilon}'_{\theta t} \\ \frac{1}{T}\sum \tilde{\epsilon}_{\theta t} x'_t & \frac{1}{T}\sum \tilde{\epsilon}_{\theta t} \tilde{\epsilon}'_{\theta t} \end{pmatrix},$$

$$Q_T = \begin{pmatrix} \frac{1}{T}\sum \psi_\theta(\epsilon_{\theta t})^2 x_t x'_t & \frac{1}{T}\sum \epsilon^*_{\theta t} \psi_\theta(\epsilon_{\theta t}) x_t z'_t \\ \frac{1}{T}\sum \epsilon^*_{\theta t} \psi_\theta(\epsilon_{\theta t}) z_t x'_t & \frac{1}{T}\sum \epsilon^{*2}_{\theta t} z_t z'_t \end{pmatrix},$$

where $\epsilon^*_{\theta t} = \epsilon_{\theta t} - E[\epsilon_{\theta t} \mid x_t]$. Under Assumption 1, one can apply the law of large numbers for mixing sequences to obtain the following:

$$M_{Tz} \xrightarrow{p} M_z = \begin{pmatrix} M_x & M_{x\epsilon} \\ M'_{x\epsilon} & M_\epsilon \end{pmatrix},$$

$$Q_T \xrightarrow{p} Q = \begin{pmatrix} \theta(1-\theta)M_x & M_{zx,\epsilon} \\ M'_{zx,\epsilon} & M_{z,\epsilon} \end{pmatrix},$$

where $M_x = \lim_{T\to\infty} E\left[\frac{1}{T}\sum x_t x'_t\right]$, $M_{x\epsilon} = \lim_{T\to\infty} E\left[\frac{1}{T}\sum x_t \tilde{\epsilon}'_{\theta t}\right]$,

$M_\epsilon = \lim_{T\to\infty} E\left[\frac{1}{T}\sum \tilde{\epsilon}_{\theta t} \tilde{\epsilon}'_{\theta t}\right]$, $M_{zx,\epsilon} = \lim_{T\to\infty} E\left[\frac{1}{T}\sum \epsilon^*_{\theta t} \psi_\theta(\epsilon_{\theta t}) x_t z'_t\right]$,

and $M_{z,\epsilon} = \lim_{T\to\infty} E\left[\frac{1}{T}\sum \epsilon^{*2}_{\theta t} z_t z'_t\right]$. Note that M_ϵ is not necessarily a diagonal matrix as in the LS framework because $E(\tilde{\epsilon}_{\theta t})$ is not necessarily zero. And $M_{zx,\epsilon}$ can be decomposed as follows:

$$M_{zx,\epsilon} = (M_{x,\epsilon} \quad M_{x\epsilon,\epsilon}),$$

where $M_{x,\epsilon} = \lim_{T\to\infty} E\left[\frac{1}{T}\sum \epsilon^*_{\theta t} \psi_\theta(\epsilon_{\theta t}) x_t x'_t\right]$ and

$M_{x\epsilon,\epsilon} = \lim_{T\to\infty} E\left[\frac{1}{T}\sum \epsilon^*_{\theta t} \psi_\theta(\epsilon_{\theta t}) x_t \tilde{\epsilon}'_{\theta t}\right]$.

Based on the previous two results, the following lemma is proposed which is useful in proving the main theorem on the asymptotic distribution of the LM statistic LM_T. In the lemma, $\mathbf{0}_{m,n}$ is the $m \times n$ matrix of zeros and I_n is the $n \times n$ identity matrix.

Lemma 1. Suppose that (i) Assumption 1 holds and (ii) $\epsilon_{\theta t}$ is heteroscedastic. Let $\hat{\gamma} = (\hat{\gamma}'_0, \hat{\rho}_1, \cdots, \hat{\rho}_p)'$. Define $\gamma = (\gamma'_0 \mathbf{0}'_p)'$ where γ'_0 is the $k \times 1$ vector such that $E[\epsilon_{\theta t} \mid x_t] = x'_t \gamma_0$. Then, the asymptotic distribution of $\hat{\gamma}$ under the null hypothesis in eq. (4.3) is given by:

$$\sqrt{T}(\hat{\gamma} - \gamma) \xrightarrow{d} N(\mathbf{0}, A + M_z^{-1} M_{z,\epsilon} M_z^{-1}),$$

where

$$A = \begin{pmatrix} A_1 + A_2 & A_3 \\ A'_3 & \mathbf{0}_{p,p} \end{pmatrix}$$

$A_1 = \theta(1-\theta)(P_0 M_x - M_x^{-1} M_{x\epsilon} PM'_{x\epsilon}) D^{-1} M_x D^{-1} (P_0 M_x - M_x^{-1} M_{x\epsilon} PM'_{x\epsilon})'$,

$A_2 = (P_0 M_x - M_x^{-1} M_{x\epsilon} PM'_{x\epsilon}) D^{-1} (P_0 M_{x,\epsilon} - M_x^{-1} M_{x\epsilon,\epsilon} PM'_{x\epsilon,\epsilon})'$,

$A_3 = -(P_0 M_x - M_x^{-1} M_{x\epsilon} PM'_{x\epsilon}) D^{-1} (-PM'_{x\epsilon} M_x^{-1} M_{x,\epsilon} + PM'_{x\epsilon,\epsilon})'$,

$P_0 = (M_x - M_{x\epsilon} M_\epsilon^{-1} M'_{x\epsilon})^{-1}$,

$P = (M_\epsilon - M'_{x\epsilon} M_x^{-1} M_{x\epsilon})^{-1}$,

$D = \lim_{T\to\infty} \frac{1}{T} \sum E[f_{\epsilon_{\theta t}}(0)^2 x_t x'_t]$.

All technical proofs are provided in the Appendix. Using Lemma 1, one can prove that the LM statistic either diverges to infinity or weakly converges to a distribution that is different from the chi-squared distribution with p degrees of freedom, depending on the heteroscedastic nature of the quantile error $\epsilon_{\theta t}$.

Theorem 1. Suppose that Assumption 1 holds.

(i) If $\epsilon_{\theta t}$ is heteroscedastic, then

$$\mathrm{LM}_T \xrightarrow{p} \infty .$$

(ii) If $\epsilon_{\theta t}$ is homoscedastic, then

$$\mathrm{LM}_T \xrightarrow{d} B'(R_1 M_z^{-1} R'_1)^{-1} B$$

where $B \sim N(\mathbf{0}_{k+p-1,1}, R_1(A + M_z^{-1} M_{z,\epsilon} M_z^{-1}) R'_1)$ and $R_1 = (\mathbf{0}_{k+p-1,1}, I_{k+p-1})$.

4.2 Correctly-sized Tests

4.2.1 QF test

In this section, an alternative test for autocorrelation is proposed, which can be used in quantile regression models without size distortion. The proposed test is the usual F-test for the null hypothesis that all of the parameters for the lagged residuals in the auxiliary regression in eq. (4.4) are jointly zero. The proposed test is called the QF test.

The test statistic (denoted by QF_T) for the QF test for this null hypothesis in eq. (4.3) is given by

$$\mathrm{QF}_T = \frac{(\sum_{t=1}^T \tilde{v}_{\theta t}^2 - \sum_{t=1}^T \hat{v}_{\theta t}^2)}{\sum_{t=1}^T \hat{v}_{\theta t}^2/(T-p-k)}, \qquad (4.7)$$

where $\hat{v}_{\theta t}$ is the residuals from the unrestricted auxiliary regression in eq. (4.4), and $\tilde{v}_{\theta t}$ is the residuals from the restricted auxiliary regression where the null hypothesis is imposed. The following theorem demonstrates that the QF statistic is asymptotically distributed as the chi-squared distribution with p degrees of freedom.

Theorem 2. Suppose that (i) Assumption 1 holds and (ii) $\epsilon_{\theta t}$ is homoscedastic. Then, we have

$$\mathrm{QF}_T \xrightarrow{d} \chi_p^2,$$

provided that the null hypothesis eq. (4.3) is correct.

Using elementary matrix manipulations, the QF statistic in eq. (4.7) can be equivalently written in a form of the Wald statistic:

$$\mathrm{QF}_T = (\sqrt{T} \boldsymbol{R}_2 \, \hat{\boldsymbol{\gamma}})(\boldsymbol{R}_2 \, \widetilde{\boldsymbol{M}}_{Tz}^{-1} \boldsymbol{R}'_2)^{-1} (\sqrt{T} \boldsymbol{R}_2 \, \hat{\boldsymbol{\gamma}})/s^2, \qquad (4.8)$$

where $\boldsymbol{R}_2 = (\boldsymbol{0}_{p,k}, \boldsymbol{I}_p)$, $\widetilde{\boldsymbol{M}}_{Tz} = \dfrac{1}{T}\sum_{t=1}^{T} \tilde{z}_t \tilde{z}'_t$, $\tilde{z}_t = (x'_t, e_{\theta t-1}, \cdots, e_{\theta t-p})'$ and $s^2 = \sum_{t=1}^{T} \hat{v}_{\theta t}^2 /(T - p - k)$. Theorem 2 is valid only under homoscedasticity. If the errors are heteroscedastic, then the correct Wald statistic (denoted as QF_T^H) is obtained using the typical robust variance-covariance estimator as follows:

$$\mathrm{QF}_T^H = (\sqrt{T} \boldsymbol{R}_2 \, \hat{\boldsymbol{\gamma}})(\boldsymbol{R}_2 \, \hat{\boldsymbol{V}} \boldsymbol{R}'_2)^{-1} (\sqrt{T} \boldsymbol{R}_2 \, \hat{\boldsymbol{\gamma}})', \qquad (4.9)$$

where $\hat{\boldsymbol{V}} = \widetilde{\boldsymbol{M}}_{Tz}^{-1} \boldsymbol{M}_{Tz,\epsilon} \widetilde{\boldsymbol{M}}_{Tz}^{-1}$, and $\boldsymbol{M}_{Tz,\epsilon} = \dfrac{1}{T}\sum_{t=1}^{T} e_{\theta t}^2 \tilde{z}_t \tilde{z}'_t$. The following theorem shows that QF_T^H converges to χ_p^2 in distribution under the null hypothesis under consideration.

Theorem 3. Suppose that (i) Assumption 1 holds and (ii) $\epsilon_{\theta t}$ is heteroscedastic. Then, we have

$$\mathrm{QF}_T^H \xrightarrow{d} \chi_p^2,$$

provided that the null hypothesis eq. (4.3) is correct.

Note that, although Theorem 3 is stated and proved under heteroscedasticity, it is still valid even under homoscedasticity because the difference between the two variance-covariance terms in eq. (4.8) and eq. (4.9) (i.e. $\boldsymbol{R}_2 \boldsymbol{M}_{Tz}^{-1} \boldsymbol{R}'_2$ and $\boldsymbol{R}_2 \boldsymbol{M}_{Tz}^{-1} \boldsymbol{M}_{Tz,\epsilon} \boldsymbol{M}_{Tz}^{-1} \boldsymbol{R}'_2$) becomes negligible as the sample size increases.

4.2.2 The QR-LM Test

For simplicity, let us assume that the function in eq. (4.1) is linear;

Chapter 4 Quantile Regression Serial Correlation Tests   79

$h(x_t, \boldsymbol{\beta}_\theta) = x'_t \boldsymbol{\beta}_\theta$. Assuming some regularity conditions, Kim and White (2003) proved that

$$T^{-1/2} \sum_{t=1}^{T} x_t \psi_\theta(e_{\theta t}) = o_p(1), \qquad (4.10)$$

where $e_{\theta t} = y_t - x'_t \hat{\boldsymbol{\beta}}_\theta$, $\hat{\boldsymbol{\beta}}_\theta$ is the θth quantile estimator, and $\psi_\theta(z) = \theta - 1_{[z \leq 0]}$. The result in eq. (4.10) can be considered as the orthogonality condition between the regressor x_t and the transformed residuals $\psi_\theta(e_{\theta t})$. Given such an orthogonality condition, an argument in Weiss (1990, pp137) can be used to consider the following auxiliary regression:

$$\psi_\theta(e_{\theta t}) = x'_t \tilde{\boldsymbol{\beta}} + \tilde{\rho}_1 e_{\theta t-1} + \tilde{\rho}_2 e_{\theta t-2} + \cdots + \tilde{\rho}_p e_{\theta t-p} + \tilde{\eta}_t. \qquad (4.11)$$

The modified auxiliary regression in eq. (4.12) is the same as eq. (4.4) except that the dependent variable is not the residual itself $e_{\theta t}$, but the transformed residual $\psi_\theta(e_{\theta t})$. The LM statistic is given by $T \times R^2$ where R^2 is the R-square from the modified auxiliary regression in eq. (4.12). The new LM test is called as the QR-LM test. Under the null hypothesis that $\rho_1 = \rho_2 = \cdots = \rho_p = 0$, it can be shown that the QR-LM statistic follows asymptotically the chi-squared distribution with p degrees of freedom. ①

---

① It can be shown that the QR-LM statistic ($T \times R^2$) can be numerically the same as the following statistic (denoted as QLM):

$$QLM = S(\theta)' I(\theta)^{-1} S(\theta),$$

where

$$S(\theta) = \begin{pmatrix} \sum_{t=1}^{T} x_t \psi_\theta(e_{\theta t}) \\ \sum_{t=1}^{T} \tilde{e}_t \psi_\theta(e_{\theta t}) \end{pmatrix},$$

$$I(\theta) = \begin{pmatrix} \sum_{t=1}^{T} \psi_\theta(e_{\theta t})^2 x'_t x_t & \sum_{t=1}^{T} \psi_\theta(e_{\theta t})^2 x'_t \tilde{e}_t \\ \sum_{t=1}^{T} \psi_\theta(e_{\theta t})^2 \tilde{e}'_t x_t & \sum_{t=1}^{T} \psi_\theta(e_{\theta t})^2 \tilde{e}'_t \tilde{e}_t \end{pmatrix},$$

$$\tilde{e}_t = (e_{\theta t-1}, \cdots, e_{\theta t-p})'.$$

4.3 Monte-Carlo Simulations

In this section, the finite sample properties of the proposed test is investigated. And the proposed test will be camparded with an extension of the test for autocorrelation proposed in Weiss (1990). Although Weiss (1990) focuses on both the LAD regression with $\theta = 0.5$ and AR(1) errors, one can conjecture that his test can be straightforwardly extended to quantile regression models by simply replacing the sign function in his argument with our step function $\psi_\theta(e_{\theta t})$. Based on Weiss (1990), consider the following modified auxiliary regression:

$$\psi_\theta(e_{\theta t}) = x'_t \tilde{\gamma}_0 + \tilde{\rho}_1 e_{\theta t-1} + \tilde{\rho}_2 e_{\theta t-2} + \cdots + \tilde{\rho}_p e_{\theta t-p} + \tilde{\eta}_t. \quad (4.12)$$

A test whose test statistic is given by $T \times R^2$, where R^2 is the R-square from the modified auxiliary regression in eq. (4.12), is called the QR-LM test. Under the null hypothesis that $\rho_1 = \rho_2 = \cdots = \rho_p = 0$, Weiss(1990) shows that the QR-LM statistic with $\theta = 0.5$ follows asymptotically the chi-squared distribution with p degrees of freedom. Our simulations indicates that the asymptotic distribution is the same for other values of $\theta \in (0,1)$.

For comparability, the identical simulation set-up as in the previous section is implied. The simulation results for the proposed QF test for the two DGPs (i) the static DGP in eq. (4.5) and (ii) the dynamic DGP in eq. (4.5) are shown in table 4.4 and table 4.5, respectively, along with its counterpart in LS regression. It is clearly demonstrated that the QF test does not show any sign of size distortion for all three error distributions. As before, the effect of changing p is also simulated, and the results based on the static DGP only shown in table 4.6 confirm the desired invariance property of the QF test with respect to the number of lagged residuals in the auxiliary regression. The results of the QR-LM test for the two DGPs (i) the static DGP in eq. (4.5) and (ii) the dynamic DGP in eq. (4.6) are reported in table 4.7 and table 4.8, respectively. As shown in the two tables, the QR-LM test performs quite well in terms of size, regardless of the choice of quantile index or error distribution. The desired invariance property with respect to p for the QR-LM test based on the static DGP is demonstrated in table 4.9. It can be concluded that the two tests are comparable in terms of size.

Table 4.4 Rejection frequencies(%) of the QF test($p=2$, size)

T	OLS	$\theta=$ 0.05	$\theta=$ 0.1	$\theta=$ 0.25	$\theta=$ 0.5	$\theta=$ 0.75	$\theta=$ 0.9	$\theta=$ 0.95
$N(0,1)$								
50	5.4	5.3	5.8	5.2	5.2	5.3	4.5	5.3
300	4.9	4.5	4.8	5.0	4.8	4.7	5.3	4.9
500	5.2	5.3	5.4	5.2	5.3	5.1	5.3	5.1
1,000	4.5	4.8	4.8	4.4	4.5	4.5	4.6	4.8
3,000	4.6	4.6	4.6	4.6	4.5	4.6	4.6	4.7
5,000	5.6	5.8	5.7	5.7	5.5	5.6	5.4	5.5
$t(5)$								
50	4.0	3.5	4.3	3.6	3.9	4.0	4.1	3.7
300	4.3	4.7	4.5	4.4	4.4	4.3	4.7	4.7
500	5.0	5.0	5.1	4.5	4.8	5.2	4.9	5.2
1,000	5.3	5.4	5.3	5.3	5.3	5.3	5.1	4.8
3,000	5.4	5.3	5.2	5.1	5.5	5.3	5.3	5.3
5,000	5.2	5.2	5.2	5.2	5.0	5.2	5.1	5.3
$LN(1,0.4)$								
50	5.0	4.5	4.7	4.5	4.7	4.7	4.7	4.0
300	4.3	4.3	4.2	4.2	4.6	4.5	4.3	4.4
500	4.8	5.0	5.0	4.8	4.7	4.9	5.2	4.5
1,000	4.9	5.0	5.3	5.2	5.0	4.9	5.1	4.9
3,000	4.8	5.1	4.9	5.0	4.9	5.0	4.9	4.7
5,000	5.4	5.4	5.4	5.4	5.3	5.2	5.2	5.2

Table 4.5 Rejection frequencies(%) of the QF test($p=2$, size)

T	OLS	$\theta=$ 0.05	$\theta=$ 0.1	$\theta=$ 0.25	$\theta=$ 0.5	$\theta=$ 0.75	$\theta=$ 0.9	$\theta=$ 0.95
$N(0,1)$								
50	4.8	4.6	5.0	4.4	4.2	4.6	4.9	4.3

Continued

T	OLS	$\theta = 0.05$	$\theta = 0.1$	$\theta = 0.25$	$\theta = 0.5$	$\theta = 0.75$	$\theta = 0.9$	$\theta = 0.95$
				$N(0,1)$				
300	4.9	4.9	4.5	4.7	4.7	4.8	4.8	4.7
500	4.5	4.5	4.8	4.5	4.4	4.2	4.3	4.4
1,000	5.4	5.4	5.3	5.5	5.3	5.2	5.3	5.5
3,000	5.0	5.0	5.1	5.0	4.8	4.8	5.1	5.0
5,000	5.5	5.2	5.4	5.4	5.3	5.4	5.5	5.5
				$t(5)$				
50	4.1	4.6	3.9	4.1	4.2	4.2	4.4	4.8
300	4.8	4.8	4.7	4.9	4.8	5.2	5.0	5.0
500	4.3	4.5	4.3	4.4	4.4	4.2	4.2	4.5
1,000	4.8	4.7	4.8	4.7	4.8	4.8	4.9	4.9
3,000	4.4	4.4	4.4	4.7	4.6	4.3	4.3	4.3
5,000	4.8	5.1	5.1	4.8	4.9	4.8	4.8	4.7
				$LN(1,0.4)$				
50	4.2	3.8	3.7	4.0	4.1	4.1	4.4	4.9
300	4.5	4.9	4.8	4.8	4.6	4.4	5.1	4.7
500	3.7	4.1	4.0	4.1	3.8	3.8	3.8	4.1
1,000	5.6	5.5	5.4	5.4	5.5	5.6	5.6	5.8
3,000	5.2	5.3	5.3	5.3	5.1	5.2	5.2	5.1
5,000	5.0	5.0	5.0	5.1	5.0	5.0	4.9	5.2

Table 4.6 Rejection frequencies(%) of the QF test(size)

T	OLS				Quantile regression($\theta = 0.9$)			
	$p=1$	$p=2$	$p=4$	$p=12$	$p=1$	$p=2$	$p=4$	$p=12$
				$N(0,1)$				
50	5.0	5.4	5.1	2.2	4.8	4.5	4.5	1.9

Continued

T	OLS				Quantile regression ($\theta = 0.9$)			
	$p=1$	$p=2$	$p=4$	$p=12$	$p=1$	$p=2$	$p=4$	$p=12$
	$N(0,1)$							
300	5.4	4.9	4.8	3.9	5.2	5.3	5.1	4.0
500	4.8	5.2	5.8	4.6	5.0	5.3	5.7	4.5
1,000	5.2	4.5	3.9	4.9	5.2	4.6	3.7	5.1
3,000	4.5	4.6	4.2	4.3	4.4	4.6	4.5	4.4
5,000	4.7	5.6	6.3	3.9	4.8	5.4	6.3	3.8
	$t(5)$							
50	3.8	4.0	3.2	2.4	3.8	4.1	3.4	2.2
300	4.8	4.3	4.3	3.6	4.8	4.7	4.4	3.5
500	6.1	5.0	5.2	5.0	6.5	4.9	5.2	4.6
1,000	5.3	5.3	4.6	4.6	5.1	5.1	4.4	4.5
3,000	3.7	5.4	4.7	3.9	3.8	5.3	4.7	4.0
5,000	4.4	5.2	3.7	4.4	4.4	5.1	3.8	4.4
	$LN(1,0.4)$							
50	4.3	5.0	4.6	2.0	3.8	4.7	3.5	2.0
300	4.6	4.3	5.1	2.6	4.9	4.3	4.9	3.0
500	4.4	4.8	4.3	4.5	4.7	5.2	4.3	4.2
1,000	4.8	4.9	4.9	4.9	4.9	5.1	4.6	4.6
3,000	5.0	4.8	4.7	4.2	5.1	4.9	5.1	4.5
5,000	4.0	5.4	5.3	4.2	3.9	5.2	5.3	4.0

Table 4.7 Rejection frequencies(%) of the QR-LM test(size)

T	$\theta=0.05$	$\theta=0.1$	$\theta=0.25$	$\theta=0.5$	$\theta=0.75$	$\theta=0.9$	$\theta=0.95$
	$N(0,1)$						
50	6.2	6.0	6.5	7.1	6.5	6.1	5.9
300	5.3	5.6	5.3	4.9	5.1	5.5	3.8

Continued

T	$\theta = 0.05$	$\theta = 0.1$	$\theta = 0.25$	$\theta = 0.5$	$\theta = 0.75$	$\theta = 0.9$	$\theta = 0.95$
$N(0,1)$							
500	5.9	4.7	5.5	4.5	7.0	5.1	5.6
1,000	5.9	5.1	5.1	6.0	4.7	5.4	5.4
3,000	6.6	4.3	4.2	3.6	4.4	4.8	5.7
5,000	4.8	4.3	5.3	5.1	4.9	4.9	4.9
$t(5)$							
50	7.6	5.3	5.7	5.2	6.3	6.7	7.6
300	4.7	5.3	4.3	4.8	6.0	4.2	5.0
500	4.0	5.5	5.9	4.6	5.4	4.1	4.4
1,000	5.2	4.4	5.2	5.3	5.3	5.7	6.4
3,000	5.5	4.8	5.0	4.7	5.1	4.8	6.1
5,000	5.9	4.6	5.9	4.9	5.6	5.2	4.0
$LN(1,0.4)$							
50	8.1	7.0	6.6	7.3	6.6	5.0	4.2
300	6.3	6.4	5.3	5.3	5.1	4.9	3.5
500	6.0	4.9	5.2	5.5	6.6	5.1	5.7
1,000	5.2	6.3	4.1	5.3	4.2	4.9	5.1
3,000	6.4	4.8	4.1	3.8	4.6	4.7	6.4
5,000	4.9	4.3	5.4	5.7	4.9	5.2	5.0

Table 4.8 Rejection frequencies (%) of the QR-LM test ($p=2$, size)

T	$\theta = 0.05$	$\theta = 0.1$	$\theta = 0.25$	$\theta = 0.5$	$\theta = 0.75$	$\theta = 0.9$	$\theta = 0.95$
$N(0,1)$							
50	9.2	6.8	6.0	5.3	6.9	8.7	8.7
300	5.2	5.2	5.2	4.3	4.8	4.9	5.5
500	5.2	5.2	4.9	6.4	4.9	4.1	5.4
1,000	4.1	3.4	4.8	5.2	4.8	5.9	4.3

Continued

T	$\theta = 0.05$	$\theta = 0.1$	$\theta = 0.25$	$\theta = 0.5$	$\theta = 0.75$	$\theta = 0.9$	$\theta = 0.95$
$N(0,1)$							
3,000	4.8	5.1	4.7	5.0	4.0	4.8	4.7
5,000	5.1	6.0	5.8	4.2	4.7	4.5	4.8
$t(5)$							
50	10.3	9.1	7.1	6.7	7.5	7.9	10.1
300	5.6	4.8	4.5	5.4	5.2	6.5	5.1
500	4.7	4.6	6.0	4.4	4.9	5.5	4.9
1,000	5.5	5.0	3.7	5.4	5.8	5.6	5.0
3,000	4.4	4.7	3.5	4.6	4.5	6.5	6.0
5,000	5.6	4.8	4.6	4.8	4.2	4.4	4.9
$LN(1,0.4)$							
50	8.9	8.7	5.9	5.4	6.3	9.3	9.2
300	5.9	5.1	5.6	4.9	5.0	5.6	6.2
500	5.4	4.6	5.2	5.2	4.2	4.8	5.1
1,000	4.4	4.4	4.6	5.4	4.4	5.5	4.6
3,000	4.8	5.3	4.3	5.2	4.9	5.1	5.3
5,000	5.4	6.4	6.2	5.0	4.4	4.8	4.9

Table 4.9 Rejection frequencies(%) of the QR-LM test($\theta=0.9$, size)

T	$p = 1$	$p = 2$	$p = 4$	$p = 12$
$N(0,1)$				
50	6.7	6.1	5.1	2.6
300	4.4	5.5	5.2	4.1
500	5.0	5.1	5.2	3.3
1,000	4.4	5.4	5.4	5.2
3,000	6.3	4.8	4.4	4.4
5,000	4.0	4.9	5.5	5.8

Continued

T	p = 1	p = 2	p = 4	p = 12
		t(5)		
50	7.0	6.7	5.6	3.1
300	5.0	4.2	2.9	3.9
500	4.3	4.1	5.5	4.6
1,000	6.3	5.7	5.8	4.7
3,000	4.6	4.8	6.9	4.8
5,000	5.6	5.2	4.8	4.9
		LN(1,0.4)		
50	5.5	5.0	4.4	2.1
300	4.5	4.9	5.3	4.1
500	5.0	5.1	4.8	4.2
1,000	5.2	4.9	5.2	5.1
3,000	5.6	4.7	4.8	4.9
5,000	4.6	5.2	5.8	5.1

We now compare the two tests in terms of power. The simulation set-up is identical to the previous cases, except that the error $\epsilon_{\theta t}$ follows an AR(1) process:

$$\epsilon_{\theta t} = \rho \epsilon_{\theta t-1} + \eta_t, \qquad (4.13)$$

where η_t is drawn from previous three distributions [$N(0,1)$, $t(5)$, and LN(1,0.4)].

Table 4.10 and table 4.11 show the rejection probabilities of the QF test ($p = 2$) with $\rho = 0.4$ and $\rho = 0.8$, respectively. Table 4.10 shows that the rejection frequencies for the three distributions are quite similar and all the rejection frequencies quickly increase to 100% as the sample size increases from $T = 50$ to $T = 300$. The more correlated case with $\rho = 0.8$ is reported in table 4.11, and, as expected, fairly high rejection frequencies are shown even for the smallest sample size of $T = 50$.

The analogous results for the QR-LM test are displayed in table 4.12 with $\rho = 0.4$ and table 4.13 with $\rho = 0.8$. It is clearly seen in table 4.12

that the QR-LM test is inferior to the QF test in terms of power. The rejection frequencies of the QR-LM test are incommensurably smaller than those of the QF test. For example, the rejection probability of the QR-LM test for the $t(5)$ case with $\theta = 0.05$ and $T = 100$ is 29.1%, while the QF test delivers 91.7% for the same case. It is interesting to note that the QR-LM test tends to be more powerful at the middle quantiles than at either lower or upper quantiles. For example, the rejection probability of the QR-LM test for the $t(5)$ case with $T = 100$ increases from 29.1% to 87.2% when θ changes from 0.05 to 0.5. However, the rejection probabilities of the QR-LM test even at the middle quantiles are much smaller than the corresponding rejection probabilities of the QF test.

Table 4.10 Rejection frequencies(%) of the QF test
($p = 2$ & $\rho = 0.4$, power)

T	OLS	$\theta =$ 0.05	$\theta =$ 0.1	$\theta =$ 0.25	$\theta =$ 0.5	$\theta =$ 0.75	$\theta =$ 0.9	$\theta =$ 0.95
				$N(0,1)$				
50	58.3	56.5	57.4	58.7	58.2	58.2	56.3	56.4
100	94.2	93.1	94.2	93.8	93.9	93.5	93.1	93.1
200	100.0	100.0	100.0	100.0	100.0	100.0	100.0	100.0
300	100.0	100.0	100.0	100.0	100.0	100.0	100.0	100.0
				$t(5)$				
50	61.0	55.8	58.0	60.0	60.3	59.9	58.4	55.3
100	94.0	91.7	93.1	93.4	93.9	93.3	93.6	92.1
200	99.7	99.7	99.7	99.7	99.7	99.7	99.7	99.7
300	100.0	100.0	100.0	100.0	100.0	100.0	100.0	100.0
				$LN(1,0.4)$				
50	56.9	57.3	58.1	57.9	57.3	55.6	53.6	50.4
100	93.9	93.9	93.8	93.7	93.9	93.1	92.4	89.4
200	100.0	100.0	100.0	100.0	100.0	100.0	100.0	99.9
300	100.0	100.0	100.0	100.0	100.0	100.0	100.0	100.0

Table 4.11 Rejection frequencies(%) of the QF test
($p=2$ & $\rho=0.8$, power)

T	OLS	$\theta=$ 0.05	$\theta=$ 0.1	$\theta=$ 0.25	$\theta=$ 0.5	$\theta=$ 0.75	$\theta=$ 0.9	$\theta=$ 0.95
				$N(0,1)$				
50	99.8	99.6	99.8	99.8	99.8	99.9	99.7	99.5
100	100.0	100.0	100.0	100.0	100.0	100.0	100.0	100.0
200	100.0	100.0	100.0	100.0	100.0	100.0	100.0	100.0
300	100.0	100.0	100.0	100.0	100.0	100.0	100.0	100.0
				$t(5)$				
50	99.5	99.6	99.4	99.5	99.4	99.5	99.4	99.3
100	100.0	100.0	100.0	100.0	100.0	100.0	100.0	100.0
200	100.0	100.0	100.0	100.0	100.0	100.0	100.0	100.0
300	100.0	100.0	100.0	100.0	100.0	100.0	100.0	100.0
				$LN(1,0.4)$				
50	99.9	99.7	99.9	99.8	99.8	99.9	99.7	99.4
100	100.0	100.0	100.0	100.0	100.0	100.0	100.0	100.0
200	100.0	100.0	100.0	100.0	100.0	100.0	100.0	100.0
300	100.0	100.0	100.0	100.0	100.0	100.0	100.0	100.0

Table 4.12 Rejection frequencies(%) of the QR-LM test
($p=2$ & $\rho=0.4$, power)

T	OLS	$\theta=$ 0.05	$\theta=$ 0.1	$\theta=$ 0.25	$\theta=$ 0.5	$\theta=$ 0.75	$\theta=$ 0.9	$\theta=$ 0.95
				$N(0,1)$				
50	60.2	13.1	19.8	36.0	40.2	34.0	18.4	16.1
100	94.3	28.9	43.2	70.5	77.1	70.6	47.5	32.2
200	100.0	62.9	82.2	97.5	99.0	96.2	80.7	61.1
300	100.0	83.5	95.8	100.0	100.0	99.9	95.6	81.9

Continued

T	OLS	$\theta = 0.05$	$\theta = 0.1$	$\theta = 0.25$	$\theta = 0.5$	$\theta = 0.75$	$\theta = 0.9$	$\theta = 0.95$
				$t(5)$				
50	62.5	12.6	20.5	39.8	51.8	39.6	21.2	13.6
100	94.3	29.1	44.6	76.7	87.2	76.8	47.8	31.2
200	99.7	51.8	80.1	98.6	99.7	98.3	80.6	51.5
300	100.0	71.4	94.2	99.8	100.0	99.7	93.9	71.0
				LN(1,0.4)				
50	58.3	8.8	16.3	44.0	51.1	36.4	21.3	17.2
100	94.3	33.1	63.4	88.3	89.0	68.5	41.5	30.4
200	100.0	86.7	98.1	99.8	99.7	96.2	69.7	47.7
300	100.0	99.2	100.0	100.0	100.0	99.7	86.5	60.7

Table 4.13 Rejection frequencies(%) of the QR-LM test ($p=2$ & $\rho=0.8$, power)

T	OLS	$\theta = 0.05$	$\theta = 0.1$	$\theta = 0.25$	$\theta = 0.5$	$\theta = 0.75$	$\theta = 0.9$	$\theta = 0.95$
				$N(0,1)$				
50	99.8	39.7	65.2	94.5	97.5	92.7	66.4	42.3
100	100.0	89.9	98.7	99.9	100.0	100.0	98.8	89.7
200	100.0	99.9	100.0	100.0	100.0	100.0	100.0	99.8
300	100.0	100.0	100.0	100.0	100.0	100.0	100.0	100.0
				$t(5)$				
50	99.5	40.0	64.8	94.0	98.3	93.6	66.6	40.7
100	100.0	86.5	98.0	100.0	100.0	99.9	98.3	87.2
200	100.0	99.4	100.0	100.0	100.0	100.0	100.0	100.0
300	100.0	100.0	100.0	100.0	100.0	100.0	100.0	100.0
				LN(1,0.4)				
50	99.9	37.9	66.0	97.2	98.3	93.9	66.4	45.0

T	OLS	$\theta = 0.05$	$\theta = 0.1$	$\theta = 0.25$	$\theta = 0.5$	$\theta = 0.75$	$\theta = 0.9$	$\theta = 0.95$
				LN(1,0.4)				
100	100.0	92.4	99.7	100.0	100.0	100.0	97.5	85.1
200	100.0	100.0	100.0	100.0	100.0	100.0	100.0	98.9
300	100.0	100.0	100.0	100.0	100.0	100.0	100.0	100.0

4.4 An Empirical Example

Fama and French (1996) proposed a three-factor model to eliminate anomalies in CAPM model as follows

$$(r_A - r_f) = \alpha_A + \beta_A(r_M - r_f) + s_A \text{SMB} + h_A \text{HML} + e, \quad (4.14)$$

where the three factors are excess return on a market portfolio $(r_M - r_f)$, difference between the return on a portfolio of small stocks and that of large stocks (SMB, small minus big), and difference between the return on a portfolio of low book-to-market stocks and that of high book-to-market stocks (HML, high minus low). $r_A - r_f$ is the $T \times 1$ excess return vector of an asset or a portfolio. α_A, β_A, s_A, and h_A are intercept, and coefficients for the above three factors, respectively. e is the error term.

Allen et al. (2011) applied quantile regression in Fama-French three-factor model to reveal differences between these factors at various quantiles by using a data set of 30 returns of Dow Jones Index stocks and factors in the range of 2002 to 2009[①]. Conventional LM test and two proposed serial correlated tests for autocorrelation in quantile regression will be applied into Fama-French Model to investigate the existence of serial correlation in this quantile model, and therefore to see whether the quantile estimates are efficient.

---

① The data is downloaded from the data library of Ken French's: http://mba.tuck.dartmouth.edu/pages/faculty/ken.french/data_library.html.

The data set is constructed by monthly return of Microsoft Corporation (MSFT) in Nasdaq(r_A) from yahoo finance website[①], three factors($r_M - r_f$, SMB, HML) collected from Ken French's data library and 3-month treasury bill as risk free rate(r_f) downloaded from Federal Reserve Bank of St. Louis site[②], over the period from July, 2006 to June, 2012, that is, 72 observations for each variable. Quantile regression estimates, statistics and the p-values of tests are displayed in table 4.14, along with OLS results as a comparison. [③]

[①] http://finance.yahoo.com/.

[②] http://research.stlouisfed.org/fred2/series/WTB3MS?cid=116.

[③] It is noted that the test results perform differently with respect to different lag lengths p. In order to decide the proper lag length for autocorrelation test, Akaike information criterion (AIC) and Bayesian information criterion (BIC) with different lag lengths are commonly used as fit measures for model selection besides adjusted R^2. For the residuals of θ-quantile regression, e_θ, AIC and BIC are calculated as [Greene(2003) and Hayashi(2000)].

$$\text{AIC} = \ln(e_{\theta'}e_\theta / \tilde{T}) + 2(k+p)/\tilde{T}$$

$$\text{BIC} = \ln(e_{\theta'}e_\theta / \tilde{T}) + (k+p)\ln(\tilde{T})/\tilde{T}$$

where $\tilde{T} = T - p$, k is the number of regressors in eq. (4.14) and equals to 4, including intercept, therefore $k+p$ stands for the number of these regressors and up to p^{th} lagged residuals of eq. (4.14), which appear in the auxiliary model as independent variables. We assume the influence would not last more than one year, i.e. the biggest p equals to 12 and then compute the AIC and BIC for $p = 1, 2, \cdots, 12$. The appropriate lag length, denoted as $\hat{p}_{\text{AIC}}$ and $\hat{p}_{\text{BIC}}$, would be determined by the corresponding p of the minimum value of AIC and BIC respectively. Based on our calculation, for most of quantile cases, $\hat{p}_{\text{AIC}} = \hat{p}_{\text{BIC}} = 1$, whereas $\hat{p}_{\text{AIC}} = 4$ as $\theta = 0.9$ and $\theta = 0.95$, therefore the appropriate lag length is considered as $\hat{p}_{\text{AIC}} = \hat{p}_{\text{BIC}} = 1$ for the auxiliary regression of QR-LM test. The results with $p = 4$ are also shown in table 4.11 as a comparison.

Table 4.14 QR application to Fama French Model (72 Observations)

Items	OLS	$\theta = 0.05$	$\theta = 0.10$	$\theta = 0.25$	$\theta = 0.50$	$\theta = 0.75$	$\theta = 0.90$	$\theta = 0.95$
				Quantile estimate of coefficients				
β	1.1148	1.0209	1.2454	1.1325	0.9428	1.1361	0.9949	0.9155
s	-0.2575	-0.8273	-0.7291	-0.7272	-0.3897	0.0559	0.1677	0.6085
h	-0.1605	0.3592	0.1245	-0.0410	0.2436	-0.2948	-0.3536	-0.7212
intercept	0.3770	-6.2329	-4.9197	-3.1117	0.0297	3.9406	5.3457	8.7135
				$p = 1$				
LM stat.	1.0913	9.1255	6.4235	3.9166	5.3538	1.9412	3.2296	13.1499
p-value	0.2962	0.0025	0.0113	0.0478	0.0207	0.1635	0.0723	0.0003
F stat.	1.0084	0.8619	1.3569	1.1463	0.6847	0.9445	0.6572	0.3884
p-value	0.3190	0.3566	0.2483	0.2882	0.4110	0.3347	0.4205	0.5353
QR-LM stat.	Na	3.3787	0.9190	3.3380	1.4393	1.8434	5.0179	4.6803
p-value	Na	0.0660	0.3377	0.0677	0.2302	0.1745	0.0251	0.0305
				$p = 4$				
LM stat.	8.3804	12.9819	10.8495	10.5307	10.3244	9.2772	11.2645	20.6249
p-value	0.0786	0.0114	0.0283	0.0324	0.0353	0.0545	0.0237	0.0004
F stat	2.1003	1.3715	1.5176	2.0459	1.5542	2.1347	2.3658	2.6770
p-value	0.0919	0.2545	0.2085	0.0993	0.1982	0.0875	0.0629	0.0402
QR-LM stat	Na	11.1700	7.1447	6.9767	4.8389	6.9404	7.5786	7.5865
p-value	Na	0.0247	0.1284	0.1371	0.3042	0.1391	0.1083	0.1080

The top panel in table 4.14 displays the OLS and quantile regression estimates, which verify the differences of the coefficient estimates across different quantiles. When the main regression is carried out by LS regression with $p = 1$, both LM test and F-test accept null hypothesis of none autocorrelation in error term, based on the significant level of 5%. Whereas the main regression is carried out by quantile regression, conventional LM test accepts the null at $\theta = 0.75, 0.90$ only, while F-test never rejects and QR-LM rejects at $\theta = 0.90, 0.95$ only. The conventional LM test obviously rejects the null more frequently, compared to F-test and QR-LM test, which also can be observed in the third panel ($p = 4$). The application results of the tests are consistent with the simulations that conventional LM test results in potentially large size distortions, however, F-test and QR-LM test perform fairly well, of which F-test is the better.

4.5 Conclusion

Although quantile regression has been increasingly employed in the context of time-series data, no formal investigation of testing for autocorrelation in quantile regression models has been proposed in the literature. In this chapter, it demonstrates the phenomenon of spurious autocorrelation that occurs when the conventional LM test is blindly applied in quantile regression models. One can find that the size distortion problem is more pronounced in either low or high quantiles than middle quantiles. Then an alternative testing procedure (the QF test) that is free of size distortion is introduced. The asymptotic distribution of the proposed test statistic is derived then, and Monte Carlo simulations show that the proposed test works well and has good sizes and power properties even in finite samples.

4.6 Appendix

Proof of Lemma 1: Note that the OLS estimator $\hat{\gamma}$ from the auxiliary regression in eq. (4.4) can be written as:

$$\hat{\gamma} = (\sum \tilde{z}_t \tilde{z}'_t)^{-1} \sum \tilde{z}_t e_{\theta t}$$

$$= (\sum z_t z'_t)^{-1} \sum z_t \{\epsilon_{\theta t} - x'_t(\hat{\boldsymbol{\beta}}_\theta - \boldsymbol{\beta}_\theta)\} + o_p\left(\frac{1}{\sqrt{T}}\right)$$

$$= (\sum z_t z'_t)^{-1} \{\sum z_t \epsilon_{\theta t} - \sum z_t x'_t D_T^{-1} \sum x_t \psi_\theta(\epsilon_{\theta t})\} + o_p\left(\frac{1}{\sqrt{T}}\right),$$

where $D_T = \frac{1}{T} \sum E[f_{\epsilon_{\theta t}}(0)^2 x_t x'_t]$. The second equality uses $\frac{1}{T} \sum \tilde{z}_t \tilde{z}'_t = \frac{1}{T} \sum z_t z'_t + o_p(\frac{1}{\sqrt{T}})$ and Assumption 1(iii). The last equality is obtained by applying Lemmas 8 and 9 and the proof of theorem 4 of Komunjer (2005) to our linear quantile regression case where $A_t(y) = \frac{1}{\theta(1-\theta)} y$ and $q_t(x_t) = x'_t \boldsymbol{\beta}_\theta$. That is, assumption 1 satisfies all the conditions of theorem 7.2 in Newey and McFadden (1994). Thus, using $\gamma = (\sum z_t z'_t)^{-1} \sum z_t E[\epsilon_{\theta t} \mid x_t]$, we can obtain that

$$\sqrt{T}(\hat{\gamma} - \gamma) = \begin{pmatrix} -D_T^{-1}(\frac{1}{T}\sum z_t x'_t)'(\frac{1}{T}\sum z_t z'_t)^{-1} \\ (\frac{1}{T}\sum z_t z'_t)^{-1} \end{pmatrix}' \begin{pmatrix} \frac{1}{\sqrt{T}}\sum x_t \psi_\theta(\epsilon_{\theta t}) \\ \frac{1}{\sqrt{T}}\sum z_t \epsilon^*_{\theta t} \end{pmatrix} + o_p(1).$$

(4.15)

Since $\psi_\theta(\epsilon_{\theta t})$ is a measurable function of $(x_t, \epsilon_{\theta t})$, it is also mixing with the same mixing coefficients according to theorem 14.1 of Davidson (1994). Therefore, under assumption 1, we can apply the central limit theorem for mixing processes to the second term in eq. (4.15) using theorem 5.20 of White(2001) to obtain the following:

$$\begin{pmatrix} \frac{1}{\sqrt{T}}\sum x_t \psi_\theta(\epsilon_{\theta t}) \\ \frac{1}{\sqrt{T}}\sum z_t \epsilon^*_{\theta t} \end{pmatrix} \xrightarrow{d} W \sim N(\boldsymbol{0}, \boldsymbol{Q}),$$

where Q is given in section 2. Using theorem 3.49 of White(2001) and the point wise continuous mapping theorem, we can also easily show the probability limit of the first term in eq. (4.15):

$$\begin{pmatrix} -D_T^{-1}(\frac{1}{T}\sum z_t x'_t)'(\frac{1}{T}\sum z_t z'_t)^{-1} \\ (\frac{1}{T}\sum z_t z'_t)^{-1} \end{pmatrix} \xrightarrow{p} \Lambda = \begin{pmatrix} -D^{-1} M'_{zx} M_z^{-1} \\ M_z^{-1} \end{pmatrix}.$$

Hence, we obtain

$$\sqrt{T}(\hat{\gamma} - \gamma) \xrightarrow{d} N(0, \Lambda'Q\Lambda).$$

We note that $\Lambda'Q\Lambda$ can be rewritten as

$$\begin{aligned}\Lambda'Q\Lambda &= \theta(1-\theta)M_z^{-1}M_{zx}D^{-1}M_xD^{-1}M'_{zx}M_z^{-1} - M_z^{-1}M_{zx,\epsilon}D^{-1}M'_{zx}M_z^{-1} \\ &\quad - M_z^{-1}M_{zx}D^{-1}M'_{zx,\epsilon}M_z^{-1} + M_z^{-1}M_{z,\epsilon}M_z^{-1} \\ &= C_1 - C'_2 - C_2 + M_z^{-1}M_{z,\epsilon}M_z^{-1},\end{aligned} \quad (4.16)$$

where the last identity defines C_1 and C_2. Comparing the conclusion of Lemma 1 and the above result in eq. (4.16), the only step needed to complete the proof is to show that $A = C_1 - C_2 - C'_2$. For this, we first obtain

$$M_z^{-1} = \begin{pmatrix} P_0 & -M_x^{-1}M_{x\epsilon}P \\ -PM'_{x\epsilon}M_x^{-1} & P \end{pmatrix},$$

by using the inverse formula of a partitioned matrix. Hence, we have

$$M_z^{-1}M_{zx} = \begin{pmatrix} P_0 M_x - M_x^{-1}M_{x\epsilon}PM'_{x\epsilon} \\ 0_{p,k} \end{pmatrix},$$

which implies

$$\begin{aligned}C_1 &= \theta(1-\theta)\begin{pmatrix} P_0 M_x - M_x^{-1}M_{x\epsilon}PM'_{x\epsilon} \\ 0_{p,k} \end{pmatrix} D^{-1} M_x D^{-1} \begin{pmatrix} P_0 M_x - M_x^{-1}M_{x\epsilon}PM'_{x\epsilon} \\ 0_{p,k} \end{pmatrix}' \\ &= \begin{pmatrix} A_1 & 0_{k,p} \\ 0_{p,k} & 0_{p,p} \end{pmatrix}.\end{aligned}$$

We also note that

$$\begin{aligned}M_z^{-1}M_{zx,\epsilon} &= \begin{pmatrix} P_0 & -M_x^{-1}M_{x\epsilon}P \\ -PM'_{x\epsilon}M_x^{-1} & P \end{pmatrix} \begin{pmatrix} M_{x,\epsilon} \\ M'_{x\epsilon,\epsilon} \end{pmatrix} \\ &= \begin{pmatrix} P_0 M_{x,\epsilon} - M_x^{-1}M_{x\epsilon,\epsilon}PM'_{x\epsilon,\epsilon} \\ -PM'_{x\epsilon}M_x^{-1}M_{x,\epsilon} + PM'_{x\epsilon,\epsilon} \end{pmatrix},\end{aligned}$$

which in turn implies that

$$\begin{aligned}C_2 &= \begin{pmatrix} P_0 M_x - M_x^{-1}M_{x\epsilon}PM'_{x\epsilon} \\ 0_{p,k} \end{pmatrix} D^{-1} \begin{pmatrix} P_0 M_{x,\epsilon} - M_x^{-1}M_{x\epsilon,\epsilon}PM'_{x\epsilon,\epsilon} \\ -PM'_{x\epsilon}M_x^{-1}M_{x,\epsilon} + PM'_{x\epsilon,\epsilon} \end{pmatrix}' \\ &= \begin{pmatrix} A_2 & A_3 \\ 0_{p,k} & 0_{p,p} \end{pmatrix}.\end{aligned}$$

Therefore, $A = C_1 - C_2 - C'_2$, which completes the proof of Lemma 1. QED.

Proof of theorem 1(i): We first note that LM_T can be rewritten as

$$\text{LM}_T = \frac{(\sum_{t=1}^{T} \hat{\tilde{e}}_{\theta t}^2 - \sum_{t=1}^{T} \hat{v}_{\theta t}^2)}{\sum_{t=1}^{T} \hat{v}_{\theta t}^2 / (T - p - k)}, \qquad (4.17)$$

where $\hat{v}_{\theta t}$ is as defined in eq. (4.4), and $\hat{\tilde{e}}_{\theta t}$ is the deviation of $e_{\theta t}$ from its sample mean. Hence, we have

$$\begin{aligned}
\text{LM}_T &= (\sqrt{T} R_1 \hat{\gamma})' (R_1 M_{T_z}^{-1} R'_1)^{-1} (\sqrt{T} R_1 \hat{\gamma})/s^2 + o_p(1) \\
&= (\sqrt{T} R_1 (\hat{\gamma} - \gamma))' (R_1 M_{T_z}^{-1} R'_1)^{-1} (\sqrt{T} R_1 (\hat{\gamma} - \gamma))/s^2 + \\
&\quad T(R_1 \gamma)' (R_1 M_{T_z}^{-1} R'_1)^{-1} (R_1 \gamma)/s^2 + \\
&\quad 2\sqrt{T}(R_1 \gamma)' (R_1 M_{T_z}^{-1} R'_1)^{-1} (\sqrt{T} R_1 (\hat{\gamma} - \gamma))/s^2 + o_p(1).
\end{aligned} \qquad (4.18)$$

where $s^2 = \frac{1}{T - k - p} \sum_{t=1}^{T} \hat{v}_{\theta t}^2$. We can apply the law of large numbers for mixing sequence to obtain (i) $R_1 M_{T_z} R'_1 \xrightarrow{p} R_1 M_z R'_1$ and (ii) $s^2 \xrightarrow{p} \sigma^2$. Hence, these results together with Lemma 1 imply that

$$(\sqrt{T} R_1 (\hat{\gamma} - \gamma))' (R_1 M_{T_z}^{-1} R'_1)^{-1} (\sqrt{T} R_1 (\hat{\gamma} - \gamma))/s^2 = o_p(1),$$
$$T(R_1 \gamma)' (R_1 M_{T_z}^{-1} R'_1)^{-1} (R_1 \gamma)/s^2 = o_p(T),$$
$$\sqrt{T}(R_1 \gamma)' (R_1 M_{T_z}^{-1} R'_1)^{-1} (\sqrt{T} R_1 (\hat{\gamma} - \gamma))/s^2 = o_p(\sqrt{T}),$$

which delivers the desired result. QED.

Proof of theorem 1(ii): Under homoscedasticity, $\gamma_0 = (\mu_{\epsilon_\theta}, \mathbf{0}'_{k-1,1})'$ with $\mu_{\epsilon_\theta} = E(\epsilon_{\theta t})$ so that $R_1 \gamma = \mathbf{0}_{p+k-1,1}$. Hence, the second and third terms in eq. (4.18) disappear. Consequently, by applying Lemma 1,

$$\sqrt{T} R_1 (\hat{\gamma} - \gamma) \Rightarrow B,$$

where $B \sim N(\mathbf{0}_{k+p-1,1}, R_1 (A + M_z^{-1} M_{z,\epsilon} M_z^{-1}) R'_1)$ and $R_1 = (\mathbf{0}_{k+p-1,1}, I_{k+p-1})$. Hence, the proof is now completed. QED.

Proof of theorems 2 & 3: We first consider the heteroscedasticity case in which the relevant statistic is given by

$$\text{QF}_T^H = (\sqrt{T} R_2 \hat{\gamma})' (R_2 \hat{V} R'_2)^{-1} (\sqrt{T} R_2 \hat{\gamma}),$$

where $\hat{V} = \widehat{M}_{Tz}^{-1} M_{Tz,\epsilon} \widehat{M}_{Tz}^{-1}$, and $M_{Tz,\epsilon} = \frac{1}{T} \sum_{t=1}^{T} e_{\theta t}^2 \tilde{z}_t \tilde{z}'_t$. Since $R_2 \gamma = 0_{p,1}$ and $R_2 A R'_2 = 0_{p,p}$, we can apply Lemma 1 to obtain that $R_2 \hat{\gamma} = R_2(\hat{\gamma} - \gamma) \xrightarrow{d} N(0_{p,1}, R_2 M_z^{-1} M_{z,\epsilon} M_z^{-1} R'_2)$. Hence, we have $QF_T^H \xrightarrow{d} x_p^2$. If $\epsilon_{\theta t}$ is homoscedastic, then the proof is analogous to the heteroscedasticity case, except $(M_{Tz}^{-1} M_{Tz,\epsilon} M_{Tz}^{-1}) \xrightarrow{p} M_z^{-1}/\sigma^2$ because $M_{z,\epsilon} = \sigma^2 M_z$ under homoscedasticity, which again implies that $QF_T \xrightarrow{d} x_p^2$.

References

[1] Abrevaya J., Dahl C. M. 2008. The effects of birth inputs on birthweight: evidence from quantile estimation on panel data. *Journal of Business and Economic Statistics*, 26:379 – 397.

[2] Allen D. E., Singh A. K., Powell R. 2011. Asset pricing, the Fama-French factor model and the implications of quantile regression analysis in *Financial Econometrics Modeling: Market Microstructure, Factor Models and Financial Risk Measures*. Editors: Greg N. Gregoriou and Razvan Pascalau, pages 176 – 193, Springer.

[3] Cho J. S, Kim T. – H., Shin Y. 2015. Quantile cointegration in the autoregressive distributed-lag modeling framework. *Journal of Econometrics*, 188:281 – 300.

[4] Davidson J. 1994. Stochastic limit theory: an introduction for econometricians. Oxford University Press.

[5] Davis R. A., Dunsmuir W. T. M. 1997. Least absolute deviation estimation for regression with ARMA errors. *Journal of Theoretical Probability*, 10:481 – 497.

[6] Fama E. F., French K. R. 1996. Multifactor explanations of asset pricing anomalies. *Journal of Finance*, 51:55 – 84.

[7] Furno M. 2000. LM tests in the presence of non-normal error distributions. *Econometric Theory*, 16:249 – 261.

[8] Galvao A. F. 2009. Unit root quantile autoregression testing using

covariates. Journal of Econometrics, 152:165 – 178.

[9] Galvao A. F. 2011. Quantile regression for dynamic panel data with fixed effects. *Journal of Econometrics*, 164:142 – 157.

[10] Galvao A. F. , Montes – Rojas G. , Olmo J. 2011. Threshold quantile autoregressive models. *Journal of Time Series Analysis*, 32:253 – 267.

[11] Galvao A. F. , Montes – Rojas G. , Park S. Y. 2009. Quantile autoregressive distributed lag model with an application to house price returns. *Oxford Bulletin of Econometrics and Statistics*, 75: 307 – 321.

[12] Geraci M. , Bottai M. 2007. Quantile regression for longitudinal data using the asymmetric Laplace distribution. *Biostatistics*, 8: 140 – 154.

[13] Greenwood-Nimmo M. , Kim T – H. , Shin Y. , Treeck T. 2011. Fundamental asymmetries in US monetary policymaking: evidence from a nonlinear autoregressive distributed lag quantile regression model. Discussion Paper.

[14] Koenker R. 2004. Quantile regression for longitudinal data. *Journal of Multivariate Analysis*, 91:74 – 89.

[15] Koenker R. 2005. Quantile Regression. Cambridge University Press.

[16] Koenker R. , Bassett G. 1978. Regression quantiles. *Econometrica*, 46:33 – 50.

[17] Koenker R. , Xiao Z. 2004. Unit root quantile autoregression inference. *Journal of the American Statistical Association*, 99: 775 – 787.

[18] Komunjer I. 2005. Quasi-maximum likelihood estimation for conditional quantiles. *Journal of Econometrics*, 128:137 – 164.

[19] Komunjer I. , Vuoung Q. 2010. Efficient estimation in dynamic conditional quantile models. *Journal of Econometrics*, 157: 272 – 285.

[20] Koul H. , Mukherjee K. 1994. Regression quantiles and related

processes under long range dependent errors. *Journal of Multivariate Analysis*,51:318 – 337.

[21] Koul H., Saleh A. K. 1995. Autoregression quantiles and related rank score processes. *Annals of Statistics*,23:670 – 689.

[22] Lamarche C. 2010. Robust penalized quantile regression estimation and inference for panel data. *Journal of Econometrics*, 157: 396 – 408.

[23] Newey W. K., McFadden D. L. 1994. Chapter 36 Large sample estimation and hypothesis testing. *Handbook of Econometrics*, 4: 2111 – 2245, Elsevier Science.

[24] Weiss A. A. 1990. Least absolute error estimation in the presence of serial correlation. *Journal of Econometrics*,44:127 – 158.

[25] Weiss A. A. 1991. Estimating nonlinear dynamic models using least absolute error estimation. *Econometric Theory*,7:46 – 68.

[26] White H. 2001. Asymptotic theory for econometricians. Academic Press.

[27] Xiao Z. 2009. Quantile cointegrating regression. *Journal of Econometrics*,150:248 – 260.

Chapter 5
Growth Empirics Based on IV Panel Quantile Regression

5.1 Economic Growth Convergence

Whether poor countries can catch up with rich ones, i.e. whether convergence exists, has been the central topic and main controversy among recent economic growth debates. Solow model (Solow, 1956) predicted that an economy's growth rate is positively related to the distance between the economy's level of output per capita and its steady state. Lots of studies focused on β-convergence, which implies a phenomenon that a poor economy tends to grow faster than a rich one, therefore the poor country tends to catch up with the rich one in terms of levels of per capita income or product (Barro and Sala-i-Martin, 2003).[①] This negative relationship between the initial level of income and the subsequent growth rate without controlling any other characteristics of

---

[①] Many researchers on economic growth are also interested in the shape of the whole income distribution. If the cross-section variance of log output per capita, $\sigma^2_{\ln y_t}$, holds the property $\sigma^2_{\ln y_T} < \sigma^2_{\ln y_t}$, for $t < T$, it gives rise to the other convergence concept, σ-convergence, see Friedman (1994), Quah (1993a, 1993b), etc. β-convergence will only be investigated in this chapter, since it not only is a necessary but not sufficient condition of σ-convergence, but also provides information of structural parameters of growth models as Islam (2003) pointed. In the following context, "convergence" represents "β-convergence."

economies is called *absolute convergence*. However, it was also illustrated that absolute convergence may be applied for regions in one country, like U. S. states, or a small group of similar countries, like OECD, but not for a broad cross section of countries. The reason of absolute convergence's invalidation lies in the unrealistic assumption of the common steady state among various countries. This brought forth another concept, *conditional convergence*, which allows the differences of steady states across economies. As the neoclassical growth theory predicted, conditional convergence is a phenomenon that lower starting initial income per capita economies grow at a higher rate after controlling the determinants of the steady state.

Mounting evidence from previous studies of convergence shows that the presence or absence of convergence depends on the sample of economies. Baumol(1986) verified the existence of absolute convergence among OECD countries and the absence of absolute convergence among 72 countries. Barro(1991) set up a cross-section data set of 98 countries in the range of 1960 to 1985 and found the evidence of conditional convergence among a broad sample of countries. A positive relationship between growth rate and initial human capital was also found in his study. Barro (1992) confirmed the existence of convergence again by using 48 U. S states from 1840 to 1988. An excellent work on conditional convergence was done by Mankiw, Romer, and Weil(1992) (hereinafter MRW, 1992). They provided an explicit formulation of conditional convergence theoretically and tested the convergence prediction by setting up cross-section datasets of three sub-groups of countries (non-oil, intermediate, and OECD countries) in the range of 1960 to 1985 empirically. Considering that their implied convergence rate is much smaller, which is only 0.6% for non-oil countries, than the rate of 2% in textbook Solow model, they proposed to include human capital into regression, along with saving rate and population growth rate, to form an augmented Solow model. Strong evidence of conditional convergence was verified in MRW(1992).

However, there have been two major problems in earlier literature using cross-section models. The first problem is that the different country-specific effects in technology and preference have not been accounted for, which leads to omitted variable bias in estimations. The issue of omitted variable bias in the cross-section approach was investigated in Canova and Marcet(1995) using a Bayesian method. They rejected the hypothesis of the common steady-state level among regions or countries in their study. Islam(1995) proposed to use a panel model allowing for individual country effects. Under the assumption of heterogeneous intercepts and homogeneous slopes, the estimated convergence rate becomes larger(for instance, from 0.005 to 0.05 for the non-oil country group), and more realistic estimates for the elasticity of output with respect to capital are obtained(for example, from 0.83 to 0.43 for the non-oil country group). The second problem is the issue of endogeneity induced in dynamic panel models, which also leads to biased estimates. Caselli et al. (1996) employed the GMM panel procedure in Arellano and Bond(1991) to overcome the endogeneity problem in which lagged level variables are used as instruments. Their estimation results showed a faster convergence rate than previous results without accounting for endogeneity. They also rejected the augmented Solow model proposed by Mankiw et al. (1992) similarly to Islam(1995). [1] On the other hand, Bond et al. (2001) advocated using a system GMM panel data approach, in which all lagged first differences are also used as instruments in addition to lagged levels, which can result in more efficient estimations. Panel data approach allows heterogeneous country effects but assumes homogeneity of technology growth and therefore the same speed of

---

[1] We have also tried to estimate the augmented Solow model. Estimation results show that the estimated coefficient for human capital is either insignificant or wrongly signed, which is consistent with Islam(1995). Therefore, we will employ the original Solow model only in our empirical study.

convergence, which is the main controversy of economic growth issue between panel data advocates and time series advocates. Allowing for the heterogeneity of technology growth across countries or regions, time series analysis is applied broadly (see Bernard and Durlauf, 1995, 1996; Pesaran and Smith, 1995; Lee, Pesaran and Smith, 1997, 1998; Binder and Pesaran, 1999). Lee, Pesaran, and Smith (1997) rejected the hypothesis of a common steady state and the same speed of convergence across countries, and found a large increase of the implied convergence rate, which was highly suspicious. Stochastic convergence was considered in Bernard and Durlauf (1995, 1996), where the hypothesis of convergence was rejected by using cointegration techniques. Pesaran (2007) defined output convergence by probability deviations and rejected log per capita output convergence by pair-wise approach test. However, the time series approach to convergence theory was also problematic and was questioned by Islam (2003) because of the improper assumption that saving rate and population rate are constant over time. Durlauf (2005) objectively summarized the trade-off between panel data methods' efficiency and time series methods' robustness and listed some difficulties existing in practice for time series approaches, like the lack of reliable data, little time variation for some key growth determinants, measurement error problem when log output is trend stationary, short-run output instability, and so on. Islam (2003) and Temple (1999) deemed that dynamic panel data approaches might be the best way to analyse growth convergence issues.

Since there was no guarantee of common surface across countries, Harberger (1987) believed that parameter heterogeneity is present, which was also verified by some empirical studies on a semiparametric linear, partially linear or nonlinear version of Solow regression model (see Liu and Stengos, 1999; Durlauf, Kourtellos and Minkin, 2001; Banerjee and Duflo, 2003; Canova and Marcet, 1995 and Maddala and Wu, 2000; Durlauf and Johnson, 1995; Lee, Pesaran and Smith, 1997; Durlauf and

Johnson, 1995, etc.). Durlauf, Kourtellos, and Minkin (2001) found the evidence of country-specific heterogeneity, especially for poor countries, and suggested that a local Solow model better fits countries than the usually used global one. Liu and Stengos (1999) employed a semiparametric approach and found that convergence hypothesis holds for the countries with more than $1,800 initial per capita GDP. But they did not provide the explicit performance and comparison of convergence rates across countries. Higher convergence rates are found in Maddala and Wu (2000) using a hierarchical Bayesian method, compared to those obtained from pooled regression under the assumption of homogeneity. They also discovered high convergence rates in European countries after World War II, which were consistent with the finding of MRW (1992) and Islam (1995), etc.

In order to control unobserved individual heterogeneity, Koenker (2004) further proposed a general approach to estimate static quantile regression models for longitudinal data with fixed effects, which leads to the interests of panel data analysis for QR. Koenker and Xiao (2006) analysed a dynamic quantile autoregression that captured a systematic interaction of the location, scale and shape of conditional distribution responses. Chernozhukov and Hansen (2005) developed the quantile treatment effects (QTE) in the presence of endogenous by using the usual method—instrumental variables (IV), to reduce the bias. Chernozhukov and Hansen (2006) further proposed an instrumental variable quantile regression (IV-QR) estimator and a robust inference approach for treatment effects, along with a class of tests based on IV-QR for examining numerous interesting hypotheses. Based on previous existing researches, Galvao (2011) did extended research on quantile regression dynamic panel model (QRP) with fixed effects and turned to use the instrumental variables approach to reduce the bias caused by the presence of lagged dependent variables.

5.2 Quantile Regression for Panel Data Model with Fixed Effects

As an alternative approach of allowing for parameter heterogeneity, quantile regression(Koenker and Bassett,1978) estimates the conditional quantile models, instead of classical least square estimation of conditional mean model, and becomes a plausible procedure to growth convergence study. First, since the assumption of Gaussian error is too strict and hard to obtain, quantile regression estimators are more efficient than OLS estimators. Second, quantile regression estimators are more robust to outliers in the data. Last but not least, quantile regression provides an alternative perspective to parameter heterogeneity, which is the central controversy in the growth convergence study. It flexibly allows researchers to investigate the relationship between economic variables not only at the centre but also over the entire conditional distribution of the dependent variable, especially at tails of the distribution. The empirical example in Koenker and Machado(1999) used the similar data and the same model in Barro and Sala-i-Martin's(2003) to estimate the quantile regression effect of initial GDP per capita on GDP growth, which is relatively constant over various quantiles, with perhaps a slightly stronger effect in the upper tail. Canarella and Pollard (2004) applied quantile regression to MRW's augmented Solow model (1992) and found the evidence of parameter heterogeneity, which showed that convergence phenomenon did not take place at lower quantiles but at the middle and higher quantiles. Ram (2008) identified the different convergence rates between the bottom quartile and the top quartile by quantile regression and the convergence rate for the top quartile countries is much bigger than that for the bottom quartile countries.

Considering that previous researches on growth convergence by quantile regression were based on cross-section data only, which obviously suffered from omitted variable bias and endogeneity problem as mentioned previously, an approach, which is robust, possible to avoid omitted variable bias and capable of solving the endogeneity problem, is needed. Galvao (2011) extended the research of Koenker (2004) on quantile panel data regression and the work of Chernozhukov and Hansen (2005) on quantile regression for treatment effects with endogeneity into quantile regression for dynamic panel data instrument variables (QRPIV) with fixed effects, which provided a methodology support in theory for convergence study.

In order to discover the convergence rate at various quantiles in the economic growth model, QRPIV approach is used in this chapter. Considering that the demeaning method to get rid of time effects used in Islam (1995), CEL (1996), and Bond, Hoeffler, and Temple (2001) will not work for quantile regression, the whole problem has to be dealt with. Both country dummies and time dummies will be introduced into regression to set up the QRPIV with two-way effects approach. The results of QRPIV demonstrate the parameter heterogeneity in linear Solow model and show the implied speeds of convergence at various quantiles.

5.3 Growth Convergence at the Conditional Mean

As explained in the previous section, the panel data approach for studying growth convergence has the main advantage of allowing for individual country-specific effects. The classical growth equation derived by Mankiw et al. (1992) has been reformulated by Islam (1995) so that it can be readily adapted to the dynamic panel framework. The growth model is based on the Cobb-Douglas production function with labor-augmenting technological process as follows:

$$Y(t) = K(t)^\alpha (A(t)L(t))^{1-\alpha}, \qquad (5.1)$$

where $Y(t)$ is the output at time t, $K(t)$ is the capital, $A(t)$ is the technology, $L(t)$ is the labor, and α is the elasticity of output with respect to the capital satisfying $0 < \alpha < 1$. Note that $A(t)L(t)$ is typically called "effective labor" in the growth literature. It is assumed that $A(t)$ and $L(t)$ grow exogenously over time t at some given rates n and g as follows:

$$A(t) = A(0)e^{gt},$$
$$L(t) = L(0)e^{nt},$$

where $A(0)$ and $L(0)$ are the initial values of the technology and the labor. It is also assumed that (i) the capital is depreciated at rate δ and (ii) the output is saved and re-invested at rate s. Starting with the production function in eq. (5.1), Islam (1995) derives the following growth equation:

$$\ln y(t_2) = e^{-\lambda\tau}\ln y(t_1) + (1 - e^{-\lambda\tau})\frac{\alpha}{1-\alpha}\ln(s) -$$
$$(1 - e^{-\lambda\tau})\frac{\alpha}{1-\alpha}\ln(n + g + \delta) +$$
$$(1 - e^{-\lambda\tau})\ln A(0) + g(t_2 - e^{-\lambda\tau}t_1), \quad (5.2)$$

where $y(t)$ is the per capita income ($Y(t)/L(t)$), $\lambda = (n + g + \delta)(1 - \alpha)$, and $\tau = t_2 - t_1$. As noted in Islam (1995), if the term $(1 - e^{-\lambda\tau})\ln A(0)$ in eq. (5.2) is treated as the time-invariant individual country-effect term, the growth eq. (5.2) can be framed as a dynamic panel data model as follows:

$$y_{it} = \beta^* y_{i,t-1} + \gamma_1^* x_{1,it} + \gamma_2^* x_{2,it} + \eta_i + \xi_t + u_{it}, \quad (5.3)$$

where $y_{it} = \ln y(t_2)$, $y_{i,t-1} = \ln y(t_1)$, $\beta^* = e^{-\lambda\tau}$, $x_{1,it} = \ln(s)$, $x_{2,it} = \ln(n + g + \delta)$, $\gamma_1^* = (1 - e^{-\lambda\tau})\frac{\alpha}{1-\alpha}$, $\gamma_2^* = -(1 - e^{-\lambda\tau})\frac{\alpha}{1-\alpha}$, $\eta_i = (1 - e^{-\lambda\tau})\ln A(0)$, $\xi_t = g(t_2 - e^{-\lambda\tau}t)$, and u_{it} is the error term. The panel model eq. (5.3) uses the level of the per capita income, y_{it}, as the dependent variable, but the model can be rewritten such that the growth rate of the per capita income, Δy_{it}, is the dependent variable as follows:

$$\Delta y_{it} = b^* y_{i,t-1} + \gamma_1^* x_{1,it} + \gamma_2^* x_{2,it} + \eta_i + \xi_t + u_{it}, \quad (5.4)$$

where $b^* = \beta^* - 1$. Note that there exists a natural restriction between some coefficients in eq. (5.3); that is, $\gamma_2^* = -\gamma_1^*$. Therefore, a

restricted version imposing this restriction is given by:
$$\Delta y_{it} = b^* y_{i,t-1} + \gamma_1^* (x_{1,it} - x_{2,it}) + \eta_i + \xi_t + u_{it}. \quad (5.5)$$

It is typically assumed in the literature that g and δ are constant across countries during the whole period, and that the sum $g + \delta$ equals to 0.05 (see Mankiw et al., 1992, and Islam, 1995). In this chaper, the same value for the sum is used. Therefore, the variation in $x_{2,it}$ solely comes from n. In estimation, replace n with n_{it}, labor growth rate at time t and for country i. Also replace s with s_{it}, the saving rate at time t and for country i, for estimation. The parameter λ in the growth equation is the convergence rate by which the output level of an economy converges to its own steady state level. It can be indirectly estimated once β^* is estimated because $\lambda = -\ln(\beta^*)/\tau$. The textbook Solow model predicts that the convergence rate is 0.02. The elasticity of output with respect to capital α can be also indirectly estimated since it is given by $\alpha = \dfrac{\gamma_1^*}{1 - \beta^* + \gamma_1^*}$ from eq. (5.3). The predicted value for α by the Solow model is approximately 1/3.

We have briefly mentioned the term $(1 - e^{-\lambda \tau})\ln A(0)$ in the growth equation in eq. (5.2) above. Mankiw et al. (1992) pointed out that "the $A(0)$ term reflects not only the technology but also resource endowments, climate, institutions and so on; it may therefore differ across countries" and assumed that
$$\ln A(0) = a + \epsilon_i,$$
where a is a constant and ϵ_i is the country-specific shift or shock term. Islam (1995) advocated that a panel data framework can provide a better explanation of technology shift term ϵ_i. The term $(1 - e^{-\lambda \tau})\ln A(0)$ can be regarded as time-invariant country-specific fixed effects in the dynamic panel data framework. Such a fixed-effect model would be more suitable for the dynamic growth convergence situation than a random-effect model because of the dependence between lagged dependent variable and country-specific intercepts (see Islam, 1995; Caselli et al., 1996;

Durlauf et al. , 2005 for details). We also note that the term $g(t_2 - e^{-\lambda\tau}(t_1))$ in eq. (5.2) represents time effects in the model. Therefore, the panel data model in eq. (5.3) is a two-way effect model.

When the growth equation in eq. (5.3), eq. (5.4) or eq. (5.5) is estimated by least squares(LS) method or a variant such as instrumental variable(IV) and generalized method of moments(GMM) estimation, it is implicitly implied that researchers focus on the convergence issue only at the conditional mean of GDP growth rate. Therefore, such empirical results cannot provide a satisfactory answer to what can happen to the issue if the growth rate is far from the conditional mean level. For example, the world economy has been experiencing a low GDP growth rate as a whole after the 2008 Global Crisis, which is usually termed[①] "Great Recession. " Do we still have economic growth convergence? Is the convergence speed the same in this low growth era, compared to previous normal periods? To answer these potentially interesting questions, quantile regression is proposed to be used here as explained in detail in the next section.

5.4 Growth Convergence at Different Conditional Quantiles

Since the pathbreaking work of Koenker and Bassett(1978), the literature on quantile regression has grown rapidly in many interesting areas in economics, finance, and other academic fields. Unlike LS-type regression focusing on the conditional mean, quantile regression is highly flexible in that it allows researchers to investigate the issue at hand when the dependent variable(i. e the growth rate in our study) is far below or above

---

① The "Great Recession" termed in (Stock and Watson, 2012) is different from previous postwar recessions because (i) it is persistent; (ii) it has a lower mean growth rate, and (iii) it shows very slower recovery.

the conditional mean level. In other words, quantile regression focuses on the impact of covariates not only on the central part but also at the tail areas of the whole distribution. As explained before, panel models were typically used in the growth convergence literature, but it is in only recent years that quantile regression has been applied to the panel data framework.

The panel quantile regression literature starts with Koenker (2004), which proposed a general approach to estimate static quantile regression models for longitudinal data with fixed effects in order to control the unobserved individual heterogeneity. When LS – type regression is used, both the country-specific effects η_i and the period-specific effects ξ_t in eq. (5.4) are eliminated by using the relevant demeaning procedure. However, demeaning does not work for quantile regression because quantiles are not invariant with respect to the demeaning procedure. Not like LS-type regression, in which linear transformations work very well, quantile regression does not hold this property. This problem was noticed by Abrevaya and Dahl (2008), among others, and has been clarified by Koenker and Hallock (2001): "Quantiles of convolutions of random variables are rather intractable objects, and preliminary differencing strategies familiar from Gaussian models have sometimes unanticipated effects." Hence, the relevant dummy variables (i.e., country dummy and time dummy variables) are used in panel quantile regression models.

Chernozhukov and Hansen (2005, 2006) have made a significant contribution to the way we deal with endogeneity in quantile regression models. Chernozhukov and Hansen (2005) established the identification condition for the quantile treatment effects (QTE) in the presence of endogenous variables while Chernozhukov and Hansen (2006) further proposed an instrumental variable quantile regression estimator to estimate such quantile treatment effects. However, only recent years we have witnessed the substantial extension of the quantile regression method into panel data models with endogeneity, particularly by the work of Galvao(2011) who has combined the previous panel quantile regression literature with the work of Chernozhukov and Hansen (2005, 2006) to propose a method that enables researchers to estimate dynamic panel quantile regression models contaminated with endogeneity. We employ this new method denoted as "Instrumental Variable Quantile Regression with Dummy Variables (IVQRDV)" in our empirical study. We first briefly explain how this new method can be employed to estimate a quantile version of the growth equation.

We will assume that for a given quantile index $\theta \in (0,1)$, all of the coefficients in the growth convergence equation are allowed to change with θ. Therefore, the quantile version of the growth equation in

$$\Delta y_{it} = b_\theta^* y_{i,t-1} + \gamma_{1\theta}^* x_{1,it} + \gamma_{2\theta}^* x_{2,it} + \eta_{i\theta} + \xi_{t\theta} + u_{it\theta}, \quad (5.6)$$
$$= b_\theta^* y_{i,t-1} + x'_{it} \gamma_\theta^* + \eta_{i\theta} + \xi_{t\theta} + u_{it\theta},$$

where $x_{it} = (x_{1,it}, x_{2,it})'$ and $\gamma_\theta^* = (\gamma_{1\theta}^*, \gamma_{2\theta}^*)'$. Of course, the corresponding quantile versions of eq. (5.4) and eq. (5.5) can be written analogously. As explained before, the relevant dummy variables are used to estimate both the country-specific effects $\eta_{i\theta}$ and the period-specific effects $\xi_{t\theta}$ in the quantile growth eq. (5.6). If there is no endogeneity, then the quantile coefficients eq. (5.6) can be estimated by

$$(\hat{\eta}, \hat{\xi}, \hat{\beta}, \hat{\gamma}) = \operatorname{argmin}_{\eta, \xi, \beta, \gamma} \sum_{i=1}^{N} \sum_{t=1}^{T} \rho_\theta (\Delta y_{it} - b_\theta y_{i,t-1} -$$
$$x'_{it} \gamma_\theta - \eta_{i\theta} - \xi_{t\theta} - \kappa_\theta w_{i\theta}), \quad (5.7)$$

where ρ_θ is the usual "check function" defined as $\rho_\theta(z) = z \varphi_\theta(z)$ with $\varphi_\theta(z) = (\theta - I_{[z<0]})$. However, $y_{i,t-1}$ is endogenous and some variables in x_{it} may be endogenous either. Therefore, we will employ the IVQRDV method proposed by Galvao(2011) as explained below. We will assume just for clarity and simplicity that only $y_{i,t-1}$ is endogenous, and it is further assumed that a set of instrument variables are available and is collected in a vector w_{it}. [①] κ_θ is the vector of coefficients on instrumental variables w_{it}.

The first step to implement the IVQRDV method is to obtain some prior guess on the value of the parameters corresponding to the endogenous variables (b_θ^* in our case). Based on this prior value, an interval (denoted by B) sufficiently large enough to include the true value is selected as a basis for a grid search. For a grid point $b \in B$, one can compute the variable $\Delta y_{it} - b y_{i,t-1}$ and use it as the dependent variable in the following quantile regression where explanatory variables are x_{it}, the relevant dummy variables, and the instrument variables:

$$\min_{\gamma_\theta,\eta_{i\theta},\xi_{t\theta},\kappa_\theta} \sum_{i=1}^{N} \sum_{t=1}^{T} \rho_\theta(\Delta y_{it} - b_\theta y_{i,t-1} - x'_{it}\gamma_\theta - \eta_{i\theta} - \xi_{t\theta} - \kappa_\theta w_{it}).$$

(5.8)

Hence, the resulting estimators are functions of b; thus, they are denoted as $\hat{\gamma}_\theta(b_\theta), \hat{\eta}_{i\theta}(b_\theta)$, and $\hat{\xi}_{t\theta}(b_\theta)$. The true coefficient ($\kappa_\theta^*$) on w_{it} in the quantile regression should be zero if w_{it} is a valid instrument because it must be independent of the error term in eq. (5.6). Therefore, one can consider estimating b_θ^* by minimizing a norm of the estimate $\hat{\kappa}_\theta(b_\theta)$ with respect to b_θ as follows:

$$\min_{b_\theta} \| \hat{\kappa}_\theta(b_\theta) \|_A \quad (5.9)$$

where $\| z \|_A = \sqrt{z'Az}$ and A is a positive definite matrix. Since $\hat{\kappa}_\theta(b_\theta)$ is a scalar in our case, we simply take the absolute value of $\hat{\kappa}_\theta(b_\theta)$ as its norm to be minimized. The solution $\hat{b}_\theta$ from eq. (5.9) is taken as an estimator for b_θ^*. All of the remaining estimators are obtained by plugging $\hat{b}_\theta$ into the solutions of eq. (5.8), i.e. $\hat{\gamma}_\theta(\hat{b}_\theta), \hat{\eta}_{i\theta}(\hat{b}_\theta)$, and $\hat{\xi}_{t\theta}(\hat{b}_\theta)$. Readers can refer to Galvao (2011) for a more detailed discussion.

[①] Following the convention in the literature, the lagged values of explanatory variables are used as instrumental variables in our empirical study below; specifically, we use the first lagged values as our instruments.

5.5 Empirical Results from 86 Non-oil Countries

5.5.1 Data and Samples

The sample of countries investigated in this section is similar to those non-oil countries collected in Mankiw et al. (1992) and Islam (1995). The sample includes a panel of annual observations for 86 non-oil countries over the sample period from 1960 to 2005. ① Islam (1995) used five-year intervals, since yearly time spans might be too short for studying growth convergence. Following Islam (1995), the sample period 1960 – 2005 is transferred into 10 time points with five-year time intervals. When $t = 1975$, for example, then $t - 1$ is 1970 so that y_{it} and its lagged value $y_{i,t-1}$ represent per worker GDP in 1975 and 1970, respectively while the saving rate s_{it} and the working population growth rate n_{it} are the averages over the period of 1970 – 1974. Among the three explanatory variables $y_{i,t-1}$, s_{it} and n_{it}, the first one surely causes endogeneity, but whether the other two are endogenous is not obvious and hence can be empirically determined. Therefore, we have conducted the Hausman-Taylor test for endogeneity whose results show that there is no evidence for endogeneity in these two variables. To account for the endogeneity bias caused by $y_{i,t-1}$, the first lagged values of $y_{i,t-1}$, s_{it}, and n_{it} are used as instrument variables. As a result, the total of 8 observations only is available in the time dimension in the panel.

Following Mankiw et al. (1992) and Islam (1995), real GDP per worker, y_{it}, and the investment share of GDP per capita, s_{it}, are collected from Penn World Table 7.0. ② The growth rate of working

---

① Mankiw et al. (1992) excluded oil producers from their data set because the major portion of their recorded GDP is from the extraction of oil resource, and as a result the standard growth theory fails to explain their GDP growth.

② http://pwt.econ.upenn.edu/php_site/pwt_index.php.

population, n_{it}, is calculated as follows:

$$n_{it} = \frac{p_{it}\,c_{it} - p_{i,t-1}\,c_{i,t-1}}{p_{i,t-1}\,c_{i,t-1}},$$

where p_{it} is the percentage of working population out of the total population and c_{it} is the percentage of age group of 15 to 64 out of the total population. These data are available in the World Bank website. As mentioned before, we also take $(g + \delta)$ to be equal to 0.05 for all countries and at all times as in Mankiw et al. (1992) and Islam (1995). Table 5.1 reports the sample means (denoted as $\overline{\Delta y_i}, \overline{s_i}$ and $\overline{n_i}$) of $\Delta y_{it}, s_{it}$ and n_{it} averaged over the 8 time-series observations for each country. Botswana has the largest mean growth rate 6% while Malawi and Kenya have the highest mean saving rate and working population growth rate, respectively. The corresponding histograms for $\overline{\Delta y_i}, \overline{s_i}$ and $\overline{n_i}$ over the 86 countries are shown in figures 5.1 – 5.3, which gives some idea of the whole distribution of each variable.

Table 5.1 Sample means of $\Delta y_{it}, s_{it}$ and n_{it}

Country	$\overline{\Delta y_i}$	$\overline{s_i}$	$\overline{n_i}$	Country	$\overline{\Delta y_i}$	$\overline{s_i}$	$\overline{n_i}$
Argentina	0.79	0.21	0.01	Kenya	0.18	0.14	0.04
Australia	1.86	0.22	0.02	Korea, Rep. of	4.53	0.31	0.02
Austria	2.57	0.23	0.01	Sri Lanka	3.09	0.29	0.02
Burundi	0.74	0.10	0.02	Morocco	2.75	0.29	0.03
Belgium	2.42	0.24	0.00	Madagascar	−0.32	0.15	0.03
Benin	1.20	0.23	0.02	Mexico	1.12	0.20	0.03
BurkinaFaso	1.22	0.17	0.02	Mali	1.33	0.19	0.02
Bangladesh	0.70	0.15	0.03	Mozambique	1.44	0.12	0.02
Bolivia	0.38	0.13	0.02	Mauritania	1.82	0.31	0.03
Brazil	1.43	0.21	0.03	Mauritius	2.15	0.32	0.02
Botswana	6.00	0.37	0.03	Malawi	1.37	0.49	0.03

Continued

Country	$\overline{\Delta y_i}$	$\overline{s_i}$	$\overline{n_i}$	Country	$\overline{\Delta y_i}$	$\overline{s_i}$	$\overline{n_i}$
CentralAfr. Rep.	−1.23	0.09	0.02	Malaysia	3.80	0.29	0.03
Canada	1.42	0.18	0.02	Niger	−0.83	0.16	0.03
Switzerland	1.20	0.27	0.01	Nigeria	0.14	0.06	0.02
Chile	1.91	0.21	0.02	Netherlands	1.63	0.19	0.01
Cameroon	1.01	0.17	0.03	Norway	2.52	0.27	0.01
Congo, Peop. Rep.	2.26	0.22	0.03	Nepal	1.09	0.16	0.02
Colombia	1.42	0.20	0.03	New Zealand	0.74	0.18	0.02
CostaRica	0.69	0.17	0.03	Pakistan	2.23	0.23	0.03
Denmark	2.00	0.20	0.00	Panama	2.05	0.21	0.03
DominicanRep.	1.89	0.17	0.03	Peru	0.45	0.25	0.03
Algeria	0.07	0.34	0.03	Philippines	1.09	0.21	0.03
Ecuador	1.21	0.33	0.03	Papua New Guinea	2.03	0.15	0.03
Egypt	3.03	0.19	0.03	Portugal	2.90	0.25	0.01
Spain	2.90	0.24	0.01	Paraguay	0.92	0.20	0.03
Ethiopia	0.61	0.19	0.03	Senegal	0.11	0.14	0.03
Finland	2.70	0.25	0.01	Singapore	4.02	0.44	0.03
France	2.37	0.20	0.01	El Salvador	0.79	0.14	0.02
United Kingdom	2.00	0.15	0.00	Sweden	2.04	0.19	0.00
Ghana	0.95	0.39	0.03	Syrian Arab Rep.	1.59	0.16	0.03
Greece	3.15	0.25	0.01	Chad	1.34	0.09	0.02
Guatemala	1.27	0.17	0.03	Togo	−0.24	0.22	0.03
Hong Kong	4.37	0.35	0.02	Thailand	4.06	0.35	0.03
Honduras	0.72	0.20	0.03	Trinidad + Tobago	1.90	0.25	0.02
Haiti	−0.44	0.08	0.02	Turkey	3.09	0.15	0.02
Indonesia	2.94	0.26	0.02	Tanzania	1.59	0.18	0.03
India	2.82	0.20	0.02	Uganda	1.19	0.11	0.03
Ireland	3.22	0.22	0.01	Uruguay	1.25	0.16	0.01
Israel	2.25	0.27	0.03	UnitedStates	1.69	0.18	0.01
Italy	2.82	0.24	0.01	Venezuela	−0.37	0.22	0.03
Jamaica	0.82	0.25	0.02	S. Africa	0.70	0.23	0.03
Jordan	0.69	0.43	0.05	Zambia	−0.47	0.15	0.03
Japan	3.57	0.29	0.01	Zimbabwe	−1.11	0.19	0.03

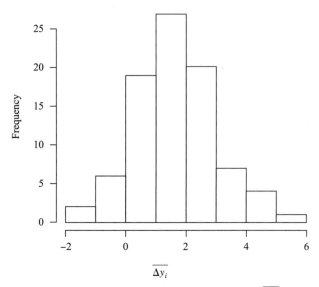

Figure 5.1 Cross-sectional Histogram of $\overline{\Delta y_i}$

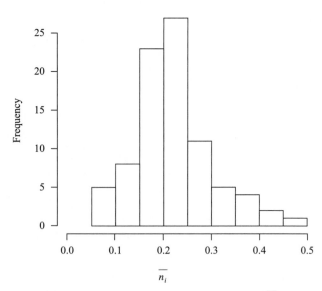

Figure 5.2 Cross-sectional Histogram of $\overline{n_i}$

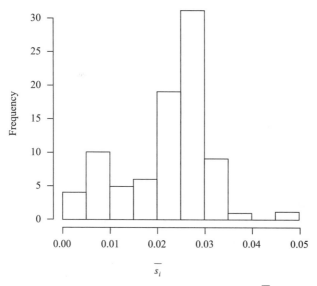

Figure 5.3 Cross-sectional Histogram of $\bar{s}_i$

5.5.2 Empirical Results

Based on the growth equation in section 2 and the data described in the previous section, we have carried out various types of both mean regression and quantile regression. We first discuss the empirical results from mean regression.

The results for estimating the unrestricted Solow model in eq. (5.4) and the restricted model in eq. (5.5) by various LS-type mean regressions are shown in table 5.2. We have employed four different mean regression methods: (i) pooled least squares (LS); (ii) pooled two-stage least squares (2SLS); (iii) least squares with dummy variables (LSDV), and (iv) two-stage least squares with dummy variables (2SLSDV). The last four columns in table 5.2 correspond to these four regression methods.

Table 5.2 LS-type mean regression results for 86 non-oil countries

Dependent variable: the growth rate of per working-age person				
Item	LS	2SLS	LSDV	2SLSDV
Unrestricted regression				
b^*	-0.01 ***	-0.02 ***	-0.24 ***	-0.25 ***
s. e.	(0.01)	(0.01)	(0.02)	(0.03)
γ_1^*	0.11 ***	0.11 ***	0.15 ***	0.15 ***
s. e.	(0.01)	(0.01)	(0.02)	(0.02)
γ_2^*	-0.18 ***	-0.19 ***	-0.13 *	-0.13 *
s. e.	(0.04)	(0.04)	(0.06)	(0.06)
Implied λ	0.003,0	0.003,7	0.054,7	0.057,3
s. e.	(0.001,1)	(0.001,1)	(0.005,9)	(0.007,0)
Adj $- R^2$	0.10	0.11	0.17	0.17
Restricted regression				
b^*	-0.01 ***	-0.01 ***	-0.24 ***	-0.25 ***
s. e.	(0.00)	(0.00)	(0.02)	(0.03)
γ_1^*	0.11 ***	0.11 ***	0.15 ***	0.15 ***
s. e.	(0.01)	(0.01)	(0.02)	(0.02)
Implied λ	0.002,2	0.002,8	0.054,8	0.057,9
s. e.	(0.001,0)	(0.001,0)	(0.058,7)	(0.007,0)
Implied α	0.91	0.89	0.38	0.38
s. e.	(0.03)	(0.03)	(0.03)	(0.03)
Adj $- R^2$	0.10	0.10	0.17	0.17
Wald test of restriction				
p-value	0.07	0.04	0.72	0.75

Note: (i) Figures in parentheses are standard errors.
(ii) Constant estimates are omitted in this table.
(iii) Significant coefficients are marked by ** (1%), * (5%).

The pooled LS regression results are similar to the corresponding regression results for non-oil countries reported in table 5.2 of Islam

(1995). All of the estimated coefficients are significant and have the sign predicted by the Solow model (i.e., b^* is negative, γ_1^* is positive, and γ_2^* is negative). Especially, whether growth convergence occurs crucially depends on the negativeness of b^*. The estimated value for b^* is -0.01 both from the unrestricted model and from the restricted model, which is highly significant. The estimated value of the implied convergence rate λ is 0.003 from the unrestricted model and 0.002 from the restricted model, both of which are much smaller than predicted by the Solow model.① The predicted value is 0.02. On the other hand, the estimated value of the implied capital share in income α is 0.908, which is far larger than the predicted value of 1/3 by the Solow model. All of these estimates from LS are qualitatively unchanged when 2SLS is employed instead. Of course, these estimates from both LS and 2SLS may not be reliable because they do not account for country-specific effects and time-specific effects, which might explain why the estimates for λ and α seem far away from their Solow model predicted values.

We now turn to the remaining two regressions, LSDV and 2SLSDV, which correct country-specific effects and time-specific effects. The last two columns in table 5.2 show the results. All of the estimates from LSDV are statistically significant. The estimated values for the convergence rate λ from unrestricted and restricted models are both 0.055, respectively, which are similar to the corresponding results in Islam(1995). Compared to the previous two pooled regression methods, the estimated value of the elasticity of output with respect to capital α becomes plausible; it is 0.384, which is quite close to the predicted value 1/3. When using 2SLSDV to correct endogeneity, the results shown in the last column in table 5.2 hardly change in terms of sign, magnitude and the statistical significance of all coefficients.

---

① When we compute λ from β^* using the equation $\lambda = -\ln(\beta^*)/\tau$, we set $\tau = 5$ given that five-year time intervals are used in estimation.

Comparing pooling regression methods (LS, 2SLS) with panel regression methods (LSDV, 2SLSDV), it is obvious that panel regressions can lead to higher convergence rates and more empirically plausible estimates of the elasticity of output with respect to capital. The difference between pooling regression and panel regression methods can be taken as the evidence supporting that different $A(0)$ among countries plays an indispensable role in the Solow model, and is an important component characterizing the steady state level along with the differences in investment and population. We have also carried out the Wald test for the restriction $\gamma_2^* = -\gamma_1^*$. When based on LS and 2SLS, the restriction is rejected at the 10% significant level. However, the null hypothesis is not rejected when the Wald test is based on the two panel regression methods, that is LSDV and 2SLSDV.

Four different types of quantile regression are analyzed here, which are completely analogous to the previously used four mean regression methods: (i) pooled quantile regression (QR); (ii) pooled instrumental variable quantile regression (QR); (iii) panel quantile regression with dummy variables (QRDV), and (iv) panel instrumental variable quantile regression with dummy variables (IVQRDV).

The estimation results based on QR are shown in table 5.3 where we report the estimated coefficients at selected quantiles ($\theta = 0.1, 0.2, \cdots, 0.9$) with the 90% confidence intervals in parentheses.① Analyzing the unrestricted quantile model first, we note that the coefficient estimate for b_θ^* decreases monotonically as θ moves from low to higher quantiles. The sign of the estimated coefficient is positive (actually, almost zero) for $\theta = 0.1$, but it becomes negative for all of higher quantiles. It is interesting to note that the coefficient b_θ^* is not significant at lower quantiles estimates;

---

① Confidence intervals are constructed by taking the relevant percentiles from 1,000 bootstrapping replications. In implementing the bootstrap procedure, the index of country is randomly selected in each replication. Once a country is sampled out, the whole data period of the country will be counted in.

Table 5.3 Pooling quantile regression – 86 non-oil countries (86)

Dependent variable: growth rate of GDP per working-age person

Unrestricted

θ	b^*		γ_1		γ_2		λ		Wald test p-value
0.1	0	(−0.03, 0.02)	0.06	(0.02, 0.14)	−0.36	(−0.52, −0.18)	−4e−04	(−0.004, 0; 0.005, 9)	0
0.2	−0.01	(−0.02, 0.01)	0.09	(0.04, 0.13)	−0.34	(−0.41, −0.16)	0.002, 3	(−0.001, 6; 0.004, 6)	0
0.3	−0.01	(−0.02, 0)	0.09	(0.06, 0.13)	−0.25	(−0.36, −0.13)	0.001, 9	(−4e−04; 0.004, 8)	0.04
0.4	−0.01	(−0.02, 0)	0.10	(0.08, 0.14)	−0.21	(−0.30, −0.10)	0.002, 4	(1e−04; 0.004, 9)	0.10
0.5	−0.01	(−0.02, 0)	0.12	(0.08, 0.14)	−0.15	(−0.26, −0.08)	0.002, 2	(5e−04; 0.005, 0)	0.55
0.6	−0.02	(−0.03, −0.01)	0.11	(0.08, 0.15)	−0.15	(−0.20, −0.08)	0.003, 7	(0.001, 4; 0.005, 1)	0.37
0.7	−0.02	(−0.03, −0.01)	0.12	(0.08, 0.16)	−0.12	(−0.18, −0.05)	0.004, 8	(0.002, 5; 0.006, 7)	0.94
0.8	−0.03	(−0.05, −0.02)	0.13	(0.09, 0.18)	−0.10	(−0.19, 0)	0.006, 4	(0.003, 0; 0.010, 3)	0.61
0.9	−0.04	(−0.06, −0.03)	0.15	(0.10, 0.19)	−0.04	(−0.16, 0.04)	0.008, 5	(0.005, 3; 0.012, 8)	0.11

Restricted

θ	b^*		γ_1		λ		α	
0.1	0.02	(0, 0.03)	0.08	(0.04, 0.15)	−0.004, 7	(−0.006, 4; 0.001, 0)	1.41	(0.92, 2.18)

Continued

Dependent variable: growth rate of GDP per working-age person

Restricted

θ	b^*		γ_1			λ		α
0.2	0.01	(0, 0.02)	0.1	(0.06, 0.15)	-0.002,1	(-0.004,0; 0.001,0)	1.12	(0.96, 1.4)
0.3	0	(-0.01, 0.01)	0.11	(0.07, 0.14)	3e-04	(-0.002,7; 0.003,0)	0.99	(0.90, 1.21)
0.4	-0.01	(-0.02, 0.01)	0.11	(0.08, 0.15)	0.001,1	(-0.001,1; 0.003,7)	0.95	(0.88, 1.07)
0.5	-0.01	(-0.02, 0)	0.11	(0.09, 0.14)	0.001,6	(0, 0.003,3)	0.93	(0.88, 1.00)
0.6	-0.01	(-0.02, -0.01)	0.11	(0.08, 0.15)	0.002,9	(0.001,1; 0.004,9)	0.88	(0.84, 0.94)
0.7	-0.02	(-0.03, -0.01)	0.12	(0.09, 0.16)	0.004,7	(0.002,7; 0.006,9)	0.84	(0.80, 0.89)
0.8	-0.03	(-0.05, -0.02)	0.13	(0.09, 0.17)	0.006,9	(0.003,5; 0.010,4)	0.80	(0.73, 0.85)
0.9	-0.05	(-0.07, -0.03)	0.15	(0.09, 0.19)	0.010,7	(0.006,5; 0.015,0)	0.74	(0.65, 0.81)

Note: Intervals in parentheses are 90% confidence intervals constructed by bootstrapping.

that is, there is no significant convergence phenomenon at lower quantiles. From the 60th quantile to 90th quantile, the convergence phenomenon appears significantly, and the rate of convergence λ_θ monotonically increases from 0.002 to 0.008 for the unrestricted model. The estimates of $\gamma_{1\theta}^*$ and $\gamma_{2\theta}^*$ are significant with the expected signs at all different quantiles. The results for the restricted model in the bottom panel of table 5.3 show that significant convergence happens again from the 60th quantile to upper quantiles, and convergence rate also monotonically increases from 0.003 at the 60th quantile to 0.011 at the 90th quantile. The coefficients $\gamma_{1\theta}^*$ of $\ln(s) - \ln(n + g + \delta)$ are significantly positive as expected at all quantiles. The estimates for α_θ are unrealistically large for all quantiles, especially for low quantiles, which might be caused by the omitted variable bias in pooling regression. The Wald test shows that the restricted Solow model is rejected at low quantiles, but accepted at middle and high quantiles. The results based on pooled instrumental variable quantile regression (IVQR) are shown in table 5.4. It is evidently shown in the table that the use of instrumental variables does not seem to change the results substantially; all of point estimates and their confidence intervals are quite similar to those in table 5.3.

If we believe in the above empirical results (i.e. the insignificance of b_θ^* for low quantiles and its monotonicity for middle and high quantiles), then we can conclude that the phenomenon of economic growth convergence is not likely to occur when the GDP growth rate is low, as in recessions, conditional on the included covariates such as the saving rate, depreciation rate, and the growth rates in both population and technology.① On the other hand, we can achieve growth convergence when the GDP growth rate is either at the middle or high quantiles. Our

---

① It is important to note that the type of convergence under consideration is "conditional convergence" as we control all of the included covariates which can be important determinants of the steady state level for an economy.

interpretations are based on the growth eq. (5.4) because the dependent variable is the growth rate Δy_{it} in eq. (5.4). An alternative way of interpreting the quantile regression results can come from the observation that estimating the growth equations in eq. (5.3) and eq. (5.4) by quantile regression (also by least squares regression) gives the numerically identical estimation results, except of course the coefficients for $y_{i,t-1}$. Since eq. (5.3) and eq. (5.4) provide the same estimation results and eq. (5.3) has the income level y_{it} as its dependent variable, we can interpret low quantiles as corresponding to "low income levels" or "low income countries," likewise, high quantile as corresponding to "high income levels" or "high income countries" over the whole conditional income distribution. Therefore, the empirical results can be alternatively interpreted as indicating that there is no convergence in low income countries whereas we do achieve convergence among high income countries. This way of interpreting the results is consistent with the findings from the parametric heterogeneity research in Durlauf et al. (2001) and Liu and Stengos (1999). They found that the estimated coefficient of initial log income per capita was positive (i.e. no convergence) for low income countries but negative for higher ones. Canatella and Rollard (2004) provided similar quantile regression results by pooling the observations from 86 countries using the sample period from 1960 to 2000. They reported that the coefficient of the initial income at the lower quantiles is not significant, and the rate of convergence monotonically increases.

Now we turn to panel quantile regression, QRDV, and IVQRDV, to correct country-specific effects and time-specific effects. The results are reported in table 5.5 for QRDV and in table 5.6 for IVQRDV. As shown in table 5.5 after controlling country-specific and period-specific effects, the estimated value for b_θ^* is significantly negative for all quantiles, which indicates that there exists strong evidence in support of economic growth convergence in all quantiles. This is a sharp contrast with the previous

Table 5.4 IV—QR86 non-oil countries

Dependent variable: growth rate of GDP per working-age person

Unrestricted

θ	b^*		γ_1		γ_2		λ	Wald test p-value
0.1	0	$(-0.04, 0.02)$	0.06	$(0.02, 0.15)$	-0.36	$(-0.56, -0.17)$	0	$(-0.004, 0; 0.008, 2)$	0
0.2	-0.01	$(-0.03, 0.01)$	0.09	$(0.03, 0.14)$	-0.34	$(-0.43, -0.14)$	$0.002, 0$	$(-0.002, 0; 0.006, 1)$	0
0.3	-0.01	$(-0.03, 0)$	0.09	$(0.05, 0.14)$	-0.26	$(-0.38, -0.12)$	$0.002, 0$	$(0, 0.006, 1)$	0.04
0.4	-0.01	$(-0.03, 0)$	0.11	$(0.07, 0.15)$	$-0.220, 0$	$(-0.34, -0.10)$	$0.002, 0$	$(0, 0.006, 1)$	0.09
0.5	-0.01	$(-0.03, 0)$	0.12	$(0.08, 0.15)$	-0.16	$(-0.29, -0.08)$	$0.002, 0$	$(0, 0.006, 1)$	0.46
0.6	-0.02	$(-0.03, -0.01)$	0.11	$(0.08, 0.16)$	-0.16	$(-0.23, -0.08)$	$0.004, 0$	$(0.002, 0; 0.006, 1)$	0.28
0.7	-0.03	$(-0.04, -0.01)$	0.12	$(0.08, 0.17)$	-0.12	$(-0.22, -0.05)$	$0.006, 1$	$(0.002, 0; 0.008, 2)$	0.95
0.8	-0.04	$(-0.06, -0.02)$	0.13	$(0.09, 0.20)$	-0.13	$(-0.21, 0)$	$0.008, 2$	$(0.004, 0; 0.012, 4)$	0.89
0.9	-0.05	$(-0.07, -0.03)$	0.15	$(0.09, 0.20)$	-0.07	$(-0.20, 0.05)$	$0.010, 3$	$(0.006, 1; 0.014, 5)$	0.22

Restricted

θ	b^*		γ_1		λ		α	
0.1	0.02	$(-0.01, 0.03)$	0.08	$(0.03, 0.15)$	$-0.004, 0$	$(-0.005, 9; 0.002, 0)$	1.36	$(0.9, 1.9)$

Continued

Dependent variable: growth rate of GDP per working-age person

Restricted

θ	b^*		γ_1		λ		α
0.2	0.01	(−0.01, 0.02)	0.10	(0.06, 0.15)	−0.002,0	(−0.004,0; 0.002,0)	1.12	(0.94, 1.43)
0.3	−0.01	(−0.02, 0.01)	0.11	(0.07, 0.15)	0.002,0	(−0.002,0; 0.004,0)	0.92	(0.87, 1.16)
0.4	−0.01	(−0.02, 0)	0.12	(0.08, 0.15)	0.002,0	(0, 0.004,0)	0.92	(0.86, 1.00)
0.5	−0.01	(−0.02, 0)	0.12	(0.09, 0.15)	0.002,0	(0, 0.004,0)	0.92	(0.86, 1.00)
0.6	−0.02	(−0.03, −0.01)	0.12	(0.09, 0.16)	0.004,0	(0.002,0; 0.006,1)	0.85	(0.82, 0.92)
0.7	−0.02	(−0.04, −0.02)	0.12	(0.09, 0.17)	0.004,0	(0.004,0; 0.008,2)	0.86	(0.78, 0.88)
0.8	−0.04	(−0.06, −0.02)	0.14	(0.09, 0.18)	0.008,2	(0.004,0; 0.012,4)	0.77	(0.72, 0.85)
0.9	−0.06	(−0.07, −0.03)	0.15	(0.10, 0.20)	0.012,4	(0.006,1; 0.014,5)	0.71	(0.63, 0.80)

Note: Intervals in parentheses are 90% confidence intervals constructed by bootstrapping.

Table 5.5 QRP with two-way effects—non-oil countries (86)

Dependent variable: log difference GDP per working-age person

Unrestricted

θ	$y_{i,t-1}$		$\ln(s_{i,t-1})$		$\ln(n_{i,t-1}+g+\delta)$		λ		Wald test p-value
0.1	-0.242,6	(-0.354,6; -0.152,4)	0.128,0	(0.033,2; 0.225,2)	-0.056,7	(-0.346,9; 0.108,0)	0.055,6	(0.033,1; 0.087,6)	0.570,3
0.2	-0.241,6	(-0.305,0; -0.164,7)	0.128,0	(0.057,7; 0.204,8)	-0.115,6	(-0.362,9; 0.066,0)	0.055,3	(0.036,0; 0.072,8)	0.914,4
0.3	-0.223,9	(-0.283,1; -0.168,5)	0.131,6	(0.069,9; 0.192,6)	-0.154,9	(-0.327,5; 0.015,3)	0.050,7	(0.036,9; 0.066,6)	0.791,7
0.4	-0.204,0	(-0.260,4; -0.157,4)	0.128,8	(0.074,5; 0.187,8)	-0.167,6	(-0.284,0; -0.021,5)	0.045,6	(0.034,2; 0.060,3)	0.567,7
0.5	-0.191,5	(-0.237,3; -0.143,4)	0.124,1	(0.083,0; 0.179,3)	-0.204,8	(-0.294,7; -0.055,2)	0.042,5	(0.031,0; 0.054,2)	0.215,6
0.6	-0.203,1	(-0.26,0; -0.143,4)	0.111,7	(0.072,5; 0.170,5)	-0.131,3	(-0.291,9; -0.020,2)	0.045,4	(0.031; 0.060,2)	0.755,4
0.7	-0.220,3	(-0.284,6; -0.145,7)	0.116,4	(0.074,7; 0.188,5)	-0.096,8	(-0.269,4; 0.019,5)	0.049,8	(0.031,5; 0.067,0)	0.757,0
0.8	-0.242,6	(-0.337,7; -0.149,4)	0.136,9	(0.061,8; 0.233,8)	-0.089,9	(-0.300,7; 0.034,5)	0.055,6	(0.032,4; 0.082,4)	0.543,5
0.9	-0.282,7	(-0.408,1; -0.134,9)	0.139,1	(0.041,5; 0.271,8)	-0.218,9	(-0.414,8; 0.093,2)	0.066,5	(0.029,0; 0.104,9)	0.511,5

Continued

Dependent variable: log difference GDP per working-age person

Restricted

θ	$y_{i,t-1}$		$\ln(s_{i,t-1}) - \ln(n_{i,t-1} + g + \delta)$		λ		α	
0.1	−0.251, 0	(−0.359, 4; −0.151, 3)	0.115, 7	(0.031, 3; 0.218, 8)	0.057, 8	(0.032, 8; 0.089, 1)	0.315, 5	(0.130, 6; 0.492, 7)
0.2	−0.243, 3	(−0.304, 9; −0.158, 8)	0.126, 0	(0.061, 3; 0.193, 4)	0.055, 8	(0.034, 6; 0.072, 7)	0.341, 2	(0.214, 0; 0.473, 7)
0.3	−0.220, 2	(−0.279, 6; −0.164, 5)	0.132, 2	(0.071, 7; 0.187, 9)	0.049, 7	(0.036, 0; 0.065, 6)	0.375, 1	(0.237, 1; 0.476, 8)
0.4	−0.200, 6	(−0.256, 0; −0.156, 2)	0.133, 7	(0.079, 7; 0.185, 0)	0.044, 8	(0.034, 0; 0.059, 2)	0.399, 9	(0.273, 1; 0.498, 8)
0.5	−0.198, 5	(−0.237, 1; −0.135, 7)	0.134, 9	(0.086, 6; 0.183, 0)	0.044, 3	(0.029, 2; 0.054, 1)	0.404, 6	(0.300, 3; 0.538, 4)
0.6	−0.200, 0	(−0.262, 2; −0.143, 4)	0.120, 0	(0.077, 8; 0.170, 7)	0.044, 6	(0.031, 0; 0.060, 8)	0.375, 0	(0.265, 1; 0.496, 7)
0.7	−0.217, 9	(−0.281, 5; −0.142, 5)	0.115, 2	(0.072, 8; 0.187, 1)	0.049, 2	(0.030, 7; 0.066, 1)	0.345, 8	(0.252, 8; 0.490, 5)
0.8	−0.244, 0	(−0.330, 4; −0.146, 7)	0.130, 1	(0.059, 3; 0.226, 4)	0.055, 9	(0.031, 7; 0.080, 2)	0.347, 8	(0.202, 7; 0.511, 9)
0.9	−0.296, 5	(−0.417, 7; −0.138, 7)	0.138, 7	(0.038, 5; 0.269, 1)	0.070, 3	(0.029, 9; 0.108, 1)	0.318, 7	(0.123, 5; 0.534, 4)

Note: Intervals in parentheses are 95% confidence intervals constructed by bootstrapping.

results based on QR and IVQR in which there is no convergence in low quantiles. It seems that the omitted variable bias plays an important role when investigating the issue of economic growth convergence and hence it should be accounted for. Based on the unrestricted model, the estimated value for the convergence rate λ_θ starts at 0.056 at the 10th quantile, then gradually decreases to 0.042 at the 50th quantile, and then rises again to 0.067 at the 90th quantile. The nearly U-shaped rate of convergence indicates the heterogeneous speed by which economies converge to their own steady state levels, depending on the conditions of the economies. Intuitively speaking, the results show that economic growth convergence occurs at a faster rate during either boom or recession periods than the normal times when investment rate, population growth, country-specific and period-specific effects are properly controlled. We will term this finding as the "smile effect." This smile effect is graphically presented in figure 5.4 with 90% confidence intervals. Thus, our data and samples indicate that growth convergence is likely to occur during the Great Recession and it occurs even at a faster rate than the normal times. Another interesting finding from our study is about the implied output elasticity with respect to capital α_θ. The estimates of α_θ at various quantiles show that, as θ moves from lower (10%) to middle (50%) quantiles, α_θ increases first from 0.32 to 0.40, which reaches the highest value. Then, it starts to decreases back to its initial level 0.32 at the 90th quantile. This inverted U-shape pattern for α_θ will be called the "inverse smile effect." When basing our quantile interpretation on the growth equation in eq. (5.3), the inverse smile effect can indicate that countries with a higher convergence rate have lower output elasticity with respect to capital, whereas countries with lower convergence rate achieve higher output elasticity with respect to capital, which is consistent with the study in Islam(1995, p. 1,162), in which the estimated values of implied α are 0.4398, 0.4575, and 0.2047 for non-oil, intermediate, and OECD countries, respectively, and the country group with a higher convergence rate has lower output elasticity with respect to capital. The inverse smile effect also corroborates the analysis of Mankiw et al. (1992), which argues that an economy will converge to its steady state level fast and capital accumulation is small if the economy is far away from its steady state level. This mechanism also causes rich countries with the fastest rate converging to their steady state to share the lowest estimates of α_θ. Capital accumulation is often equated to investment or savings. The higher the rate of saving, the richer the country [see Mankiw et al. (1992) for more details]. The results for the restricted model are reported in the bottom panel in table 5.5. Both the smile effect and the inverse smile effect are as pronounced as before. The Wald test fails to reject the restricted Solow model at all quantiles.

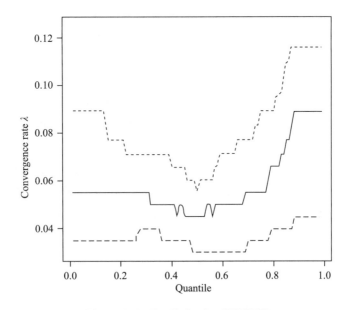

Figure 5.4 Implied λ by IVQRDV

Finally, the results based on IVQRDV to correct the endogeneity bias are shown in table 5.6. All of the results are qualitatively similar to those reported in table 5.6 with some minor changes in the estimated value for b_θ^* at high quantiles. Both the simile and inverse smile effects are present. Basing our quantile interpretation on the growth equation in eq. (5.3), the smile effect can be also taken as evidence to support that either low or high income countries tend to converge to the steady state level at a faster rate than middle income countries, which is typically argued in the growth literature. It has been argued, for example in Mankiw et al. (1992) and Islam (1995), that OECD countries, which are considered as high income (non-oil) countries in our data, tend to converge faster than whole non-oil countries. One empirical result in Islam (1995) and other recent growth literature indicated that slow conditional convergence is usually found among countries in larger samples. However, this opinion is not accurate based on the results. The slower convergence rate in a larger sample of countries does not depend on the size of sample, but on whether middle income countries are included in the samples or not, who converge slowest and make the mean-based convergence rate estimates smaller. The result that the fastest rate of convergence happens at the highest quantile is consistent with the previous findings of MRW (1992), Islam (1995), etc. MRW (1992) gave a plausible explanation for the highest convergence rate for OECD countries as that "The Second World War surely caused large departures from the steady state, and it surely had larger effects on the OECD than on the rest of the world." Table 5.7 summarizes the implied estimates of convergence rate, λ, in this section.

Table 5.6 QRPIV with two-way effects—non-oil countries (86)

Dependent variable: log difference GDP per-working age person

Unrestricted

θ	$y_{i,t-1}$		$\ln(s_{i,t-1})$		$\ln(n_{i,t-1}+g+\delta)$		λ		Wald test p-value
0.1	−0.24	(−0.36; −0.14)	0.128,2	(0.038,6; 0.229,9)	−0.053,7	(−0.356,1; 0.109,4)	0.054,9	(0.030,2; 0.089,3)	0.557,4
0.2	−0.24	(−0.32; −0.16)	0.128,3	(0.059,9; 0.207,9)	−0.117,4	(−0.359,7; 0.057,3)	0.054,9	(0.034,9; 0.077,1)	0.922,5
0.3	−0.24	(−0.3; −0.18)	0.136,5	(0.069,5; 0.190,1)	−0.158,8	(−0.333,3; 0.010,7)	0.054,9	(0.039,7; 0.071,3)	0.800,9
0.4	−0.22	(−0.3; −0.16)	0.128,2	(0.078,1; 0.18,7)	−0.157,2	(−0.281,1; −0.011,9)	0.049,7	(0.034,9; 0.071,3)	0.669,7
0.5	−0.20	(−0.26; −0.14)	0.120,4	(0.081,8; 0.183,9)	−0.196,8	(−0.289,2; −0.050,6)	0.044,6	(0.030,2; 0.060,2)	0.245,9
0.6	−0.22	(−0.3; −0.16)	0.118,6	(0.076,1; 0.177,6)	−0.134,5	(−0.288,4; −0.015,8)	0.049,7	(0.034,9; 0.071,3)	0.804,3
0.7	−0.24	(−0.34; −0.16)	0.126,5	(0.076,1; 0.194,7)	−0.095,4	(−0.278,9; 0.005,2)	0.054,9	(0.034,9; 0.083,1)	0.635,5
0.8	−0.28	(−0.38; −0.16)	0.142,8	(0.060,5; 0.243,1)	−0.115,3	(−0.299,8; 0.021,6)	0.065,7	(0.034,9; 0.095,6)	0.732,5
0.9	−0.36	(−0.48; −0.18)	0.130,6	(0.043,3; 0.276,7)	−0.163,6	(−0.412; 0.057,8)	0.089,3	(0.039,7; 0.130,8)	0.780,8

Continued

Dependent variable: log difference GDP per-working age person							
Restricted							
θ	$y_{i,t-1}$		$\ln(s_{i,t-1}) - \ln(n_{i,t-1}+g+\delta)$		λ		α
0.1	−0.26	(−0.38; −0.14)	0.118,1	(0.034,6; 0.230,1)	0.060,2	(0.030,2; 0.095,6)	0.312,4	(0.030,2; 0.089,3)
0.2	−0.26	(−0.32; −0.18)	0.121,2	(0.068,9; 0.201,6)	0.060,2	(0.039,7; 0.077,1)	0.317,9	(0.034,9; 0.077,1)
0.3	−0.24	(−0.30; −0.18)	0.137,3	(0.079,1; 0.195,8)	0.054,9	(0.039,7; 0.071,3)	0.363,9	(0.039,7; 0.071,3)
0.4	−0.22	(−0.30; −0.16)	0.132,4	(0.079,5; 0.194,2)	0.049,7	(0.034,9; 0.071,3)	0.375,7	(0.034,9; 0.071,3)
0.5	−0.20	(−0.26; −0.14)	0.131,4	(0.084,3; 0.186,8)	0.044,6	(0.030,2; 0.060,2)	0.396,5	(0.030,2; 0.060,2)
0.6	−0.20	(−0.30; −0.16)	0.120,3	(0.076,7; 0.179,4)	0.044,6	(0.034,9; 0.071,3)	0.375,6	(0.034,9; 0.071,3)
0.7	−0.24	(−0.32; −0.16)	0.120,5	(0.078,1; 0.189,2)	0.054,9	(0.034,9; 0.077,1)	0.334,3	(0.034,9; 0.077,1)
0.8	−0.28	(−0.38; −0.18)	0.141,0	(0.067,7; 0.235,6)	0.065,7	(0.039,7; 0.095,6)	0.334,9	(0.039,7; 0.095,6)
0.9	−0.38	(−0.48; −0.20)	0.134,4	(0.050,5; 0.271,3)	0.095,6	(0.044,6; 0.130,8)	0.261,3	(0.044,6; 0.130,8)

Table 5.7 Summary of the implied estimates of convergence rate, λ

Item	θ = 0.1	θ = 0.2	θ = 0.3	θ = 0.4	θ = 0.5	θ = 0.6	θ = 0.7	θ = 0.8	θ = 0.9	Mean-based regression
Unrestricted regression										
QR	-4e-04	0.002,3	0.001,9	0.002,4	0.002,2	0.003,7	0.004,8	0.006,4	0.008,5	0.003,0
IV - QR	0	0.002,0	0.002,0	0.002,0	0.002,0	0.004,0	0.006,1	0.008,1	0.010,3	0.003,7
QRP	0.055,6	0.055,3	0.050,7	0.045,6	0.042,5	0.045,4	0.049,8	0.055,6	0.066,5	0.054,7
QRPIV	0.054,9	0.054,9	0.054,9	0.049,7	0.044,6	0.049,7	0.054,9	0.065,7	0.089,3	0.057,3
Restricted regression										
QR	-0.004,7	-0.002,1	3e-04	0.001,1	0.001,6	0.002,9	0.004,7	0.006,9	0.010,7	0.002,2
IV - QR	-0.004,0	-0.002,0	0.002,0	0.002,0	0.002,0	0.004,0	0.004,0	0.008,2	0.012,4	0.002,8
QRP	0.057,8	0.055,8	0.049,7	0.044,8	0.044,3	0.044,6	0.049,2	0.055,9	0.070,3	0.054,8
QRPIV	0.060,2	0.060,2	0.054,9	0.049,7	0.044,6	0.044,6	0.054,9	0.065,7	0.095,6	0.057,9

5.5.3 Conclusion

We have revisited the important issue of economic growth convergence in this section. Our investigation into the issue is based on employing a newly developed econometric technique, "instrumental variable panel quantile regression." There are two distinct advantages of this new method. First, it allows researchers to investigate the issue at hand when the growth rate is far below or above the conditional mean level, which is not possible in the traditional LS-type regression method. Secondly, the new method provides a solution to the endogeneity problem that has been a serious obstacle to applying quantile regression to the panel data framework. Using the new method and an extensive dataset on 86 non-oil countries, some quite interesting findings are discovered: (i) economic growth convergence does take place at all quantiles; (ii) but the rate of convergence does depend on the condition of the economy over the whole distribution; especially, it can be found that growth convergence occurs even with a faster rate at either low or high quantiles than the normal times indicated by the middle quantiles. In summary, the application of the instrumental variable panel quantile regression method provides a richer description about the issue of economic growth convergence than the previously employed econometric methods.

5.6 Evidence from China Provincial Panel Data

5.6.1 Literature on China's Regional Economic Development

The report of the 19th National Congress of the Communist Party of China pointed out that the current major contradictions in our society have been transformed into between the people's growing needs for a better life and the development of inadequate imbalances. As China's economy enters a new era, China's economic development faces a complex situation abroad, and the domestic situation presents new features. Currently, the problem of uneven development between regions remains outstanding, i. e. some aspects of economic development in the central and western regions are far less than that in the eastern region. Achieving regional coordinated development is not only a great strategy for promoting the construction of a modern economic system but also an inevitable requirement for maintaining sustained and healthy economic development. Therefore, the following part studies the balance of regional economic development in China and reveals the factors that affect the imbalance of development among regions.

Uneven Development is among regions of China. The coordination and balance of China's regional economic development have received a lot of attention from researchers. Based on the space-time evolution characteristics of China's eastern, middle, and western regions, Peng and Liu(2010) studied regional economic disparity in China and found the club convergence in regions. Qin et al. (2012), taking the Yangtze River Delta as an example, discovered the existence of spacial club convergence at the convergence rate of 1.57%, by introducing factors of spacial spillovers into the research on regional economic growth. Zhu et al. (2014) applied the provincial dynamic panel data model from 1952 to 2008 to find that there has no economic growth convergence but found the existence of economic convergence in the central and western regions. From multi-dimensional research on the quality of economic growth, Xiao et al. (2016) found that there was no economic growth convergence in the whole country, but several economic growth convergences in several different regions. Zhang and Guo (2017), by using the inter-provincial data, found that the economic growth rate of lower-developing provinces was faster than that of developed provinces and the convergence rate had experienced the characteristics of first accelerating and then slowing down.

In practice, economists and policymakers concerned about the situation of slow-growing and fast-growing regions. Compared to mean-based regression methods, quantile regression has a more robust estimation result and highlights the correlation of variables at tails. Koenker and Machado(1999) used quantile regression and found that at most of the quantiles, GDP per capita showed no significant negative correlation with its initial value. While corresponding to high-income countries, the negative correlation becomes stronger at high quantiles. Focusing on the advantages of the distribution tail based on quantile regression, Ram (2008) used cross-sectional data for quantile regression to find that high-income countries were much faster than low-income countries.

China's relatively slow-growing central and western regions are crucial areas for China's future high-quality economic growth. Most Researches on the Convergence of China's Economic Growth ignore the entire distribution, due to applying mean-based regression, or suffer from omitted variable bias, due to the use of cross-sectional data and ignoring the fixed effects of different provinces. There are several papers that applied quantile regression to analyze China's economic convergence. Zhu et al. (2010) discovered different characteristics of stages in China Economic Growth, by using Bayesian quantile regression. This part applies panel data quantile regression, from the perspective of overall distribution, to investigate the convergence of economic growth in different economic development areas, thus avoiding the omitted variable bias and analyzing the factors that affect economic growth more accurately.

Status of China's Regional Economic Growth since the market reform and opening policy in 1978: China has achieved remarkable results. However, the development among regions is imbalanced and performs that the eastern region developed at a relatively faster rate and the average income in the eastern region was obviously higher than in central and western regions.① Figure 5.5 shows GDP per capita from 1978 to 2016②. It can be seen that the income per capita of the three regions are significantly different. In 2000, GDP per capita in the central region was about 6,000 yuan, which is only equivalent to that of the eastern region around 1995. In 2016, the ratio of GDP per capita in the eastern, middle, and western regions was 1.86:1.21:1, which demonstrates that there are still large differences in the level of economic development among regions in China and the living standards of the people in the eastern region are much higher than those in the central and western regions.

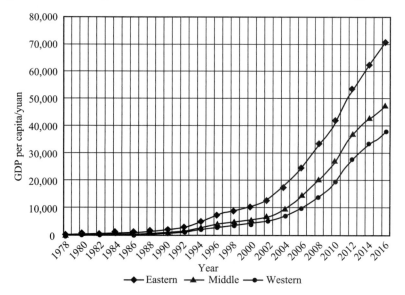

Figure 5.5 GDP per capita(RMB) in eastern, middle, and western regions from 1978 – 2016

---

① The eastern, central and western regions are divided as follows: Eastern Region: Beijing, Tianjin, Hebei, Liaoning, Shanghai, Jiangsu, Zhejiang, Fujian, Shandong, Guangdong, Guangxi, Chongqing, Hainan, Shenzhen; Central Region: Shanxi, Inner Mongolia, Jilin, Heilongjiang, Anhui, Jiangxi, Henan, Hubei, Hunan; Western regions: Sichuan, Guizhou, Yunnan, Tibet, Shaanxi, Gansu, Qinghai, Ningxia, Xinjiang.

② Data in this part is collected from New China 60 Years Statistical Data Collection and from the official website of National Bureau of Statistics.

Figure 5.6 shows the regional GDP share in the eastern, middle, and western regions of China from 1978 to 2016. East share, which rose from 52.0% in 1978, reached a peak in 2003 of about 61.5%, and then dropped slightly to 57.8% in 2016. The GDP shares in the central and western regions demonstrated a trend of a slight increase after the decline from 1978 to 2004. Although the GDP share in the east region is much higher than that of the central and western regions in recent years, the GDP share in central and western regions has been expanding year by year.

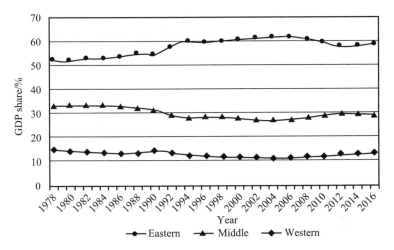

Figure 5.6 GDP share in eastern, middle, and western regions from 1978 – 2016

Figure 5.7 shows the fixed asset investment in the eastern, central and western regions from 1978 to 2016. The nation's total fixed asset investment has increased from 8.8 billion yuan in 1978 to more than 60 billion yuan in 2016, which is 680 times that of 1978. The ratio of eastern, central, and western regions in 1978 was 2.39: 1.94: 1, while the ratio extended to 5.18 : 1.89 : 1 in 1995. Thanks to the reform and opening up policy, the eastern coastal received policy support to establish special economic zones and grew rapidly. Under the guidance of the rise of the central region and the western development strategy, the ratios of investment in the central and western regions have been expanded.

However, there are still large differences among investment regions. The fixed asset investment in the western region is much lower than that in the central and eastern regions. However, the gaps among regions are shrinking.

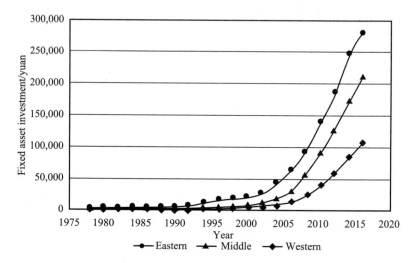

Figure 5.7 Fixed asset investment (RMB) in the eastern, middle, and western regions from 1978 – 2016

The average years of schooling in the western region are relatively low, and the regional differences are huge. The average years of schooling is a common indicator measuring the average quality of the population[①]. Figure 5.8 shows the trend of schooling in the eastern, middle, and western regions. In 1989, the average years of schooling were 6.26 years, which was only the level of primary school education; and it

---

① The human capital, h_{it}, is measured by the years of schooling based on the yearly census. The conversion formula is: years of schooling = (population of primary education × 6 + population of junior high school education × 9 + population of high school education × 12 + population of college education × 15 + population of university undergraduate × 16 + population of graduates × 19)/population of censuses in province i year t. Since the schooling data collected from 1987, the results related to the return of human capital was from 1987 to 2016.

rose to the junior high school graduation level of 9.07 years by 2016, which demonstrated the remarkable results of Nine-year Compulsory Education Policy. The schooling in the western region increased from 4.8 years in 1987 to 8.05 years in 2016, however, it was still rather lower, compared with the eastern and central regions. Since the labor force flowed into Beijing, Shanghai and Tianjin, the years of schooling of these three cities are more than 10 years in 2016. Comparing the schooling in Beijing(12.39 years) and Guizhou Province(7.73 years), the gap of 4.6 years is very huge.

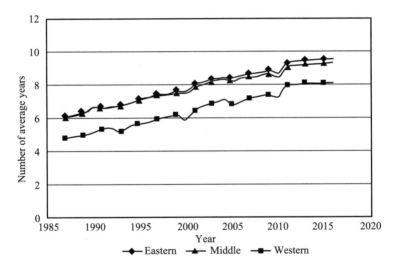

Figure 5.8 Average years of schooling in eastern, middle, and western regions from 1987 - 2016

Overall, China's economic development has achieved remarkable results since the reform and opening up, but regional development is still uneven. The eastern region has developed more rapidly and the living standard is significantly higher than in other regions. However, the central and western regions have a tendency to rise slowly year by year. The education level in the western region is lower than that in the eastern and central regions, and the differences among provinces are obvious.

5.6.2 Model and Data

Based on Islam(1995) and Koenker(2004), the quantile panel data with fixed effect can be expressed as:

$$\hat{\beta} = \underset{\beta_0,\beta_1,\beta_2,\beta_3}{\operatorname{argmin}} \sum_{i=1}^{N} \sum_{t=1}^{T} \rho_\theta(\Delta y_{it} - \beta_0 - \beta_1 \ln(y_{i,t-1}) - \beta_2 \ln\left(\frac{I_{it}}{Y_{it}}\right) - \beta_3 \ln(n_{it} + g + \delta) - u_i) \qquad (5.10)$$

where Y_{it} is GDP per capita of province i in year t, and the dependent variable $\delta \ln(Y_{it})$ represents the growth rate of GDP per capita; $\frac{I_{it}}{Y_{it}}$ denotes the fixed assets investment in province i year t. The proportion of n_{it} denotes population growth rate in province i year t. If the estimate of the coefficient β_1 of the lag term $\ln(Y_{i,t-1})$ is significantly negative, there exists convergence of economic growth, and the convergence rate is $\lambda = -(\ln(1-\beta_1))/t$. Considering human capital, the fixed-effect panel quantile regression is estimated as

$$\hat{\beta} = \underset{\beta_0,\beta_1,\beta_2,\beta_3}{\operatorname{argmin}} \sum_{i=1}^{N} \sum_{t=1}^{T} \rho_\theta(\Delta y_{it} - \beta_0 - \beta_1 \ln(y_{i,t-1}) - \beta_2 \ln\left(\frac{I_{it}}{Y_{it}}\right) - \beta_3 \ln(n_{it} + g + \delta) - \beta_4 \ln(h_{it}) - u_i) \qquad (5.11)$$

where h_{it} denotes the years of schooling in province i year t. Annual data in 31 provinces and municipalities from 1978 to 2016 are collected from New China 60 Years Statistical Data Collection and National Bureau of Statistics.

5.6.3 Empirical Results

Table 5.8 shows the panel quantile regression results in three periods of China's economic development path, i.e. 1978 – 1990, 1990 – 2004, 2004 – 2016. In the early days of China's reform and opening up policy, from 1978 to 1990, China experienced a transition period from a planned economy and gradually got rid of the traditional development model and the economic system. Regression (1) shows the results of the corresponding period, and it is not difficult to find that China's economic growth has not exhibited significant convergence. The coefficient of $\ln(Y_{i,t-1})$ is negative at the low quantile, but not statistically significant, since China was at the transition stage from the planned economy to market economy and the results of reform and opening up did not appear immediately. However, the investment-to-GDP ratio shows a significant positive correlation with the economic level at most of the quantiles. It can be seen that in the early days of China's reform and opening up policy, investment has played a significant role in promoting economic development.

From 1990 to 2004, China has established an overall market economic system, and gradually broke the stalemate of the planned economic system, with increasing the degree of marketization. From the results of regression (2), it can be seen that except for the 90th quantile, the regression coefficients of $\ln(Y_{i,t-1})$ show significant convergence, and the convergence rate at lower quantiles is higher than at higher quantiles. Specifically, the regression coefficient of $\ln(Y_{i,t-1})$ is gradually reduced from -0.0212 at $\tau = 0.1$ to -0.0104 at $\tau = 0.8$, corresponding the convergence rate from 0.021 to 0.010. It implies that the convergence rate in lower developed regions was faster than that in higher developed regions. At the same time, at most of quantiles, the effect of population growth and investment ratio on economic growth are not obvious.

When China's economy entered a period of completing the market economy system since 2005, the reform of state-owned enterprises was in-depth progress and has achieved an average annual growth rate of 9%. From the results of regression (3) in table 5.8, it can be seen that it exhibited significant convergence at all quantiles, and the convergence rate gradually decreased monotonously with the rise of quantiles. The coefficient of $\ln(Y_{i,t-1})$ decreased from -0.0612 at $\tau = 0.1$ to -0.0507 at $\tau = 0.9$ in absolute value. Except for the high quantiles $\tau = 0.8, 0.9$

Table 5.8 Panel quantile regression results for all provinces in different time periods

Quantile	Time span	1978–1990	1990–2004	2004–2016	1978–2016
Quantile estimate of coefficients					
0.1	$\ln(Y_{i,t-1})$	−0.027,50	−0.021,20***	−0.061,20***	−0.007,59**
	$\ln(I_{it}/Y_{it})$	0.013,20	−0.001,48	−0.004,60*	0.005,09
	$\ln(n_{it}+g+\delta)$	0.155,00	0.020,80	0.013,90	0.005,99
	constant	−0.376,00**	0.299,00***	0.733,00***	0.133,00***
0.2	$\ln(Y_{i,t-1})$	−0.001,51	−0.021,00***	−0.058,60***	−0.005,57***
	$\ln(I_{it}/Y_{it})$	0.016,90***	−0.004,02**	−0.005,23**	0.004,22*
	$\ln(n_{it}+g+\delta)$	−0.130,00**	0.014,90	0.013,80	0.004,51
	constant	−0.262,00	0.302,00***	0.734,00***	0.133,00***
0.3	$\ln(Y_{i,t-1})$	0.000,12	−0.019,30***	−0.057,50***	−0.007,21***
	$\ln(I_{it}/Y_{it})$	0.018,00***	−0.005,06	−0.004,89**	0.006,60***
	$\ln(n_{it}+g+\delta)$	−0.131,00*	0.014,30	0.014,00	−0.003,88
	constant	−0.262,00	0.302,00***	0.734,00***	0.137,00***
0.4	$\ln(Y_{i,t-1})$	0.001,86	−0.018,20***	−0.056,30***	−0.008,31***
	$\ln(I_{it}/Y_{it})$	0.017,00***	−0.003,02	−0.006,22***	0.007,16***
	$\ln(n_{it}+g+\delta)$	−0.131,00**	0.013,30	0.013,50	−0.010,30
	constant	−0.262,00	0.303,00***	0.734,00***	0.140,00***

Continued

Quantile	Time span	1978–1990	1990–2004	2004–2016	1978–2016
Quantile estimate of coefficients					
0.5	$\ln(Y_{i,t-1})$	0.003,59	-0.017,20***	-0.055,50***	-0.007,94***
	$\ln(I_{it}/Y_{it})$	0.016,80***	-0.002,89	-0.006,86***	0.006,59***
	$\ln(n_{it}+g+\delta)$	-0.131,00**	0.010,80	0.012,50	-0.013,70
	constant	-0.262,00	0.304,00***	0.734,00***	0.142,00***
0.6	$\ln(Y_{i,t-1})$	0.005,46	-0.015,70***	-0.054,80***	-0.006,60***
	$\ln(I_{it}/Y_{it})$	0.018,10***	-0.001,51	-0.005,24**	0.006,41***
	$\ln(n_{it}+g+\delta)$	-0.132,00**	0.009,66	0.012,00	-0.015,40
	constant	-0.261,00	0.304,00***	0.734,00***	0.142,00***
0.7	$\ln(Y_{i,t-1})$	0.007,87	-0.013,30***	-0.054,10***	-0.005,81***
	$\ln(I_{it}/Y_{it})$	0.016,70***	-0.001,58	-0.006,60*	0.005,38*
	$\ln(n_{it}+g+\delta)$	-0.134,00**	0.008,23	0.010,10	-0.021,50*
	constant	-0.261,00	0.305,00***	0.735,00***	0.144,00***
0.8	$\ln(Y_{i,t-1})$	0.010,20	-0.010,40**	-0.051,90***	-0.003,68*
	$\ln(I_{it}/Y_{it})$	0.017,90***	-0.001,71	-0.003,03	0.007,79*
	$\ln(n_{it}+g+\delta)$	-0.135,00**	0.007,53	0.011,10	-0.022,30*
	constant	-0.260,00	0.305,00***	0.734,00***	0.145,00***
0.9	$\ln(I_{it}/Y_{it})$	0.013,70	-0.006,73	-0.050,70***	-0.005,69
	$\ln(I_{it}/Y_{it})$	0.017,10***	-0.002,07	0.002,14	0.008,18***
	$\ln(n_{it}+g+\delta)$	-0.137,00**	0.006,67	0.010,20	-0.035,20**
	constant	-0.260,00	0.305,00***	0.735,00***	0.152,00***

Note: * denotes $p < 0.10$, ** denotes $p < 0.05$, *** denotes $p < 0.01$.

that the investment ratio coefficient is not significant, the impact of investment on economic growth is significantly negative, and elasticity of investment with respect to economic growth is rather small, which indicates that investment-driving economic growth mode plays a limited role in China recently.

The returns of regression (4) show the overall economic growth of China since the reform and opening up policy in 1978 until 2016. Except for highest quantile, 0.9, it exhibits significant convergence in China's economic growth at other quantiles. The investment significantly and positively impacts the economic growth at most of quantiles, which indicates that investment plays a positive role in promoting economic development, and this impact is more remarkable in the early stage of reform and opening up policy. However, with the development of the economy, the way in which investment drives the economy is no longer suitable for the needs of China's economic development.

This part analyzes the economic growth clubs in the eastern, central, and western regions. The so-called "club convergence" is a β conditional convergence, which adds the regional factors into the convergence model as control variables. Since different steady-states exist in different regions, thus there are probably different convergence rates in different regions. Due to the uncoordinated development in regions, it is crucial to analyze the economic development in different regions, i.e. eastern, central, and western regions.

Table 5.9 shows the panel quantile regression results for eastern, central, western regions and 31 provinces and municipalities as a whole. In this part, the human capital variable, $\ln(h_i)$, is considered as a factor that may affect economic growth. Firstly, from the results of the whole country data in regression (5), the estimated coefficients of $\ln(Y_{i,t-1})$ are significantly negative, which indicates that economic growth convergence exists. Except for the two lowest quantiles, $\tau = 0.1$, 0.2, the investment has a significantly positive effect on economic growth.

The last three columns of table 5.9 represent the panel quantile regression results for the eastern, central, and western regions, respectively. In all of the three regions, economic growth convergence exists at almost all quantiles, and convergence rates in the central and western regions are higher than that of the whole country and the eastern region. Taking the 50th quantile as an example, the estimated coefficient is $-0.022,5$, indicating the rate of convergence at $\lambda = -\ln(1-0.025,7) = 0.026$, and is slightly smaller than the corresponding estimation coefficient in the eastern region, $\lambda = -\ln(1-0.025,7) = 0.026$, while the central and western regions are $\lambda = -\ln(1-0.031,4) = 0.032$ and $\lambda = -\ln(1-0.030,9) = 0.031$, respectively. As the quantile increases from low to high, both the central and western regions exhibit a trend of decreasing convergence rate. At lower quantiles, the corresponding slower developed region exhibits a higher rate of convergence.

The impact of investment on economic growth is more pronounced in the central and western regions than in the eastern region, which indicates that increased investment in relatively backward economic regions will promote economic growth and the improvement of people's living standards. Although education as a whole has a significant positive effect on economic growth at all quantiles, the impact of education levels in the central region is more pronounced, compared to other regions. This may be due to the fact that the education facilities in the central region are relatively better than those in the west, but the level of schooling has a greater development space than the eastern region, and the marginal effect of education will be greater, and the impact of education on economic growth will be more significant.

Table 5.9 Panel quantile regression results in different regions from 1987 to 2016

Quantile	Time span	1978−1990	1990−2004	2004−2016	1978−2016
Quantile estimate of coefficients					
0.1	$\ln(Y_{i,t-1})$	−0.019,70***	−0.025,90*	−0.034,40***	−0.037,30**
	$\ln(I_{it}/Y_{it})$	0.003,88	0.001,91	0.021,80***	0.019,80*
	$\ln(n_{it}+g+\delta)$	0.013,70	0.010,90	0.005,70	−0.008,84
	$\ln(h_{it})$	0.035,90**	0.011,40	0.126,00**	0.021,00
	constant	0.201,00***	0.315,00***	0.115,00	0.265,00***
0.2	$\ln(Y_{i,t-1})$	−0.017,40***	−0.019,10	−0.035,60***	−0.035,00**
	$\ln(I_{it}/Y_{it})$	0.003,12	0.003,49	0.013,90***	0.024,90*
	$\ln(n_{it}+g+\delta)$	0.014,50*	0.021,70*	−0.001,46	−0.005,70
	$\ln(h_{it})$	0.037,00**	0.006,60	0.129,00**	0.019,50
	constant	0.201,00***	0.310,00***	0.118,00	0.263,00***
0.3	$\ln(Y_{i,t-1})$	−0.018,20***	−0.024,50**	−0.033,20***	−0.033,70**
	$\ln(I_{it}/Y_{it})$	0.004,49*	0.003,30	0.014,90***	0.021,80
	$\ln(n_{it}+g+\delta)$	0.007,80	0.005,59	−0.000,901	−0.009,44
	$\ln(h_{it})$	0.036,60**	0.013,20	0.129,00*	0.021,30
	constant	0.204,00***	0.317,00***	0.118,00	0.265,00***

Continued

Quantile	Time span	1978–1990	1990–2004	2004–2016	1978–2016
Quantile estimate of coefficients					
0.4	$\ln(Y_{i,t-1})$	-0.020,300***	-0.024,600**	-0.032,800***	-0.032,200**
	$\ln(I_{it}/Y_{it})$	0.005,350***	0.002,620	0.013,300**	0.025,000*
	$\ln(n_{it}+g+\delta)$	-0.000,005,36	0.002,020	-0.003,360	-0.009,000
	$\ln(h_{it})$	0.040,000*	0.014,500	0.130,000**	0.019,700
	constant	0.207,000***	0.318,000***	0.119,000	0.264,000***
0.5	$\ln(Y_{i,t-1})$	-0.022,500***	-0.025,700**	-0.031,500***	-0.030,900
	$\ln(I_{it}/Y_{it})$	0.004,490**	0.006,440	0.013,000**	0.022,600
	$\ln(n_{it}+g+\delta)$	-0.008,610	-0.003,020	-0.004,070	-0.010,200
	$\ln(h_{it})$	0.043,300*	0.016,300	0.131,000*	0.021,600
	constant	0.211,000***	0.321,000***	0.119,000	0.265,000***
0.6	$\ln(Y_{i,t-1})$	-0.022,100***	-0.024,600**	-0.029,200***	-0.029,700
	$\ln(I_{it}/Y_{it})$	0.003,770	0.007,030	0.013,500***	0.021,700
	$\ln(n_{it}+g+\delta)$	-0.012,900*	-0.003,810	-0.004,730	-0.011,500
	$\ln(h_{it})$	0.043,700*	0.016,700	0.131,000**	0.022,500
	constant	0.213,000***	0.321,000***	0.119,000	0.266,000***

Continued

Quantile	Time span	1978–1990	1990–2004	2004–2016	1978–2016
Quantile estimate of coefficients					
0.7	$\ln(Y_{i,t-1})$	−0.022,10***	−0.024,00	−0.026,90***	−0.027,80***
	$\ln(I_{it}/Y_{it})$	0.005,77**	0.008,21	0.013,70***	0.022,10
	$\ln(n_{it}+g+\delta)$	−0.017,60	−0.006,22	−0.005,41	−0.012,20
	$\ln(h_{it})$	0.045,60**	0.017,40	0.132,00**	0.023,10
	constant	0.214,00***	0.322,00***	0.120,00	0.266,00***
0.8	$\ln(Y_{i,t-1})$	−0.024,30***	−0.022,80	−0.025,00***	−0.026,00**
	$\ln(I_{it}/Y_{it})$	0.004,34	0.011,40	0.013,30**	0.017,70
	$\ln(n_{it}+g+\delta)$	−0.027,40***	−0.009,50	−0.006,41	−0.016,70
	$\ln(h_{it})$	0.053,20**	0.018,60	0.132,00**	0.027,60
	constant	0.219,00***	0.323,00***	0.120,00	0.268,00***
0.9	$\ln(Y_{i,t-1})$	−0.022,10***	−0.024,80*	−0.023,20***	−0.022,90**
	$\ln(I_{it}/Y_{it})$	0.005,24*	0.013,70	0.011,90**	0.017,30*
	$\ln(n_{it}+g+\delta)$	−0.027,10***	−0.020,00	−0.008,08	−0.016,00
	$\ln(h_{it})$	0.054,60***	0.023,30	0.133,00**	0.027,40
	constant	0.220,00***	0.328,00***	0.121,00	0.268,00***
	N	90,300	33,900	29,700	26,700

Note: * denotes $p < 0.10$, ** denotes $p < 0.05$, *** denotes $p < 0.01$.

5.6.4 Conclusion from China's Empirical Results

Panel data quantile regression model is used to study China's economic convergence, and to discover that it exhibits the different characteristics of convergence in different stages of China's economic development and different regions, which is related to the imbalance of regional economic development in China. It shows that economic growth exhibits different convergence rates in different regions at different quantiles and identified the differences between the eastern and mid-west regions. Education still plays a crucial role in economic growth, especially in middle regions promoting education level can obviously improve economic development.

China's current regional development is unbalanced, and coordinating regional development is an important issue to be resolved. Based on the above research, the following policy suggestions are proposed:

(1) Developing education and providing talent support for the development of the central and western regions. The empirical results show that the level of education is still a crucial factor for high-quality economic development. The development of talents, technology, knowledge, and information largely depends on the improvement of the education level. Especially for the central and western regions, where the education level is relatively low and the education level has a significant impact on the economy, a more favorable policy of talent introduction should be adopted to improve the education level and promote the development in the central and western regions.

(2) Establishing a mechanism of cooperation to promote the development of the central and western regions. The empirical results of the different periods show that, with the continuous development of the economy, the investment in the eastern region has limited promotion effect on economic development, while in central and western regions with lower economic conditions, investment still plays a significant role on the development. Due to the advantages in terms of resources and environment

in the central and western regions, China should improve the complete and nationwide cooperation mechanism between the east and the west regions, enhance the investment and policy support further in the central and western regions, and implement relevant incentive policies such as taxation, talent introduction, and technology transfer. The technology and talent advantages of the eastern region will spillover to the west, and some measures should be implemented like complementing the resources and environment among regions, effectively driving the development of the western region and narrowing the gap among regions.

(3) Fully exploring the advantages of the central and western regions and focusing on the development of related industries. The empirical results show that there is conditional convergence in regional economic growth, and their growth converges to their steady states quickly in central and western regions, indicating that under certain conditions, the growth rates of the central and western regions are higher than that of the eastern region. The central and western regions should seize the current development opportunities and take full advantages of localities. Since the central and western regions are vast and rich in natural resources, measurements, like making full use of natural resource endowments, vigorously promoting tourism, culture, modern agriculture, creating a mid-western brand with international influence, forming a complete industrial chain of culture, tourism and surrounding industries etc, should be taken to help for providing a basis for the early realization of the three major goals of regional coordinated development.

References

[1] Abrevaya J. ,Cahl C. 2008. The effects of birth inputs on birthweight: evidence from quantile estimation on panel data. *American Statistical Association*, 26; 379 −397.

[2] Arellano M. , Bond S. 1991. Some tests of specification for panel

data: Monte Carlo evidence and an application to employment equations. *Review of Economic Studies*,58:277 −279.
[3] Banerjee A. ,Duflo E. 2003. Inequality and growth: what can the data say? *Journal of Economic Growth*,8:267 −300.
[4] Barro Robert J. 1991. Economic growth in a cross section of countries. *Quarterly Journal of Economics*,106:407 −43.
[5] Barro Robert J. 1992. Convergence. *Journal of Political Economy*, 100:223 −251.
[6] Barro Robert J. , Xavier Sala-i-Martin. 2003. Economic growth. 2nd edition. Cambridge,MA: MIT Press.
[7] Baumol W. 1986. Productivity growth convergence,and welfare: what the long-run data show. *American Economic Association*,76:1072 − 1085.
[8] Bernard A. B. , Durlauf, S. N. 1995. Convergence in international output. *Journal of Applied Econometrics*,10:97 −108.
[9] Bernard A. B. , Durlauf S. N. 1996. Interpreting tests of the convergence hypothesis. *Journal of Econometrics*,71:161 −173.
[10] Binder M. ,Pesaran M. H. 1999. Stochastic growth models and their econometric implications. *Journal of Economic Growth*, 4: 139 −183.
[11] Bond S. ,Hoeffler A. ,Temple J. 2001. GMM estimation of empirical growth models. Centre for Economic Policy Research Discussion Paper,No. 3,048.
[12] Canarella G. , Pollard, S. 2004. Parameter heterogeneity in the neoclassical growth model: a quantile regression approach. *Journal of Economic Development*,29:1 −31.
[13] Canova F. , Marcet A. 1995. The poor stay poor: non-convergence across countries and regions. CEPR Working Paper:1215.
[14] Caselli F. ,Esquivel G. ,Lefort F. 1996. Reopening the convergence debate: a new look at cross-country growth empirics. *Journal of Economic Growth*:1363 −1390.

[15] Chernozhukov V. , Hansen C. 2005. An IV model of quantile treatment effects. *Econometrica*, 73:245 −261.

[16] Chernozhukov V. , Hansen C. 2006. Instrumental quantile regression inference for structural and treatment effects models. *Journal of Econometrics*, 132:491 −525.

[17] Durflauf S. ,Johnson P. A. 1995. Multiple regimes and cross country growth behaviour. *Journal of Applied Econometrics*, 10:365 −384.

[18] Durlauf S. N. , Johnson P. A. , Temple R. W. 2005. Growth econometrics. In: Aghion P. , Durlauf S. N. Eds. Handbook of Economic Growth, Volume 1. North-Holland, Amsterdam.

[19] Durlauf S. ,Kourtellos A. ,Minikin A. 2001. The local Solow growth model. *European Economic Review*, 45:928 −940.

[20] Friedman M. 1994. Do old fallacies ever die? *Journal of Economic Literature*, 30:2129 −2132.

[21] Galvao A. 2011. Quantile regression for dynamic panel data with fixed effects. *Journal of Econometrics*, 164:142 −157.

[22] Harberger A. 1987. Comment in Fischer S. Macroeconomics Annual. MIT Press, Cambridge.

[23] Huo L. , Kim T − H. , Kim Y. 2015. Revisiting growth empirics based on IV panel quantile regression. *Applied Economics*, 47 (36):3859 −3873.

[24] Islam N. 1995. Growth empirics: a panel data approach. *Quarterly Journal of Economics*, 110:1127 −1170.

[25] Islam N. 2003. What have we learnt from the convergence debate? *Journal of Economic Surveys*, 17:309 −362.

[26] Koenker R. 2004. Quantile regression for longitudinal data. *Journal of Multivariate Analysis*, 91:74 −89.

[27] Koenker R. ,Bassett G. 1978. Regression quantiles. *Econometrica*, 46:33 −49.

[28] Koenker R. ,Hallock K. 2001. Quantile regression: an introduction. *Journal of Economic Perspectives*, 15:43 −56.

[29] Koenker R., Machado J. A. F. 1999. Goodness of fit and related inference processes for quantile regression. *Journal of American statistical Association*, 94: 1296 – 1310.

[30] Lee K., Pesaran M. H., Smith R. 1997. Growth and convergence in a multi-country empirical stochastic Solow model. *Journal of Applied Econometrics*, 12: 357 – 392.

[31] Lee K., Pesaran M. H., Smith R. 1998. Growth empirics: a panel data approach: a comment. *Quarterly Journal of Economics*, 113: 319 – 323.

[32] Liu Z., Stengos T. 1999. Non-linearities in cross country growth regressions: a semiparametric approach. *Journal of Applied Econometrics*, 14: 527 – 538.

[33] Maddala G., Wu S. 2000. Cross-country growth regression: problems of heterogeneity, stability, and interpretation. *Applied Economics*, 32: 635 – 642.

[34] Mankiw N. G., Romer D., Weil D. 1992. A contribution to the empirics of economic growth. *Quarterly Journal of Economics*, 107: 407 – 437.

[35] Pesaran M. H. 2007. A pair-wise approach to testing for output and growth convergence. *Journal of Econometrics*, 138: 312 – 355.

[36] Pesaran M. H., Smith R. 1995. Estimating long-run relationships from dynamic heterogeneous panels. *Journal of Econometrics*, 68: 79 – 113.

[37] Quah D. 1993a. Golton's fallacies and tests of the convergence hypothesis. *Scandinavian Journal of Economics*, 95: 428 – 443.

[38] Quah D. 1993b. Empirical cross-section dynamics in economic growth. *European Economic Review*, 40: 1353 – 1375.

[39] Ram R. 2008. Parametric variability in cross-country growth regressions: an application of quantile-regression methodology. *Economics Letters*, 99: 387 – 389.

[40] Solow Robert M. 1956. A contribution to the theory of economic

growth. *Quarterly Journal of Economics*, LXX:65 – 94.

[41] Stock J. H., Watson M. W. 2012. Disentangling the channels of the 2007 – 2009 recession. Brookings Papers on Economic Activity, Forthcoming.

[42] Temple J. 1999. The new growth evidence. *Journal of Economic Literature*, 37:112 – 156.

[43] 彭文斌, 刘金全. 我国东、中、西三大区域经济差距的时空演变特征[J]. 经济地理, 2010, 30(04):574 – 578.

[44] 覃成林, 刘迎霞, 李超. 空间外溢与区域经济增长趋同——基于长江三角洲的案例分析[J]. 中国社会科学, 2012. (05):76 – 94, 206.

[45] 肖攀, 李连友, 苏静. 中国省域经济增长质量测度及其收敛性分析[J]. 财经理论与实践, 2016(04):111 – 117.

[46] 张宇, 郭万山. 中国经济新常态下省际经济差距收敛性研究[J]. 统计与决策, 2017(24):111 – 114.

[47] 朱国忠, 乔坤元, 虞吉海. 中国各省经济增长是否收敛?[J]. 经济学(季刊), 2014(03):1171 – 1194.

[48] 朱慧明, 曾惠芳, 虞克明. 基于 MCMC 稳态模拟的异质性经济增长模型研究[J]. 统计研究, 2010(07):52 – 59.

Chapter 6
The Impact of FDI on Economic Growth: an Empirical Evidence from IV Panel Quantile Regression

Intense debates on the impact of Foreign Direct Investment (FDI) on domestic economies, especially on the economies of developing host countries, have been carried on for several decades and remained a hot topic till now. FDI is widely considered as a win-win co-operation between the investors and the local firms, since the investors can profit from holding a share of the foreign firms and the local firms can also acquire positive productivity spillovers like capital, technologies, and knowledge and so on. FDI plays a vital role in transferring and disseminating international technologies. Therefore, many developing countries, who believe that FDI can positively impact the economic growth, compete with each other to attract FDI by making policies such as setting up special economic zones, reducing tax, and granting subsidies. Instrumental variable quantile regression for panel data with fixed effects is used to analyze the impact of FDI on economic growth, in order to reduce the omitted variable bias, solve the potential endogeneity of FDI, and allow heterogeneity across countries. The empirical findings show that FDI positively relates to the economic growth in underdeveloped countries, and the contribution of FDI on growth in those countries is even greater than GDI.

6.1 FDI and Economic Growth

A lot of literature has emerged to discover the relationship between FDI and the economic growth in host countries. Influential work by Levine and Renelt(1992) discovers a positive and robust correlation of share of investment with both growth rate and share of trade, through Leamer's extreme bounds analysis (EBA). Some cross-sectional and time-series analysis discovered that FDI did not positively or significantly influence host countries' economies, but under some special conditions, FDI can enhance the economic growth in host countries.

Blomstrom et al. (1992) used a dataset of 78 developing and 23 developed countries from 1960 – 1985, and concluded that FDI might significantly impact the economic growth only in rather wealthier host countries, therefore, there exists a certain threshold level of income, below which FDI has no impact on growth.

Borensztein et al. (1998) separated a dataset of 69 developing countries into two periods, i. e. 1970 – 1979 and 1980 – 1989. Allowing different constants for each period but restricting identical coefficients of explanatory variables, they found that FDI itself performs a positive but insignificant effect on economic growth, however, under the condition that if a host country has a minimum threshold stock of human capital, FDI has a positive and determinant effect on developing host countries and the effect is shown to be more contributing than domestic investment. Furthermore, they also found a crowding-in effect of FDI on domestic investment, which means FDI increases the total investment more than one for one.

Balasubramanyam et al. (1996, 1999) used a cross-sectional annual dataset of 46 developing countries from 1970 to 1985, and identified the important role of the domestic market, the competitive climate in relation to local producers and FDI-labor interactions on economic growth. They concluded that FDI influences the growth rate in countries whose strategy was export promoting(EP), rather than import substituting(IS).

The empirical study of Olofsdotter(1998) investigated the impacts of FDI in 50 developed and developing countries over the period from 1980 to 1995. He found the evidence of a positive relationship between economic growth and FDI, however, the combinations of FDI with openness and human capital show no positive impacts on growth. He also discovered that FDI is still profitable for countries with a higher level of institutional capability.

However, there are some other literature such as Stocker (2000) reporting an opposite result. Stocker(2000) investigated the relationship between FDI and economic growth through both cross-section analysis with data of 72 countries over the period 1980 – 1995 and time-series analysis with data of 100 countries over the period 1970 – 1996. No reliable relationship or persistent Granger-causality between FDI and economic growth were verified.

Compared to cross-sectional or time-series approaches, panel data analysis is generally considered as a more efficient method, due to its flexibility in allowing for heterogeneity of different countries, which can help to avoid omitted variable bias induced by an underlying correlation between country-specific effects and the error term. For this reason, panel data analysis has been applied to investigate the relationship between FDI and economic growth.

Nair-Reichert and Weinhold (2001), by using a sample of 24 developing countries, proposed applying the Mixed Fixed and Random estimator to solve the heterogeneity across countries and found a causal relationship between FDI and economic growth. Furthermore, the impact of FDI is higher in more open economies. Choe(2003) set up a panel dataset of 80 countries over the period 1971 – 1995. By using a panel VAR model, he found FDI Granger-causes economic growth and vice versa, and the latter Granger-causality relation is more apparent.

Carkovic and Levine (2005) constructed a dataset consisting of 72 countries and 7 five-year periods from 1960 to 1990. Considering country-specific effects and underlying endogeneity in the model, they used GMM (generalized method of moments) panel estimator to investigate the impact of FDI on economic growth, and found that FDI inflows do not show any significant positive impacts on growth.

Since all of the different estimation methods mentioned above are based on LS-type regression, researchers are restricted to investigating the relationship between economic growth and FDI at the mean of the conditional distribution of the dependent variable, i. e. economic growth in this chapter. As an alternative approach of allowing for parameter heterogeneity, quantile regression proposed by Koenker and Bassett (1978) enables researchers to study the relationship between economic growth and FDI not only at the center but also at different parts of the entire conditional distribution. Moreover, quantile regression has additional advantages as follows. Firstly, the assumption of Gaussian error seems too strict and not common in empirical analysis, while quantile regression estimators are more efficient when the error term is not normally distributed. Secondly, quantile regression will be more robust if outliers exist in the data. Stocker (2000) demonstrated how the presence of outliers can distort the relationship between economic growth and FDI, i. e. , OLS regression using his full dataset shows a significantly negative coefficient estimate of FDI, whereas, after getting rid of 7 outliers from the regression, the effect of FDI turns to be insignificant. Thirdly, quantile regression allows heterogeneous results of most of the variables of interest, which is suitable for analyzing the relationship between FDI and growth, since the relationship may be complex and heterogeneous [see Nair-Reichert and Weinhold, 2001]. Due to these advantages, quantile regression has been already applied to the study of FDI. Dimelis and Louri (2002) used quantile regression to analyze the production efficiency of 4,056 firms in Greece in 1997 and discovered that the entry of foreign affiliates can enhance the local labor productivity, however, the impact is significant only at the median. Girma and Gurg (2005) used a dataset period from 1980 – 1992 in UK to estimate the effect of various covariates on productivity at different quantiles. They found that productivity benefits from FDI spillovers while the efficient gap is reduced to some threshold level of the establishment in the UK.

It seems that quantile regression is a suitable way to analyze the FDI and economic growth, however, this method still suffers from the problem of endogeneity, since FDI may be correlated to the country-specific error term (see Carkovic and Levine, 2005; Borensztein, 1998, etc.). This particular problem remained unresolved until the work of Galvao (2011) who extends Chernozhukov and Hansen (2005, 2006) to develop the IV (instrumental variable) panel quantile regression method. In this chapter, this novel technique is used to reinvestigate the impact of FDI on economic growth at various quantiles.

In the last 40 years, FDI has increased dramatically, and peaked at 2.356 trillion US Dollars in 2007 on a global scale. Figure 6.1 lists some area-specific FDI inflow trends over the period 1970 – 2010. It shows that the European Union enjoys the greatest amount of FDI among the areas under consideration. East Asia and Pacific area obtains the second largest amount whereas Sub-Saharan Africa acquires the least amount among the five areas and its FDI net inflows in 2007 is only about 8 percent of European Union or 20 percent of East Asia and Pacific area. There are two significant falls in Figure 6.1. The first one happened at the beginning of this century, which was largely caused by the significant drop in cross-border M&A among the industrial countries, coinciding with the correction in world equity markets (Patterson, et al., 2004). The other drop in 2008 was obviously caused by the subprime mortgage crisis.

Although low and middle-income countries possess a small share of the total FDI, the impact of FDI on their economic growth should not be neglected. During last two decades, FDI to developing countries has risen prominently, and numerous papers have studied the impact of FDI on the growth rate of host developing countries. The strong positive effect of FDI on GDP growth in the host developing countries has been repeatedly shown in the literature. As Stocker(2000) describes, although developing countries have turned out to be less integrated with the world economy, the effects of FDI flows to poor countries are significant, regardless of their economic sizes. This observation can be supported by Figure 6.1, which displays the share of FDI net inflows in GDP. In Figure 6.2, the share of FDI has fluctuated all the time and started an increasing trend from 1985. In 2007, the FDI net inflows in the Sub-Saharan Africa is about 30 billion US Dollars, while the European Union enjoys nearly forty times of FDI net inflows. However, the share of FDI in GDP in the Sub-Saharan is about 3.4, which is only a little less than that of European Union. Although a low-income area like Sub-Saharan Africa obtains small FDI net inflows, the share of FDI in GDP cannot be ignored, even in such a case.

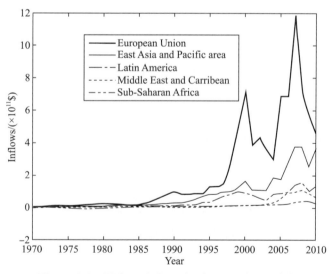

Figure 6.1 FDI net inflows(BoP, current US $)

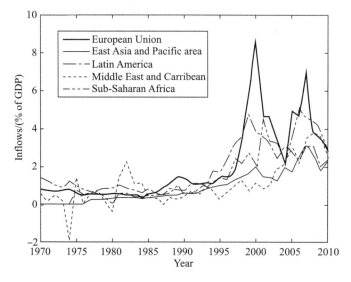

Figure 6. 2　FDI net inflows(% of GDP)

6. 2　IV Quantile Regression Model for Panel Data with Fixed Effects

While studying FDI impacts, not only country-specific effects but also time effects are considered in the model. Carkovic and Levine (2005) considered a time dummy in each period to control time effects. In this chapter, a dynamic panel model is used to control country-specific and time effects to avoid omitted variable bias. Consider a panel-based model for FDI and economic growth as follows:

$$GY_{it} = \alpha Y_{i,t-1} + \beta FDI_{it} + X'_{it}\Gamma + \eta_i + \lambda_t + u_{it},$$
$$i = 1,2,\cdots,N; t = 1,2,\cdots,T \quad (6.1)$$

where GY_{it} is the growth rate of GDP per capita in country i and year t, $Y_{i,t-1}$ is the logarithm of GDP per capita in country i and year $t-1$, FDI_{it} is FDI net inflow (% of GDP), and X'_{it} is a set of other independent variables that can influence economic growth such as government consumption, gross domestic investment (GDI), inflation, M2, quality of government and political rights. The other two terms, η_i and λ_t, are country-specific effects and year-specific effects, respectively.

Since FDI might be influenced by growth rate simultaneously, FDI may be endogenous and needs to be taken into account when estimating model (6.1). The potential problem caused by the presence of endogeneity has been considered in the FDI literature when LS-type regression was employed for estimation; see Borensztein et al. (1998), Stocker(2000), Carkovic and Levine(2005). As for quantile regression, if an endogenous variable exists, Kim and Muller (2004) showed that the estimate of quantile regression was biased. Galvao (2011) extends the work of Chernozhukov and Hansen(2005, 2006) to develop the IV (instrumental variable) panel quantile regression method. In this chapter, the IV panel quantile regression method imployed here was proposed by Galvao (2011), and the lagged values of explanatory variables are used as instruments. To enhance the quality of such instrumental variables, a sufficiently long length is applied, i.e. 1st to 5th lagged values of explanatory variables, denoted as w_{it}. For a certain quantile θ, the parameters α_θ, Γ_θ, $\eta_{i\theta}$, $\lambda_{t\theta}$, ζ_θ are estimated by

$$\mathrm{argmin}_{\alpha_\theta, \Gamma_\theta, \eta_{i\theta}, \lambda_{t\theta}, \zeta_\theta} \sum_{i=1}^{N} \sum_{t=1}^{T} \rho_\theta (GY_{it} - \alpha_\theta Y_{i,t-1} - \beta_\theta FDI_{it} - X'_{it}\Gamma_\theta - \eta_{i\theta} - \lambda_{t\theta} - w'_{it}\zeta_\theta) \quad (6.2)$$

where $\rho_\theta(u) = u(\theta - I(u<0))$. For a certain quantile θ and a certain value of $\beta_{\theta j}$ from a previously defined grid $\{\beta_\theta j, j = 1, 2, \cdots, J\}$, the estimators are $\hat{\alpha}_\theta(\beta_\theta)$, $\hat{\Gamma}_\theta(\beta_\theta)$, $\hat{\eta}_{i\theta}(\beta_\theta)$, $\hat{\lambda}_{t\theta}(\beta_\theta)$, $\hat{\zeta}_\theta(\beta_\theta)$. The true coefficients on IV, ζ_θ, should be zero, since if w_{it} is a collection of valid instruments, w_{it} must be independent of the error term u_{it} in eq. (6.1). Hence, β_θ can be estimated by making $\hat{\zeta}_\theta(\beta_\theta)$ as close to zero as possible; i.e. by the following minimizing

$$\hat{\beta}_\theta = \min_{\beta_\theta} \| \hat{\zeta}_\theta(\beta_\theta) \|_A \quad (6.3)$$

where $\|x\|_A = \sqrt{x'Ax}$, and A is a positive definite matrix. Hence, the final IV panel quantile estimators are given by $\hat{\alpha}_\theta(\hat{\beta}_\theta), \hat{\Gamma}_\theta(\hat{\beta}_\theta), \hat{\eta}_{i\theta}(\hat{\beta}_\theta),$ $\hat{\lambda}_{t\theta}(\hat{\beta}_\theta), \hat{\zeta}_\theta(\hat{\beta}_\theta)$. Readers can refer to Galvao(2011) for a more detailed discussion.

6.3 Data and Empirical Results

The data set consists of 60 developed and developing countries, and the sample period is from 1991 to 2008. FDI net inflows(% of GDP), gross domestic investment(GDI,% of GDP), GDP per capita(constant 2,000 US $), general government final consumption expenditure(% of GDP) denoted as GCE, trade(% GDP) that equals to the sum of exports and imports of goods and services, and(M2)(% of GDP) are collected from World Development Indicators. Human capital is measured by average years of male secondary schooling, which is collected from Barro and Lee (2010). Quality of Government by International Country Risk Guide is used to measure the quality of governments, which is the mean value of the ICRG variables Corruption, Law and Order and Bureaucracy Quality, and scaled 0 – 1 (Higher values indicate higher quality of government). Political rights is measured by the grade of people participating freely in the political process between 1(most free) and 7(least free) by Freedom House[1].

The impacts of FDI on economic growth are revealed by the mean-based OLS and panel data regression in table 6.1. The first column of table 6.1 displays the results of pooling OLS regression. Strongly significant and positive effects of FDI on growth are confirmed. The initial GDP significantly and negatively relates to economic growth. GDI also significantly and positively impacts economic growth and its impacts play a greater role than FDI. The significantly negative relation between

---

[1] Data on the quality of government and political rights is downloaded from http://www.qog.pol.gu.se/.

openness of trade and growth is unexpected, which might be caused by possible endogeneity in the model or omitted variable bias. Although other explanatory variables achieve ideal sign in OLS regression, their impacts on economic growth are not significant. Compared with OLS regression results, two-stage least squares regression results in column two show the influence of endogeneity of FDI, i. e. , the estimated coefficient of FDI changes from 0. 102, 7 by OLS to 0. 277, 2 by TSLS, which indicates that, without considering the potential endogeneity of FDI, OLS underestimates the impact of FDI about 170%. One still needs to keep in mind that OLS and TSLS constrain common interception for all countries, therefore neglect country-specific effects, which causes omitted variable bias.

The last two columns exhibit panel data regression results with both country-specific and period-specific effects. FDI is considered as an exogenous variable in column 3, while as an endogenous variable in column 4. In column 4, FDI significantly impacts economic growth by using IV to solve the endogenous problem, furthermore, without considering the endogeneity, the impact of FDI on growth is underestimated and not significant in column 3. The estimates of initial GDP and GDI are significant for all these regressions, which demonstrates their stable impact on growth. Compared to FDI, GDI shows a little smaller impact on GDP after solving endogeneity problems in the model, which means that FDI and GDI play very important roles for growth, and the impact of FDI is greater than GDI. In the last column, M2 and quality of government show their significant impact on growth as well. All the above mean-based regression results display the positive impacts of FDI on economic growth, which demonstrates the vital role of FDI in the recent 20 years.

Chapter 6 The Impact of FDI on Economic Growth: an Empirical Evidence from IV Panel Quantile Regression

Table 6.1 Pooling and panel regression
(dependent variable: GDP growth per capita)

Item	OLS	TSLS	PDTW	PDTWIV
ln(initial GDP)	−0.354,8 **	−0.336,2 *	−9.014,6 ***	−8.771,6 ***
	(0.131)	(0.133 4)	(1.185 6)	(1.208 1)
FDI	0.102,7 ***	0.277,2 ***	0.042,0	0.209,5 **
	(0.028,3)	(0.052,6)	(0.030,2)	(0.076,7)
GDI	0.177,3 ***	0.176,8 ***	0.169,8 ***	0.149,7 ***
	(0.019,5)	(0.019,9)	(0.029,9)	(0.031,5)
GCE	−0.028,8	−0.035,6	0.062,0	0.066,3
	(0.022,9)	(0.023,4)	(0.052,7)	(0.053,5)
Inflation rate	−7.00E−04	−7.00E−04	−5.00E−04	−5.00E−04
	(6.00E−04)	(6.00E−04)	(6.00E−04)	(6.00E−04)
Openness of trade	−0.004,1 *	−0.010,3 ***	0.006,5	0.004,8
	(0.002,3)	(0.002,8)	(0.008,4)	(0.008,5)
schooling	0.009,7	−0.070,6	0.728,2	0.441,6
	(0.132,3)	(0.136,2)	(0.637,7)	(0.658,6)
M2	0.003,0	0.002,4	−0.024,8 *	−0.027,6 **
	(0.003,3)	(0.003,4)	(0.010,5)	(0.010,7)
Political, rights	−0.058,2	−0.058,3	−0.108,0	−0.133,2
	(0.063,4)	(0.064,5)	(0.127,6)	(0.130,0)
Quality of government	1.131,5	1.184,5	4.171,9 **	3.639,0 *
	(0.831,3)	(0.846,0)	(1.434,0)	(1.473,1)
Adjust−R square	0.103,0	0.071,2	0.102,1	0.083,9

Standard errors are in parentheses. Constant estimates including the fixed effect terms are not shown. Significant coefficients are marked by *** (0.1%), ** (1%), * (5%).

Quantile regression could provide an alternative perspective to parameter heterogeneity at different quantiles, which enable us to reveal the detailed impacts of FDI on economic growth among different countries. Table 6.2 to table 6.3 exhibit quantile regression results by pooling regression, pooling regression with IV, quantile regression for panel data, and IV quantile regression for panel data. The estimated coefficients at some pre-selected quantiles ($\theta = 0.1, 0.2, \cdots, 0.9$) with 90% confidence intervals are displayed in parentheses.

Table 6.2 shows pooling quantile regression results are very different from mean-based regressions. It can be found that FDI estimates are positive at all quantiles but not significant while $\theta = 0.1$ only, which means that FDI hardly has significantly positive effects on economic growth for the lowest income growth countries. Compared to LS regression results in column 1 of table 6.1, the quantile regression results demonstrate the different impacts of FDI on growth across countries, i.e. the impacts of FDI for the lowest countries are smaller than those in the highest income growth countries. Negative relation between initial GDP and growth is not confirmed as θ is bigger than 0.4. GDI exerts strong and positive impacts on growth and its impacts in lower income growth countries are smaller than higher income growth countries. Government consumption shows its negative effects on growth while $\theta = 0.2 \sim 0.5$, which verifies the negative relationship between growth and government consumption in lower and middle income growth countries. Schooling has significantly positive impacts on growth only for the lowest income growth countries. Quality of government has significant and positive effects on growth only for lower income growth countries.

Table 6.2 Pooling quantile regression with 90% confidence interval (exogeneity)

θ	FDI	ln GDP	GDI	GCE	Inflation
0.1	0.093,9 (-0.095,4; 0.143,2)	-0.737,1 (-1.175,5; -0.423,7)	0.132,7 (0.088,8; 0.244,4)	-0.080,5 (-0.115,9; 0.012,9)	-1e-04 (-1.8e+308; -1e-04)
0.2	0.088,1 (0.042,0; 0.159,1)	-0.410,4 (-0.648,6; -0.201,6)	0.158,8 (0.115,4; 0.208,7)	-0.081,9 (-0.136,9; -0.028,8)	-4e-04 (-0.601,5; -4e-04)
0.3	0.108,2 (0.052,8; 0.158,3)	-0.290,2 (-0.470,4; -0.009,8)	0.139,8 (0.095,8; 0.182,8)	-0.100,1 (-0.152,1; -0.052,1)	-6e-04 (-0.147,0; 0.001,4)
0.4	0.117,6 (0.077,0; 0.190,7)	-0.205,8 (-0.453,5; -0.066,2)	0.158,3 (0.114,3; 0.208,6)	-0.073,7 (-0.103,9; -0.037)	-8e-04 (-0.018,1; 0.00,1)
0.5	0.131,1 (0.080,9; 0.168,4)	-0.166,4 (-0.361,7; 0.011,6)	0.181,2 (0.133,2; 0.208,1)	-0.046,4 (-0.077,9; -0.021,3)	-0.001 (-0.004,2; 7e-04)
0.6	0.107,7 (0.062,0; 0.180,7)	-0.184,4 (-0.443,8; 0.05,3)	0.175,7 (0.144,5; 0.203,1)	-0.035,8 (-0.071,8; 0.005,9)	2e-04 (-0.001,2; 0.012,4)
0.7	0.112,0 (0.068,3; 0.209,1)	-0.204,3 (-0.442,5; 0.097,1)	0.181,6 (0.153,8; 0.217,5)	-0.022,4 (-0.067,1; 0.009)	-1e-04 (-0.001,3; 0.090,5)
0.8	0.140,9 (0.057,8; 0.216,4)	0.107,3 (-0.352,2; 0.358,7)	0.218,6 (0.185,8; 0.251,3)	0.013,8 (-0.032,2; 0.043,9)	-5e-04 (-0.001,6; 0.474,3)
0.9	0.133,5 (0.091,5; 0.229,8)	0.127,0 (-0.104,5; 0.450,7)	0.223,2 (0.203,4; 0.277,1)	0.010,2 (-0.028,6; 0.062,5)	-0.001,0 (-0.001,1; 1.8e+308)

Continued

θ	Trade	Schooling	M2	Political rights	Quality of government
0.1	−0.008, 9 (−0.016, 3; −1e−04)	0.566, 1 (0.178, 4; 0.913, 8)	0.002, 5 (−0.007, 0; 0.009)	−0.184, 9 (−0.618, 6; 0.058, 7)	2.282, 7 (−1.079, 9; 4.942, 6)
0.2	2e−04 (−0.011, 0; 0.005, 7)	0.248, 3 (0.079, 6; 0.540, 9)	0.001, 1 (−0.005, 8; 0.005, 3)	−0.125, 5 (−0.313, 0; 0.043, 5)	1.623, 6 (−0.731, 0; 3.894, 0)
0.3	−0.001, 6 (−0.008, 9; 0.003, 2)	0.149, 3 (−0.042, 9; 0.311, 7)	0.001, 7 (−0.006, 6; 0.005, 8)	−0.043, 0 (−0.188, 8; 0.089, 1)	1.920, 0 (0.447, 7; 3.425, 2)
0.4	−0.003, 0 (−0.008, 6; 3e−04)	−0.002, 1 (−0.118, 4; 0.152, 4)	9e−04 (−0.002, 5; 0.005, 3)	0.029, 0 (−0.111, 2; 0.132, 4)	1.722, 2 (0.159, 0; 3.362, 2)
0.5	−0.003, 1 (−0.008, 5; 0.003, 3)	−0.104, 7 (−0.218, 4; 0.123, 2)	−2e−04 (−0.004, 6; 0.003, 8)	0.061, 8 (−0.064, 3; 0.113, 7)	1.132, 0 (−0.167, 9; 2.921, 3)
0.6	1e−04 (−0.005, 3; 0.002, 4)	−0.110, 3 (−0.293, 6; 0.078, 1)	−0.001, 2 (−0.005, 2; 0.004, 4)	0.033, 5 (−0.029, 8; 0.129)	1.464, 1 (−0.181, 3; 2.940, 5)
0.7	−5e−04 (−0.004, 1; 0.001, 9)	−0.123, 2 (−0.299, 1; −0.027, 3)	−0.002, 1 (−0.006, 0; 0.005, 6)	0.084, 1 (−0.044, 9; 0.178)	1.103, 5 (−0.395, 5; 2.462, 5)
0.8	−0.001, 9 (−0.004, 3; 0.002, 2)	−0.359, 2 (−0.452, 1; −0.123, 4)	−0.004, 5 (−0.011, 6; 0.001, 4)	0.061, 3 (−0.039, 2; 0.174, 3)	−0.864, 4 (−2.427, 6; 0.662, 5)
0.9	−8e−04 (−0.004, 8; 0.003, 4)	−0.413, 4 (−0.741, 0; −0.089, 6)	−0.006, 3 (−0.013, 2; 4e−04)	0.004, 5 (−0.072, 1; 0.152)	−1.955, 2 (−3.275, 8; −0.554, 5)

Note: 90% confidence intervals are in parentheses.

Table 6.3 displays quantile regression results while considering endogeneity of FDI in the model. Compared to table 6.2, the impacts of FDI are higher after considering the endogeneity of FDI, which confirms the bias caused by endogeneity in pooling quantile regression. GDI also plays a very important role in growth, but its impact is not as high as FDI.

After the country-specific and period-specific effects are introduced into regression to avoid the omitted variable bias, results of quantile regression for panel data are displayed in table 6.4. FDI is positively related to growth but only significant at several quantiles, i.e. $\theta = 0.3$, $0.4, 0.6$. GDI still exerts a significantly positive influence on growth, and the higher the domestic investment is, the more important the effect is. It can also be found that the evidence that schooling significantly and positively relates to growth at median income growth and higher income growth countries, and at the fastest growth countries one more year education helps GDP per capita increase by 1.5%. M2 has significantly negative impacts on growth at all countries except the richest ones. Political rights play an important role for median income growth countries, while the quality of government shows its impact on growth only in poorer economies.

The estimation results based on IV panel quantile regression are shown in table 6.5. As shown in table 6.5, FDI tends to have a positive effect on economic growth at all quantiles, but it is significant only at low quantiles between $\theta = 0.1$ and $\theta = 0.4$. The estimated coefficient for FDI starts at 0.42 at the 10th quantile and falls gradually to 0.25 at the 30th quantile. At intermediate and high quantiles, i.e. $\theta = 0.4, 0.5, \cdots, 0.9$, the positive impacts are not significant. Compared to table 6.5, the estimate results for FDI in table 6.2 and table 6.4 underestimate the effect of FDI, due to neglecting the endogeneity of FDI. While in table 6.3, although the endogeneity problem is considered, the effect of FDI is also underestimated at $\theta = 0.1$ and $\theta = 0.2$ quantiles and at $\theta = 0.3$ the

Table 6.3 Pooling quantile regression with 90% confidence intervals (endogeneity)

θ	FDI	ln GDP	GDI	GCE	Inflation
0.1	0.25 (0.07, 0.43)	−0.851,1 (−1.480,8; −0.097,6)	0.133,4 (0.036,0; 0.279,7)	−0.079,6 (−0.221,0; 0.012,5)	−1e−04 (−0.102,1; 8e−04)
0.2	0.23 (0.06, 0.48)	−0.486,2 (−0.891,1; 0.068,1)	0.167,3 (0.082,7; 0.251,6)	−0.071,7 (−0.199,5; −0.023,4)	−4e−04 (−0.049,2; 0.001)
0.3	0.26 (0.06, 0.50)	−0.251,3 (−0.678,0; 0.085,5)	0.157,5 (0.073,2; 0.258,0)	−0.120,4 (−0.178,6; −0.023,9)	−6e−04 (−0.023,4; 0.001,4)
0.4	0.32 (0.07, 0.48)	−0.208,1 (−0.580,9; 0.144,0)	0.167,2 (0.087,3; 0.253,0)	−0.061,1 (−0.148,2; −0.021,8)	−9e−04 (−0.009,4; 0.001,1)
0.5	0.26 (0.08, 0.44)	−0.117,1 (−0.514,5; 0.175,0)	0.202,4 (0.094,4; 0.249,5)	−0.053,1 (−0.118,3; −0.006,5)	−0.001 (−0.004,7; 9e−04)
0.6	0.27 (0.09, 0.44)	−0.126,9 (−0.532,1; 0.236,4)	0.177,7 (0.101,9; 0.254,1)	−0.052,2 (−0.103,7; 0.009,4)	2e−04 (−0.004,8; 0.001,4)
0.7	0.30 (0.10, 0.43)	−0.059,3 (−0.545,3; 0.441,2)	0.205,3 (0.109,5; 0.260,9)	−0.001,5 (−0.091,1; 0.033,3)	−1e−04 (−0.001,5; 0.008,4)
0.8	0.25 (0.05, 0.40)	0.165,2 (−0.514,2; 0.610,6)	0.222,0 (0.124,3; 0.263,6)	−0.009,3 (−0.077,9; 0.057,1)	−5e−04 (−0.001,7; 0.010,0)
0.9	0.25 (0.04, 0.45)	0.185,5 (−0.437,7; 0.721,2)	0.223,3 (0.131,3; 0.279,9)	0.008,2 (−0.069,3; 0.096,4)	−0.001 (−0.002,1; 0.007,8)

Continued

θ	Trade	Schooling	M2	Political rights	Quality of government
0.1	-0.018,5 (-0.034,8; -0.004,2)	0.603,1 (-0.020,5; 1.230,3)	0.004,4 (-0.007,7; 0.022,8)	-0.203,5 (-0.651,8; 0.227,1)	1.917,4 (-1.311,8; 5.376,9)
0.2	-0.006,1 (-0.023,9; 0.002,7)	0.269,9 (-0.278,9; 0.760,6)	0.001,4 (-0.008,2; 0.017,7)	-0.115,8 (-0.361,3; 0.211,6)	1.717,2 (-1.082,7; 3.996,7)
0.3	-0.008,9 (-0.023,2; 0.003,0)	0.090,3 (-0.269,3; 0.510,4)	-0.001,3 (-0.009,6; 0.015,5)	-0.061,3 (-0.252,2; 0.212,9)	1.883,5 (-0.074,9; 3.755,5)
0.4	-0.012,5 (-0.021,8; 0.003,1)	-0.047,6 (-0.300,2; 0.399,4)	-0.001,3 (-0.010,4; 0.013,8)	0.017,5 (-0.193,6; 0.201,4)	1.050,3 (-0.315,5; 3.531,8)
0.5	-0.008,8 (-0.019,8; 0.003,2)	-0.096,6 (-0.326,8; 0.303,8)	-0.003,0 (-0.010,1; 0.012,5)	0.050,5 (-0.136,0; 0.198,9)	0.965,5 (-0.476,7; 3.244,9)
0.6	-0.007,0 (-0.017,7; 0.003,5)	-0.160,9 (-0.372,3; 0.237,9)	-0.003,4 (-0.009,7; 0.011,7)	0.054,0 (-0.117,5; 0.211,3)	1.737,1 (-0.418,6; 3.292,4)
0.7	-0.007,4 (-0.015,0; 0.004,3)	-0.203,6 (-0.446,0; 0.167,9)	-0.003,3 (-0.012,1; 0.010,3)	0.055,9 (-0.152,4; 0.228,8)	-0.104,2 (-0.949,2; 2.626,4)
0.8	-0.004,0 (-0.011,3; 0.005,3)	-0.381,3 (-0.591,6; 0.094,8)	-0.006,4 (-0.015,5; 0.006,3)	0.038,6 (-0.160,5; 0.248,7)	-0.867,7 (-2.827,8; 1.409,4)
0.9	-0.004,8 (-0.012,4; 0.007,6)	-0.448,4 (-0.830,2; 0.017,1)	-0.008,5 (-0.019,8; 0.006,0)	0.047,1 (-0.217,6; 0.295,6)	-2.070,0 (-3.354,5; -0.221,2)

Note: 90% confidence intervals are in parentheses.

Table 6.4 Quantile regression for panel data with 90% confidence intervals

θ	FDI	ln GDP	GDI	GCE	Inflation
0.1	0.072, 0 (−0.003, 3; 0.152, 8)	−9.612, 1 (−15.717, 0; −3.691, 5)	0.129, 9 (−6e−04; 0.311, 4)	−0.225, 8 (−0.415, 5; 0.117, 2)	−0.001, 9 (−1.8e+308; 8e−04)
0.2	0.075, 6 (−0.012, 5; 0.140, 9)	−7.873, 9 (−12.100, 7; −5.467, 8)	0.123, 5 (0.041, 70; 0.184, 0)	−0.151, 2 (−0.329, 2; −0.004, 5)	3e−04 (−1.137, 2; 5e−04)
0.3	0.089, 5 (0.045, 1; 0.160, 1)	−8.135, 5 (−11.045, 7; −5.456, 8)	0.130, 1 (0.075, 1; 0.189, 4)	−0.138, 3 (−0.224, 5; −0.065, 6)	2e−04 (−0.185, 8; 0.001)
0.4	0.067, 3 (0.020, 9; 0.129, 5)	−7.773, 9 (−10.495, 8; −4.057, 5)	0.160, 1 (0.119, 5; 0.202, 5)	−0.134, 7 (−0.232, 3; −0.039, 5)	1e−04 (−0.033, 1; 8e−04)
0.5	0.050, 5 (−0.007, 6; 0.097, 0)	−5.971, 9 (−8.186, 9; −2.527, 0)	0.152, 1 (0.118, 0; 0.192, 0)	−0.155, 7 (−0.254, 7; −0.027, 6)	−2e−04 (−0.006, 0; 0.001, 2)
0.6	0.065, 3 (0.009, 9; 0.092, 7)	−4.295, 4 (−6.596, 0; −2.338, 6)	0.156, 2 (0.138, 2; 0.190, 9)	−0.115, 5 (−0.211, 7; −0.059, 5)	−6e−04 (−6e−04; 8e−04)
0.7	0.030, 3 (−0.003, 1; 0.077, 1)	−4.973, 9 (−5.709, 9; −2.388, 9)	0.182, 0 (0.139, 5; 0.219, 7)	−0.082, 3 (−0.172, 9; 0.003, 9)	−1e−04 (−7e−04; 0.027, 5)
0.8	0.010, 6 (−0.017, 0; 0.062, 8)	−4.515, 1 (−8.657, 7; −3.474, 9)	0.181, 9 (0.144, 3; 0.232, 7)	−0.032 (−0.183, 9; 0.075, 5)	−1e−04 (−9e−04; 0.734, 8)
0.9	0.028, 3 (−0.032, 6; 0.114, 5)	−8.524, 4 (−12.182, 2; −2.402, 7)	0.194, 2 (0.137, 6; 0.275, 7)	−0.061, 3 (−0.142, 7; 0.143, 5)	−1e−04 (−5e−04; 1.8e+308)

Chapter 6 The Impact of FDI on Economic Growth: an Empirical Evidence from IV Panel Quantile Regression   175

Continued

θ	Trade	Schooling	M2	Political rights	Quality of government
0.1	0.014,8 (−0.026,7; 0.026,7)	0.888,6 (−1.723,0; 3.357,2)	−0.039,8 (−0.097,8; −0.008,6)	0.057,9 (−0.637,8; 0.387,1)	5.869,8 (0.309,1; 11.436,6)
0.2	0.006,6 (−0.011,8; 0.026,0)	−0.047,2 (−1.201,4; 1.900,3)	−0.038,1 (−0.055,6; −0.015,6)	−0.075,8 (−0.364,6; 0.191,1)	4.243,5 (1.396,5; 8.053,5)
0.3	0.009,1 (−0.009,3; 0.026,2)	0.345,3 (−0.347,5; 1.748,3)	−0.031,0 (−0.043,4; −0.017,2)	0.042,0 (−0.173,9; 0.287,5)	2.858,8 (0.144,8; 5.687,5)
0.4	0.012,3 (−0.005,5; 0.027,2)	0.656,4 (−0.349,5; 1.658,4)	−0.024,5 (−0.044,1; −0.007,9)	0.230,6 (−0.108,8; 0.382,7)	2.890,4 (−0.439,5; 4.999,7)
0.5	0.019,3 (−0.011,5; 0.027,5)	0.682 (0.108,2; 1.470,4)	−0.020,6 (−0.035,6; −0.012,0)	0.149,2 (0.043,6; 0.364,9)	0.883,5 (−1.663,9; 3.816,6)
0.6	0.009,5 (−0.003,1; 0.024,7)	0.949,9 (0.269,0; 1.645,6)	−0.029,1 (−0.038,1; −0.015,5)	0.251,0 (0.023,6; 0.350,9)	0.097,1 (−1.201,9; 2.490,7)
0.7	0.008,0 (−0.004,1; 0.020,3)	0.925,3 (0.174,3; 1.608,6)	−0.027,0 (−0.040,2; −0.017,5)	0.187,1 (0.016,0; 0.333,4)	−0.119,4 (−1.967,8; 0.850,8)
0.8	0.005,4 (−0.007,8; 0.028,5)	0.997,4 (0.112,8; 2.373,2)	−0.026,0 (−0.035,9; −0.010,2)	0.118,6 (−0.049,8; 0.342,2)	−1.768,9 (−4.138,1; 2.010,6)
0.9	0.017,2 (−0.007,2; 0.025,2)	1.575,1 (0.094,1; 2.062,8)	−0.018,6 (−0.033,6; 0.008,4)	0.080,4 (−0.242,8; 0.312,1)	0.088,6 (−3.597,3; 3.995,6)

Note: 90% confidence intervals are in parentheses.

Table 6.5 IV panel quantile regression results with 90% confidence intervals

θ	FDI	ln GDP	GDI	GCE	Inflation
0.1	0.42 (0.02, 0.57)	−8.703, 2 (−17.150, 6; −4.276, 4)	0.074, 6 (−0.013, 9; 0.283, 6)	−0.215, 4 (−0.424, 3; 0.081, 4)	−9e−04 (−0.082, 3; 0.001, 0)
0.2	0.33 (0.04, 0.57)	−8.510, 2 (−14.224, 8; −4.389, 3)	0.070, 8 (0.014, 0; 0.217, 5)	−0.178, 3 (−0.325, 7; 0.015, 3)	3e−04 (−0.043, 4; 9e−04)
0.3	0.25 (0.07, 0.53)	−7.866, 6 (−13.047, 1; −4.657, 4)	0.112, 5 (0.048, 7; 0.207, 9)	−0.143, 2 (−0.271, 9; −0.008, 8)	2e−04 (−0.036, 2; 0.001, 2)
0.4	0.21 (0.00, 0.47)	−7.790, 3 (−12.468, 5; −3.820, 9)	0.140, 7 (0.071, 8; 0.213, 9)	−0.101, 4 (−0.279, 9; 0.006, 4)	−1e−04 (−0.025, 8; 0.001, 0)
0.5	0.17 (−0.01, 0.42)	−5.121, 3 (−11.594, 3; −2.405, 1)	0.141, 1 (0.089, 7; 0.210, 0)	−0.103, 2 (−0.265, 6; 0.028, 6)	−2e−04 (−0.016, 7; 9e−04)
0.6	0.16 (0.00, 0.35)	−4.655 (−10.413, 4; −1.854, 8)	0.146, 3 (0.101, 7; 0.203, 0)	−0.116, 8 (−0.236, 7; 0.041, 8)	−6e−04 (−0.013, 6; 7e−04)
0.7	0.13 (−0.03, 0.33)	−4.716, 7 (−9.987, 7; −1.99, 1)	0.173, 6 (0.105, 1; 0.211, 3)	−0.059, 7 (−0.227, 7; 0.075, 4)	0 (−0.014, 1; 8e−04)
0.8	0.06 (−0.08, 0.33)	−4.391, 9 (−12.005, 1; −2.636, 1)	0.175, 4 (0.106, 9; 0.227, 8)	−0.047, 8 (−0.236, 3; 0.128, 7)	−2e−04 (−0.015, 4; 6e−04)
0.9	0.17 (−0.09, 0.45)	−9.748 (−16.861, 4; −1.736, 7)	0.184, 4 (0.092, 2; 0.250, 4)	−0.022, 2 (−0.217, 8; 0.263, 0)	1e−04 (−0.019, 3; 7e−04)

Continued

θ	Trade	Schooling	M2	Political rights	Quality of government
0.1	0.003,5 (-0.028,4; 0.039,9)	-0.329,2 (-1.693,2; 2.829,1)	-0.064,3 (-0.089,7; -0.009,2)	-0.314,8 (-0.909,8; 0.289,8)	2.844,9 (-0.863,1; 10.170,4)
0.2	-0.002,0 (-0.016,0; 0.028,0)	0.221,3 (-1.420,4; 2.120,5)	-0.038,3 (-0.070,3; -0.008,1)	-0.219,2 (-0.465,5; 0.235,7)	4.266,7 (0.255,1; 7.938,2)
0.3	0.002,9 (-0.014,1; 0.025,6)	0.292,1 (-0.820,4; 1.864,5)	-0.031,0 (-0.056,9; -0.009,9)	0.053,1 (-0.246,3; 0.293,1)	3.505,5 (-0.343,6; 6.866,7)
0.4	0.008,0 (-0.013,6; 0.026,8)	0.673,1 (-0.847,2; 1.741,3)	-0.023,1 (-0.051,1; -0.004,5)	0.163,8 (-0.140,3; 0.381,8)	2.325,5 (-1.317,7; 5.475,9)
0.5	0.007,3 (-0.010,6; 0.028,8)	0.313,8 (-0.953,8; 1.774,8)	-0.023,3 (-0.047,4; -0.004,6)	0.200,7 (-0.109,6; 0.404,2)	0.552,7 (-2.239,4; 4.452,4)
0.6	0.004,6 (-0.009,5; 0.026,7)	0.852,4 (-0.609,3; 1.801,9)	-0.028,9 (-0.044,8; -0.010,2)	0.208,8 (-0.107,1; 0.366,3)	0.538,6 (-2.859,7; 3.169,9)
0.7	0.005,8 (-0.010,6; 0.026,9)	1.051,3 (-0.455,3; 1.872,5)	-0.028,8 (-0.044,0; -0.009,7)	0.201,6 (-0.127,0; 0.337,7)	-0.698,9 (-2.556,2; 2.391,8)
0.8	0.004,7 (-0.012,8; 0.033,1)	0.869,2 (-0.186,7; 2.208,2)	-0.024,6 (-0.042,1; -0.006,0)	0.118,5 (-0.186,4; 0.340,0)	-1.746,1 (-3.440,1; 2.765,3)
0.9	0.004,7 (-0.020,3; 0.036,2)	1.503,3 (-0.270,5; 2.770,5)	-0.017,8 (-0.038,0; 0.003,0)	0.118,7 (-0.292,4; 0.325,1)	0.229 (-4.509,1; 4.426,0)

Note: 90% confidence intervals are in parentheses.

effect of FDI is very close to that in table 6.5. It can be found that both endogeneity problem and omitted variable bias underestimate the effect of FDI on economic growth. The estimate results for FDI in table 6.5 indicates that FDI can be a powerful engine of those economies located at the bottom of the conditional distribution of the growth rate variable. One possible interpretation is that FDI can be more effective, especially for countries which experience a period of low economic growth relative to other countries. Usually, very under-developed countries tend to suffer from low economic growth so that FDI can be helpful in such cases.

Table 6.5 also displays that GDI has positive and significant impacts on economic growth at all quantiles, and the degree of such impact rises while the considered quantile increases. However, at lower quantiles, FDI contributes more than GDI on growth. It can be seen from table 6.5 that the income level in the last period negatively influences economic growth. GCE shows negative influences on growth, but the impacts are only significant in moderately slower and middle growth countries. The impacts of trade, schooling, political rights, and quality of government have also negative effects on growth at most quantiles as expected, but the effects are not significant. Inflation does not show any significant impacts on growth, either.

6.4 Conclusion

Our analysis on FDI is based on the novel method called the IV panel quantile regression method, which can allow for heterogenous impact of FDI on growth at different quantiles, and it can control endogeneity, country-specific and time-specific effects. Our investigation on 60 countries from the sample period from 1991 to 2008 shows significant positive impacts of FDI on economic growth at low quantiles. Either neglecting the potential endogeneity problem of FDI or existing omitted variable bias in the cross-sectional model can underestimate the impacts of FDI on growth. The IV panel quantile regression results indicate that FDI can be a powerful engine of those economies located at the bottom of the conditional distribution of the growth rate variable. One possible interpretation is that FDI can be more effective, especially for countries which experience a period of low economic growth relative to other countries. Usually, very under-developed countries tend to suffer from low economic growth so that FDI can be helpful in such cases.

6.5 Appendix

About 60 countries are investigated in this chapter:

Australia, Bahrain, Bangladesh, Bolivia, Botswana, Brazil, Canada, Chile, China, Congo Rep. , Costa Rica, Cote d'Ivoire, Cyprus, Denmark, Ecuador, Egypt, Arab Rep. , El Salvador, Finland, Gabon, Ghana, Guatemala, Honduras, Iceland, India, Indonesia, Israel, Italy, Japan, Jordan, Kenya, Korea Rep. , Malaysia, Malta, Mexico, Morocco, New Zealand, Nicaragua, Pakistan, Panama, Papua New Guinea, Paraguay, Peru, Philippines, Saudi Arabia, Senegal, Sierra Leone, Singapore, South Africa, Sri Lanka, Sudan, Sweden, Switzerland, Syrian Arab Republic, Thailand, Tunisia, Turkey, United Kingdom, United States, Uruguay, Venezuela RB.

References

[1] Balasubramanyam V. N. , Salisu M. , and Sapsford D. 1996. Foreign direct investment and growth in EP and IS countries. *The Economic Journal*, 106:92 – 105.

[2] Balasubramanyam V. N. , Salisu M. , and Sapsford D. 1999. Foreign direct investment as an engine of growth. *The Journal of International Trade & Economic Development*, 8:27 – 40.

[3] Barro R. J. , Lee J. W. 2010. A new data set of educational

attainment in the world, 1995 – 2010. *Journal of Development Economics*, 104:184 – 198.

[4] Blomström M., Lipsey R. E., and Zejan M. 1992. What explains developing country growth. NBER Working Paper, No. 4, 132.

[5] Borensztein E., Gregorio J. D. and Lee J. W. 1998. How does foreign direct investment affect economic growth? *Journal of International Economics*, 45:115 – 135.

[6] Carkovic M., and Levine R. 2005. Does foreign direct investment accelerate economic growth? in Does Foreign Investment Promote Development? ed. by Theodore H. Moran, Edward M. Graham, and Magnus Blomström. Washington: Institute for International Economics Center for Global Development:195 – 220.

[7] Chernozhukov V., Hansen C. 2005. An IV Model of quantile treatment effects. *Econometrica*, 73(1):245 – 261.

[8] Chernozhukov V., Hansen C. 2006. Instrumental quantile regression inference for structural and treatment effect models. *Journal of Econometrics*, 132(2):491 – 525.

[9] Chernozhukov V., Hansen C. 2008. Instrumental variable quantile regression: a robust inference apporach. *Journal of Econometrics*, 142:379 – 398.

[10] Choe J. I. 2003. Do foreign direct investment and gross domestic investment promote economic growth? *Review of Development Economics*, 7:44 – 57.

[11] Dimelis S. and Louri H. 2002. Foreign ownership and production efficiency: a quantile regression analysis. *Oxford Economic Papers*, 54:449 – 469.

[12] Galvao A. F. 2011. Quantile regression for dynamic panel data with fixed effects. *Journal of Econometrics*, 142:379 – 398.

[13] Girma S., Görg H. 2005. Foreign direct investment, spillovers and absorptive capacity: evidence from quantile regressions. Working Paper.

[14] Kim T. H., and Muller C. 2004. Two-stage quantile regression when the first stage is based on quantile regression. *Econometrics Journal*, 7:218 – 231.

[15] Koenker R., Bassett G. 1978. Regression quantiles. *Econometrica*, 46:33 – 50.

[16] Levine R., and Renelt D. 1992. A sensitivity analysis of cross-country growth regressions. *American Economic Association*, 82: 942 – 963.

[17] Lipsey R. E. and Sjohölm F. 2005. The impact of inward FDI on host countries: why such different answers? in Does Foreign Investment Promote Development? ed. by Theodore H. Moran, Edward M. Graham, and Magnus Blomström. Washington: Institute for International Economics Center for Global Development.

[18] Nair-Reichert U., Weinhold D. 2001. Causality tests for cross-country panels: a new look at FDI and economic growth in developing countries. *Oxford Bulletin of Economics and Statistics*, 63:153 – 171.

[19] Olofsdotter K. 1998. Foreign direct investment, country capabilities and economic growth. *Weltwirtschaftliches Archiv*, 134: 534 – 547.

[20] Patterson N., Montanjees M., Motala J., and Cardillo C. 2004. FDI-trends, data availability, concepts and recording practices. International Monetary Fund, Washington DC.

[21] Stocker H. 2000. Growth effects of foreign direct investment-myth or reality? in Foreign Direct Investment ed. by J. Chen. London and New York, MacMillan Press:115 – 137.

Chapter 7
Financial Risk Measurement: CoVaR

Financial systemic risk is a risk that a shock (coming from market failure or institute failure) can bring a chain of institute bankruptcies and market failures, causing tremendous loss and system breakdown. This chapter studies CoVaR to analyze the financial systemic risk and focuses on risk measurement. Quantile regression models are used to compute individual institute's margin risk contribution to the whole financial market and the tail risk spillover effects between every two financial subsystems. Weekly returns on the secondary market from January 2008 to March 2018 of 26 institutes are chosen from the banking industry, the security industry, the insurance industry, and the trust industry. CSI 800 index data are collected for measuring the margin risk contribution of each subsystem to the whole system and the spillover effects between subsystems.

7.1 Financial Risk Transition Mechanism and Source of Risk in China

Systemic financial risk is a series of institutional failures or market failures caused by a certain impact, causing huge financial losses or even system collapse. Systematic risk, also known as aggregate risk or undiversifiable risk, refers to the vulnerability of market participants facing the effect of aggregate results (e. g. overall revenue in financial markets, resources or storage capacity of the total economy). We can refer to an impact that all individuals in the market face as systematic risks, such as fiscal policy, monetary policy, weather or natural disasters, and the impact of international markets and this risk cannot be eliminated by diversifying investment. William Sharp defined systemic risk in his 1964 paper, which corresponds to individual risks, the latter also known as diversifiable risk or unsystematic risk.

7.1.1 The Transmission Mechanism of Financial Risk in China

Inter-bank business dealings. Inter-bank business dealings include inter-bank deposits, inter-bank lending, capital settlement, foreign exchange, and derivative exchange, etc, among which the inter-bank deposits and inter-bank lending are direct inter-bank businesses, and are also the most vulnerable segment to liquidity shortages and debt defaults. Due to the need for payment clearing and business cooperation, some non-bank financial institutions will open deposit accounts in commercial banks, which is called deposit-taking of interbank; on the other hand, commercial banks will also deposit in other institutions in the same industry due to business needs, resulting in interbank deposits. According to China's deposit reserve system, commercial banks need to deposit a certain deposit reserve in the central bank according to their own deposit amount. When the amount of deposits are changed, excess reserves or insufficient reserves happen in commercial banks, and there will be demand for interbank lending. Currently, China encourages interbank lending among banks, security institutions, and insurance institutions, which is conducive to the circulation of funds and maximizing of profits. However, it cannot eliminate the systemic financial risks brought about by direct business transactions. Ma et al. (2007), based on 2003 balance sheet information of 130 banks in China (the bank's assets and liabilities are composed of interbank deposits and lending data), used matrix algorithm to simulate the domino effect of debt defaults caused by initial bank failures under the condition of that there are inter-bank business dealings. The results showed that most banks can not cause the transmission of risk and continuous close of banks independently as an inducing factor.

Direct or indirect relationship of the balance sheet. According to a direct relationship of the balance sheet, a typical example is the mortgage business. Enterprises and individuals usually need to provide collateral to the bank as a guarantee to obtain a loan. The collateral can be a physical object or securities issued by other institutions or enterprises, after the approval of the bank, they become the bank's assets and then can be sold through asset securitization. At this point, the bank, the individual, the institution that issues the financial instrument, and the enterprise constitute a direct debt relationship on the balance sheet. Price fluctuations in the market of collateral will seriously affect the balance sheet of these banks and enterprises. Before the 2009 US subprime crisis, even the person with credit and low income can also get housing loans. Banks and other financial institutions will put housing loans with low credit into A-class financial products, then sell them to other investors in the market. Real estate price is an important pillar in supporting the quality of housing loans. Then the subsequent increase in the number of defaults on housing loans and the fall in real estate price led to a sharp drop in bond prices and a decline in bank assets, as to all institutions and investors involved in buying and selling subprime financial products face the plight of bankruptcy. Indirect balance sheet relationship refers to the existence of similar risk exposures and debt structures without direct debt relationships, such as the purchase of the same financial products. Similar risk exposures and debt structures among institutions make it possible for investors and rating agencies to have the same concerns about the assets of other institutions when one company is in crisis.

Depositor (investor) revaluation effect. When a primitive shock occurs, such as a large dip in the price of a financial asset, a liquidity shortage in a bank, or a failure of a financial institution's operations, the depositor (investor) cannot know the exact cause of the risk and the spreading extent in a short period of time. Since the acquisition of information and screening require cost, and the deterioration of credit increases the uncertainty and the cost of acquiring information. In order to avoid potential or further losses, investors need to re-evaluate other individuals immediately. At this time, due to their increased level of risk aversion, insufficient information acquired, it is easy to misjudge some institutions with good solvency and good operating status and then sell financial assets at a low price or run on banks.

7.1.2 Sources of Financial Risk in China

Regarding the theoretical sources of risk generation, scholars have done a lot of in-depth analyses. This section will combine these theoretical analyses of the actual situation in China to summarize the potential sources of systemic financial risks in China.

(1) The liquidity difficulty caused by the term mismatch of the bank deposit and loan business. Mismatching of deposit and loan term is a measurement for banks to complete resource allocation. Banks absorb depositors' short-term deposits to form bank liabilities and provide long-term loans for enterprises, financial institutions and individuals to form bank assets. In theory, as long as the average term of bank assets is less than the liability, it is able to repay the capital and interest when the deposit expires to meet the liquidity demand. However, when the average term of assets is greater than liabilities, there will be insufficient liquidity. The more serious the mismatch of terms, the greater the liquidity gap is. Qiu (2015) believes that the net interest margin of the bank's deposit-loan is affected by both the cost effect and the risk-bearing effect. Based on empirical research on 135 banks in China, Qiu (2015) concludes that the effect of overall risk-bearing on the Chinese banking industry is greater than the effect of the cost, which means that, with the increase in the risk of term mismatching, the net interest margin of

deposits and loans has a downward trend which is insufficient to compensate for the mismatch risk and increases the accumulation of risk.

(2) The moral hazard and huge non-performing loan caused by the financial system and government intervention. The reality that China's economic system has undergone tremendous changes and the market economy went through a short time of development has determined that an imperfect financial system and inappropriate government intervention will cause serious moral hazard and leave a heavy historical burden to financial institutions. Large state-owned commercial banks such as Bank of China, Industrial and Commercial Bank of China, and China Construction Bank occupy a monopoly position in terms of deposits and loans, bank assets, number of employees, and social recognition. They are also subject to explicit or implicit guarantees from the government, so the status of monopoly and government guarantees bring a lot of moral hazards in many ways.

First, because of the support of national credit, depositors realize that even if the state-owned banks are in trouble, the government will inevitably intervene to provide liquidity support to the banks, even pay the bill. In consequence, they will relax their vigilance, generate excessive trust, and send funds to these commercial banks continuously even without considering and recognizing those financial institutions whose assets have deteriorated significantly. Depositors are not worried that large commercial banks will default, and banks are not worried about a bank run due to panic among depositors, thereby steady short-term liabilities contribute to the bank's moral hazard.

Second, after the banks occupy a monopoly position, their financial strength will often be very great, so the adequate funds will make it easier for banks to make additional investments when lending to enterprises, even if the initial project investment becomes a sunk cost, and the loan companies facing soft budget constraints lead to moral hazard.

Third, for the purpose of stabilizing the economy and public confidence, the government has always guaranteed explicitly or implicitly for large commercial banks, which has enabled commercial banks to generate incentives to expand their scale to achieve big but not falling down effects and to gain the government guarantees through striving for more customers, strengthening the contact with other financial departments to cover up their own balance sheet issues.

Fourth, the government heterogeneous protections will also encourage weaker banks to take on higher risks. Wang et al. (2016), based on the empirical test on China's 159 commercial banks during 2005 to 2012 as samples, concluded that the government heterogeneous guarantee for banks will enhance the risk-taking incentives of weak banks through competitive distortions. In addition to moral hazard, the huge non-performing loans caused by the transition of the economic system are also a serious hidden danger in China's financial system. Before the establishment of the four major assets management companies and the divestiture of large non-performing assets of large commercial banks in 1999, China's large commercial banks had a total of 1.4 trillion bad debts. The balance sheet situation aroused the vigilance and pessimistic estimation of international institutions and international investors, therefore the inflow of international capital and the competitiveness of China's commercial banks reduced. A large proportion of these non-performing loans are not derived from poor business operations, but from policy loans, credit support for state-owned enterprises, and government intervention at all levels before the transition of the economic system. However, although the asset management companies have taken over non-performing loans from commercial banks such as Bank of China and Industrial and Commercial Bank of China, the funds are from the partial refinancing issued by the People's Bank of China to state-owned commercial banks and the financial debt issued by the state guaranteed asset management companies. In 2006, the asset management company's statements showed that the cash recovery rate of bad debts was only

20%, and the remaining non-performing assets still existed in China's financial system, and ultimately the taxpayers would pay.

(3) High leverage. According to the 2017 China Financial Stability Report released by the People's Bank of China, the ratio of credit to GDP has been rising since 2008, increasing from 100% to around 140%. The whole society leverage ratio rose from 130% to 240% in 2008, approaching the level of social leverage during the US subprime mortgage crisis. Under the supply-side reform of de-capacity, de-stocking, and de-leveraging, although the growth rate of debt in the corporate sector has declined, there exists a tendency to shift from corporate debt to household debt. The ratio of household debt to GDP rose from 30.7% in 2013 to 44.4% in 2016. New loans are concentrated in the real estate industry, encouraging the real estate bubble and possibly spilling over into other sub-sectors.

(4) Shadow banking business. Shadow banking business refers to non-bank financial intermediaries that provide financial services similar to traditional commercial banks and are free from normal supervision. The concept of shadow banking was first proposed by Paul McCulley, PIMCO's executive director at the 2007 Federal Reserve annual meeting.

Ben Bernanke, the former Federal Reserve Chairman, gave the definition and examples of shadow banking in 2013. He believes that asset securitization tools and asset-backed commercial papers channels, money market mutual funds, repurchase agreements, investment banks and mortgage insurance companies are all important components of the shadow banking system. According to China's actual situation, Li et al. (2015) believe that the bank's off-balance-sheet wealth management business, the trust company's wealth management business with banks and security companies, the insurance company's investment-linked insurance business, the bond repurchase, currency market fund, and asset securitization of the dealer market should be included in the shadow banking system. According to the 2014 Global Shadow Banking Report released by the Financial Stability Board, China's shadow banking has a global share of 4%, ranking third in the world. This figure shows that China's shadow banking business has developed extremely fast in recent years and cannot be ignored when financial market risks are considered. The investment targets of China's shadow banking products are mainly coal, real estate, and other industries, which are characterized by cyclical fluctuations, overcapacity, and slowdown in growth, and the price of investment targets is greatly affected by the macro-economy. Due to the long shadow banking debt chain, the complex derived relationship and the high degree of inter-mediation, the creditor's supervisory role on the debtor is weak, and investors face a high degree of information asymmetry. Li and Xue (2014) measured the systemic risk of shadow banking from 2007 to 2012 in China using an input-output method based on Markov procedure assumption of accounts. Their research results showed that the growth rate of capital in the trust industry is lower than the growth rate of assets and the dependence rate on other sectors is high, which is the main risk source of China's shadow banking. Li and Yan (2015) measured the dynamic risk spillover effects of China's shadow banking on commercial banks as a whole and as a part, based on the Copula-CoVaR model, and the results suggest that the risk spillover effect on the trust industry is the most obvious, and the spillover effect on the private lending industry is the least, and the risk spillover effect of shadow banking on joint-stock banks is the largest, followed by that of city commercial banks and state-owned banks.

(5) Accounting standards and the procyclicality of rating agencies. Accounting standards can be divided into the historical cost method and the fair value method, and the latter is based on the current market price. After the 2008 subprime crisis, financial circles had a greater arguement and intense debate for fair value accounting. Many scholars believed that the fair value method, especially the market-to-market, increased the fluctuations of the balance sheet. During the boom period, the price of

financial assets in bank trading accounts is prone to overestimation and bubbles, reflecting a considerable profit on the books, prompting banks to purchase more financial assets. During the recession, the asset bubble burst, prices have shrunk, and the statement of banks states a large number of book losses that force management to decide to sell assets at a low price, causing further depreciation of assets. The procyclicality of rating agencies is similar, i. e. the economic rating is getting better and better when the economy is good, which encourages investors' optimism, while the reversal occurs, the rating follow-up speed is very fast, and an AAA-rated company may immediately become a C-level, which will aggravate market panic.

7.2 Risk Measurements: VaR, CoVaR, and ΔCoVaR

7.2.1 Definition of VaR

Value at Risk(VaR), first proposed by the JP Morgan in the late 1980s, is a tool for measuring investment losses and estimating how much damage an investor's assets will suffer under certain periods of observation and market conditions. VaR is a risk-management technique that has been widely used to assess market risk. VaR for a portfolio is a simply estimate of a specified percentile of the probability distribution of the portfolio's value in a certain period. It can be used as a risk measurement and management of financial institutions such as banks, securities companies, insurance companies, and non-financial institutions.

If a stock's portfolio has a VaR of 5% for $1 million a day, this means that within a day, there is a 5% probability that the loss of this portfolio will equal or exceed $1 million. VaR can also be the asset price or the return on assets calculated from the asset price. A probability distribution map of the observations can be obtained, given observations in some period arranged from small to large. VaR summarizes the worst loss over a target horizon that will not be exceeded with a given level of confidence. At the confidence level c, VaR_q corresponds to the qth quantile observation at the tail level $(1-c)$ of the distribution, defined by the formula:

$$P_r(X_i \leq \text{VaR}_q) = 1 - c. \qquad (7.1)$$

From the perspective of probability theory, the formula indicates the probability that the asset price (asset return rate), X_i, less than or equal to VaR is $(1-c)$ during the given observation period. Take a 99% confidence level, i. e. $c = 0.99$, VaR then is the cut off loss such that the probability of experiencing a greater loss is less than 1%. VaR summarizes the worst loss over a target horizon that will not be exceeded with a given level of confidence.

7.2.2 Calculation of VaR

A market risk estimate can be calculated by following steps. Firstly, value the current portfolio using today's prices, the components of which are market factors. For example, the market factors that affect the value of a bond denominated in a foreign currency are the term structure of that currency's interest rate (either the zero-coupon curve or the par yield curve) and the exchange rate. Secondly, revalue the portfolio using alternative prices based on changed market factors and calculate the change in the portfolio value that would result. Thirdly, revaluing the portfolio using a number of alternative prices gives a distribution of changes in value. Given this, a portfolio VaR can be specified in terms of confidence levels. Lastly, the risk manager can calculate the maximum the firm can lose over a specified time horizon at a specified probability level.

In implementing VaR the main problem is finding a way to obtain a series of vectors of different market factors. One will see how the various methodologies try to resolve this issue for each of the three methods that can be used to calculate VaR.

The calculation method of VaR can be divided into partial evaluation method and complete evaluation method in the early stage. Partial evaluation methods such as the delta-normal evaluation method assume that the portfolio return rate follows a normal distribution and is a parametric simulation method. The first step is to list the risk factors, then represent each financial asset in a portfolio as a linear function of the risk factor, and add up the risk of each financial instrument. The second step is to estimate the covariance matrix of the risk factor and calculate the risk value of the overall portfolio. Full evaluation methods such as historical simulation and Monte Carlo simulation are nonparametric simulations. The historical simulation method relies entirely on the historical data representation of the asset or portfolio, establishes the true distribution of the rate of return, and finds the corresponding quantile value in the distribution according to the confidence level. Monte Carlo simulation first derives the risk, correlation coefficients and other parameters from the historical data and then establishes a random process such as price changes, using a stochastic process to simulate price movements.

From the perspective of the parameter setting, the VaR calculation method includes a parametric method, a semiparametric method, and a nonparametric method. As parameter methods, ARCH model and GARCH model abandon the previous assumption of independent homoskedasticity and are more suitable for the characteristics of financial time series such as heteroscedasticity, sharp peak and heavy tail. Semiparametric methods include extreme value theory EVT, CAViaR, and so on. The extreme value theory does not give the entire distribution hypothesis of the sequence but concentrates on the tail distribution. CAViaR uses the autocorrelation of VaR to establish an autocorrelation function with its lag term.

7.2.3 Definition of CoVaR and ΔCoVaR

VaR can only be used to measure the potential risks of an organization itself. In systemic financial events, direct transactions, credit risk, and liquidity spirals all lead to spillover effects among financial institutions. The VaR of a single financial institution does not necessarily reflect its risk contribution to other financial institutions or the entire financial market. In order to measure the spillover effects and marginal risk contribution, Adrian and Brunnermeier(2009) proposed CoVaR on the basis of VaR. The CoVaR of a single financial institution i is defined as the VaR of the entire financial system or another financial institution when i is in a particular event or period.

$\text{CoVaR}_q^{j|C(X_i)}$ is the VaR of the financial institution (or financial system) j, when event $C(X^i)$ happens in financial institution i. $\text{CoVaR}_q^{j|C(X_i)}$ is expressed as the qth quantile of the following conditional probability distribution:

$$P_r(X^j \mid C(X^i)) \leqslant \text{CoVaR}_q^{j|C(X_i)} = q\%. \qquad (7.2)$$

The contribution of financial institution i to j is less than or equal to VaR_q^i, and the probability of occurrence is $1 - q\%$.

The contribution of institution i to institution j is

$$\Delta\text{CoVaR}_q^{j|i} = \text{CoVaR}_q^{j|X^i=\text{VaR}_{q\%}^i} - \text{CoVaR}_q^{j|X^i=\text{VaR}_{50\%}^i}, \qquad (7.3)$$

where $\text{CoVaR}_q^{j|X^i=\text{VaR}_{50\%}^i}$ is the VaR of institution j when institution i is at a normal level. ΔCoVaR captures the increase in the tail risk of institution j when i changes from normal to an extreme event, which calculates the tail-dependent correlation of two random variables rather than the mean level.

ΔCoVaR has a direction, which means $\Delta\text{CoVaR}_q^{\text{system}|i}$ under the condition of institution i is different from the conditional $\Delta\text{CoVaR}_q^{i|\text{system}}$. Adrian and Brunnermeier defined $\Delta\text{CoVaR}_q^{i|\text{system}}$ as "Exposure – ΔCoVaR," i.e. the risk exposure of a single financial institution in the event of a financial crisis. It is the increase in the tail risk of a single financial institution i when extreme events occur in the financial system. When it comes to the risk management of an organization, this reverse direction calculation helps us to distinguish which financial institutions are the most vulnerable to systemic extreme events, and set different capital adequacy requirements, liquidity requirements or management rules for these institutions to help to reduce the possibility that an institution will be collapsed by the crisis. ΔCoVaR has a"clonal attribute," i. e. when a huge financial system is divided into n colones, CoVaR of the whole system is almost the same as the n colones.

7. 2. 4 Calculation of CoVaR

Based on quantile regression method proposed by Koenker and Bassett (1978), Adrian and Brunnermeier(2009) proposed CoVaR and ΔCoVaR to capture all forms of risk, including not only the risk of adverse asset price movements, but also funding liquidity risk. Girardi and Ergün (2013) calculated CoVaR by GARCH model. Mainik and Schaanning (2012) used the copulas method to obtain better calculation results, which showed that it can well estimate the joint distribution with heavy tails and heteroscedasticity. Bernardi et al. (2013) used the Markov transformation method to solve the heavy-tailed and nonlinear correlations with the student-t distribution.

Among Chinese scholars, Xie (2010) empirically studied the risk spillover effects among the three major Asian stock market indices with the GARCH-Copula-CoVaR model. Gao and Pan (2011) analyzed the systemic risk contribution rate of 14 listed banks in China by using their stock prices data and found that there was no significant linear relationship between banks' contribution of systemic risk and their own VaR.

Mao and Luo(2011) used CoVaR to conduct empirical research on risk spillovers between the banking industry and the security industry. Shen et al. (2014) used the GARCH-Copula-CoVaR model to measure risk spillover among the banking, insurance, security, and trust, as well as their contribution to systemic risk of the financial sector. They finally found banking industry had the greatest contribution to systemic risk, and the risk spillover effect between the banking industry and the security industry is much greater than that of other sub-markets. Bai and Shi (2014) used more than 5 years' weekly closing prices of all 27 listed companies, including banking, insurance, trust and securities, and futures industry to calculate the contribution that individual financial institution made on the financial systemic risk. Chen et al. (2015) used the CoVaR model to empirically analyze the systemic risk spillover effects among banks, securities, and insurance companies. Xie (2015) combined SQ-ARCH model, which describes the time-varying characteristics of fluctuations, and Nop-Quantile model, which constructs VaR, to establish a robust semi-parametric model.

7.2.5 CoVaR Model Based on Quantile Regression

Using a single financial institution's rate of return series as an independent variable, and the system's conditional rate of return series as a dependent variable to establish the following quantile regression model at the qth quantile:

$$X^{\text{system}|i} = \alpha_q^i + \beta_q^i X^i + \epsilon_q^i. \tag{7.4}$$

Because $\text{CoVaR}_q^{\text{system}|i}$ and VaR_q^i are quantiles in essence, then the fitted value of $\text{CoVaR}_q^{\text{system}|i}$ is

$$\text{CoVaR}_q^{\text{system}|i} = \hat{\alpha}_q^{\text{system}|i} + \hat{\beta}_q^{\text{system}|i} \text{VaR}_q^i \tag{7.5}$$

and the fitted value of $\Delta\text{CoVaR}_q^{\text{system}|i}$ is

$$\Delta\text{CoVaR}_q^{\text{system}|i} = \hat{\beta}_q^{\text{system}|i} (\text{VaR}_q^i - \text{VaR}_{50\%}^i). \tag{7.6}$$

Based on eq. (7.5) and eq. (7.6), $\Delta\text{CoVaR}_q^{\text{system}|i}$ can be obtained to generally describe the contribution of the marginal risk of a single financial institution over a period of time. In order to describe the time-varying joint distribution of X_{system} and X_i, it is necessary to introduce state variable, M_t, to set up a regression model of VaR and ΔCoVaR on a lagged state variable. To express the change in time, the above regression models can be adjusted by assigning corner mark t, and expressed as the following quantile regression model at the qth quantile

$$X_t^i = \alpha_q^{\text{system}|i} + \gamma_q^i M_{t-1} + \epsilon_{q,t}^i \qquad (7.7)$$

$$X_t^{\text{system}|i} = \alpha_q^i + \gamma_q^{\text{system}|i} M_{t-1} + \beta_q^{\text{system}|i} X_t^i + \epsilon_{q,t}^{\text{system}|i} \qquad (7.8)$$

and the corresponding fitted values

$$\text{VaR}_{q,t}^i = \hat{\alpha}_q^i + \hat{\gamma}_q^i M_{t-1} \qquad (7.9)$$

$$\text{CoVaR}_{q,t}^{\text{system}|i} = \hat{\alpha}_q^{\text{system}|i} + \hat{\gamma}_q^{\text{system}|i} M_{t-1} + \hat{\beta}_q^{\text{system}|i} \text{VaR}_{q,t}^i \qquad (7.10)$$

$$\Delta\text{CoVaR}_{q,t}^{\text{system}|i} = \hat{\beta}_{q,t}^{\text{system}|i} (\text{VaR}_{q,t}^i - \text{VaR}_{50,t}^i) \qquad (7.11)$$

7.3 Empirical Study on Systemic Financial Risks in China

7.3.1 Data Selection

According to the China Securities Regulatory Commission (CSRC) industry classification in 2012, the data from 26 financial institutions in banking, security, insurance, and asset management industry are collected, over the period from the January 4, 2008 to March 30, 2018, in order to cover the periods of the global financial crisis in 2008, the money shortage in 2013, and the domestic stock market crash in 2015. Although there are far more than 26 financial institutions in China, many institutions are listed after 2008 (including the Agricultural Bank of China), so that the observable time is short. There are a few institutions listed before 2008, but experienced a long suspension time and serious data loss. Therefore, 26 listed institutions are selected after screening. These financial institutions have been established for a long time with stable operations, solid financial strength, strong representativeness, and high market weight.

In the calculation of VaR and CoVaR, weekly return (percentile) of a single financial institution is calculated using the stock weekly closing price. Due to the lack of weekly closing prices in some institutions, 12,064 observations were obtained after eliminating these missing dates, and the data is collected from the Guo Tai'an Database. The average weight of individual financial institution in each period is calculated by the lagged proportion of the total market value, therefore constructing the weekly returns series by calculating the weighted average of each period.

7.3.2 Data Processing and Descriptive Statistics

Descriptive Statistics and Stationary Test

Due to the particularity of the financial time series, it is necessary to test the series of weekly returns for normality and stationarity before VaR and CoVaR are calculated. It has been mentioned above that the calculation of the early VaR was based on the assumption that the return rate follows a normal distribution, on the basis of which the relevant parameters are estimated. The following descriptive statistics and normality tests will visually explain why the method is no longer applicable.

Table 7.1 Descriptive statistics of weekly returns of financial institutions

Name of institution	Mean	SD	Median	Skewness	Kurtosis
Bank of China	0.03	3.46	0	0.268,2	2.862,2
ICBC	0.09	3.61	0	0.450,5	3.643,0
China Construction Bank(CCB)	0.10	4.00	−0.212,8	0.761,1	3.911,7
Bank of Communications (BoCom)	0.07	4.58	−0.241,2	0.791,4	4.389,0
Ping An Bank	0.19	5.66	−0.171,8	0.442,1	2.213,8
SPDB	0.25	5.29	−0.106,6	0.318,9	3.414,8
Hua Xia Bank(HXB)	0.13	5.10	−0.128,9	0.294,9	2.329,0
Minsheng Bank(CMSB)	0.17	4.69	−0.122,1	0.582,8	4.265,1
China Merchants Bank (CMBC)	0.23	4.90	−0.156,7	0.124,1	1.882,6
CITIC Bank	0.03	4.80	−0.216,8	0.963,7	5.970,5

Continued

Name of institution	Mean	SD	Median	Skewness	Kurtosis
Northeast Securities (NESC)	0.05	7.21	0	0.863,9	4.649,1
China Industrial Bank(CIB)	0.24	5.29	−0.293,4	0.236,8	2.198,6
Bank of Ningbo (NBCB)	0.21	5.00	0	0.617,9	2.715,2
Bank of Nanjing(BNJ)	0.26	4.58	0.033,2	0.569,0	2.239,7
Bank of Beijing(BOB)	0.12	4.36	0	0.470,2	2.098,9
China Pacific Life Insurance(CPIC)	0.10	5.29	−0.274,1	0.120,6	0.835,5
China Life Insurance (LFC)	0.02	5.39	−0.654,8	0.851,2	4.448,2
Ping An Insurance	0.22	5.29	−0.154,6	0.237,8	1.839,0
Guoyuan Securities	0.04	7.07	−0.088,4	1.156,6	6.953,4
Changjiang Securities	0.11	7.07	−0.109,0	0.784,2	3.958,4
CITIC Securities	0.16	6.63	−0.132,7	1.199,0	6.507,2
Sinolink Securities	0.17	7.28	−0.175,9	0.990,8	4.478,9
China Fortune Securities	0.41	7.07	0.584,3	0.853,9	5.613,1
Haitong Securities	0.13	6.93	0.303,8	0.684,7	6.061,6
Pacific Securities	−0.21	6.78	−0.347,7	1.744,3	12.857,3
Haide Limited	0.31	7.62	0.266,8	0.400,8	2.337,8
Data source: Guo Tai'an Database.					

As shown in table 7.1, except the Pacific Securities, the mean values of all the financial institutions are positive, the median values are mostly negative, the skewness of all returns are positive, and the series is right-biased. Among these, the skewness of the return of Guoyuan Securities, CITIC Securities, and CPIC is greater than 1 and the kurtosis is significantly greater than 3, while only CPIC's skewness and kurtosis values are relatively small. According to the results of the Jarque-Bera test, the p-value of all the return series is significantly less than 0.05, rejecting the normality hypothesis, which is consistent with the conclusion from the Q-Q plot. And the ADF unit root test shows that the p-values are all around 0.01, and rejects the null hypothesis of existing a unit at significance level 5%, so all sequences are stationary series.

It can be seen from the fluctuation of return series of all individual institutions, the return has obvious segmentation in time, and most financial institutions have large fluctuations during the period from 2008 to 2010, 2015 to 2016, while the fluctuations in other periods are relatively slight. These two characteristics are most evident in the banking and securities industries, which explains that the 2008 global financial crisis and the 2015 stock market crash have a significant impact on the stock prices of China's banking and securities institutions.

Static VaR Based on Historical Return Series

From $VaR_{0.05}$ at 5% level (table 7.2), the risk for the bank industry is relatively lower than other financial industries. The tail risk values of Bank of China, Industrial and Commercial Bank of China, Bank of Communications, and China Construction Bank are the lowest, which are no more than -7%. The performance of three insurance companies in the insurance industry is similar to that of city banks and share-holding banks. Five of the eight securities companies have a tail risk value of lower than -10%. From $VaR_{0.95}$ at 5% level, the high return rate of the banking industry is relatively lower than others, no more than 10%. Except for Pacific Securities, other securities companies' high return rate is over 10%. Haide Limited Company in the sample, the only one with capital management as core business, has the highest left-tail risk, -12%, and the highest right-tail return rate, 12.6%.

Table 7.2 Quantiles of weekly returns of financial institutions

Name of institution	$VaR_{0.05}$	$VaR_{0.1}$	$VaR_{0.95}$	$VaR_{0.95} - VaR_{0.05}$
Bank of China	−5.570,1	−3.354,9	5.786,7	11.356,8
ICBC	−5.279,4	−3.537,8	5.341,8	10.621,2
China Construction Bank(CCB)	−6.152,7	−4.101,9	6.337,4	12.490,1
Bank of Communications (BoCom)	−6.361,5	−4.579,4	7.529,4	13.890,9
Ping An Bank	−8.478,6	−5.966,0	9.793,3	18.271,9
SPDB	−7.697,4	−5.016,2	8.727,8	16.425,2
Hua Xia Bank(HXB)	−8.075,7	−5.320,1	8.384,3	16.46,0
Minsheng Bank(CMSB)	−7.012,9	−4.598,2	8.049,1	15.062,0
China Merchants Bank(CMBC)	−7.001,6	−4.571,1	8.964,4	15.966,0
CITIC Bank	−6.993,3	−5.325,8	7.761,1	14.754,4
China Industrial Bank(CIB)	−7.511,3	−5.505,4	9.695,2	17.206,5
Bank of Ningbo(NBCB)	−7.267,1	−5.558,0	8.248,0	15.515,1
Bank of Nanjing(BNJ)	−6.682,4	−4.614,9	7.155,0	13.837,4
Bank of Beijing(BOB)	−6.714,6	−4.918,5	7.859,2	14.573,8
China Pacific Life Insurance(CPIC)	−8.181,4	−6.205,5	9.071,2	17.252,6
China Life Insurance (LFC)	−7.701,7	−5.703,7	8.569,2	16.270,9
Ping An Insurance	−7.824,7	−5.520,7	8.306,8	16.131,5
Northeast Securities (NESC)	−11.342,6	−6.865,9	10.859,6	22.202,2
Guoyuan Securities	−10.176,9	−7.216,4	11.022,0	21.198,9
Changjiang Securities	−10.069,8	−7.314,4	12.731,6	22.801,4
CITIC Securities	−8.811,3	−6.860,4	10.134,6	18.945,9
Sinolink Securities	−11.252,9	−8.220,3	12.371,2	23.624,1

Continued

Name of institution	$VaR_{0.05}$	$VaR_{0.1}$	$VaR_{0.95}$	$VaR_{0.95} - VaR_{0.05}$
China Fortune Securities	−10.659,3	−7.050,5	11.637,8	22.297,1
Haitong Securities	−9.428,7	−6.545,5	11.485,7	20.914,4
Pacific Securities	−9.760,2	−6.906,5	9.070,2	18.830,4
Haide Limited	−12.022,4	−7.942,5	12.625,3	24.647,7

Data source: Guo Tai'an Database.

Static ΔCoVaR

The weekly return series of the financial market is a weighted sum of individual institutions, with market value proportion as the weight, which implies that the institution with a larger market capitalization has a stronger effect on the performance of the current financial market. This is consistent with the actual situation that the larger the financial institutions, the more complex the business relationship network, the wider the impact of their states of business in the market. However, since the purpose of ΔCoVaR is to quantify the tail dependence between the two variable distributions, the relationship between the institution and the market cannot be simply determined by the weight but can be determined by the static marginal risk contribution of individual institutions to the whole system, by computing the tail correlation coefficient $\beta_q^{system|i}$. The 5th quantile is selected when calculating ΔCoVaR, and the results are shown in table 7.3.

Table 7.3 β and static ΔCoVaR for financial institutions

Name of institution	$\beta_q^{system|i}$	$\Delta CoVaR_{0.05}$	$VaR_{0.05}$
Bank of China	0.752,5	−4.191,43	−5.570,1
ICBC	0.716,9	−3.785,23	−5.279,4
China Construction Bank(CCB)	0.674,6	−4.007,12	−6.152,7
Bank of Communications(BoCom)	0.549,1	−3.360,49	−6.361,5

Continued

Name of institution	$\beta_q^{system|i}$	$\Delta CoVaR_{0.05}$	$VaR_{0.05}$
Ping An Bank	0.402,1	−3.341,45	−8.478,6
SPDB	0.460,2	−3.492,92	−7.697,4
Hua Xia Bank(HXB)	0.457,7	−3.638,72	−8.075,7
Minsheng Bank(CMSB)	0.534,8	−3.684,77	−7.012,9
China Merchants Bank(CMBC)	0.547,6	−3.745,58	−7.001,6
CITIC Bank	0.433,8	−2.936,83	−6.993,3
China Industrial Bank(CIB)	0.425,4	−3.071,39	−7.511,3
Bank of Ningbo(NBCB)	0.472,1	−3.432,17	−7.267,1
Bank of Nanjing(BNJ)	0.526,4	−3.532,14	−6.682,4
Bank of Beijing(BOB)	0.425,4	−2.854,43	−6.714,6
China Pacific Life Insurance(CPIC)	0.428,2	−3.387,06	−8.181,4
China Life Insurance(LFC)	0.428,2	−3.018,81	−7.701,7
Ping An Insurance	0.430,6	−3.330,27	−7.824,7
Northeast Securities(NESC)	0.265,2	−3.007,4	−11.342,6
Guoyuan Securities	0.240,9	−2.430,68	−10.176,9
Changjiang Securities	0.278,7	−2.773,07	−10.069,8
CITIC Securities	0.364,9	−3.167,33	−8.811,3
Sinolink Securities	0.266,9	−2.954,58	−10.659,3
China Fortune Securities	0.164,5	−1.848,98	−10.659,3
Haitong Securities	0.350,6	−3.411,34	−9.428,7
Pacific Securities	0.330,7	−3.111,89	−9.760,2
Haide Limited	0.141,2	−1.735,4	−12.022,4
Data source: Guo Tai'an Database.			

According to the formula $\Delta CoVaR_q^{system|i} = \hat{\beta}_q^{system|i}(VaR_q^i - VaR_{50\%}^i)$, the marginal risk contribution of an individual financial institution, $\Delta CoVaR_{0.05}$, is determined by the difference between its $VaR_{0.05}$ and $VaR_{0.5}$, and the coefficient $\beta^{system|i}$. The values of $\beta^{system|i}$ for 14 banks are all greater than 0.4, of which the Bank of China and Industrial and

Commercial Bank of China have a beta of about 0.7. The beta of the four insurance institutions is around 0.4. The beta values of most brokers are less than 0.3, and the coefficients of China Fortune Securities and Haide Limited are only 0.1645 and 0.1412, respectively.

The difference of institution itself's $VaR_{0.05}$ and $\Delta CoVaR_{0.05}$ indicates that institutions with higher risk at their tails do not necessarily contribute to the marginal risk of the entire financial system. Among the 26 institutions, four institutions, which are Haide Limited, China Fortune Securities, Guoyuan Securities, and Changjiang Securities, had the lowest $\Delta CoVaR_{0.05}$ values, while their $VaR_{0.05}$ of institutions are very high. As systemically important banks, Bank of China, Industrial and Commercial Bank and Construction Bank have the lowest value of $VaR_{0.05}$ and the highest value of $\Delta CoVaR_{0.05}$. Overall, the $\Delta CoVaR_{0.05}$ of the banking and insurance industries are significantly higher than that of the securities industry.

7.3.3 Identification of Systemically Important Financial Institutions

Systemically important financial institutions (SIFIs) mean financial institutions with large business scale, high business complexity, hurting regional or global financial system once a risk incident happens in the institutions. The Financial Stability Board (FSB) publishes a list of systemically important banks each year, dividing the banks into different levels based on additional capital requirements. Up to 2017, four banks in China have entered the list and China is the only developing countries entering the list. It can be seen that identifying systemically important institutions is an important part of financial stability.

Based on the above data processing results, we can draw the following conclusions about systemically important financial institutions:

(1) Most of the banks' own tail risk values and high return values are lower, the distributions of the return are quite stable, while the return of

the securities company fluctuates greatly, and the insurance company's fluctuation of the rate of return is moderate. This reflects that China's banking industry has higher requirements for stable asset prices and stricter control. Among them, Bank of China, Industrial and Commercial Bank, Construction Bank and Bank of Communications have the lowest tail risk value.

(2) The relationship between the banking industry and the financial system's tail risk is stronger than other industries, followed by the insurance industry, while the securities industry reflects the weakest correlation. Bank of China, Industrial and Commercial Bank of China and China Construction Bank have the largest beta coefficient and the highest $\Delta CoVaR_{0.05}$ value. They have the strongest spillover effect on the tail risk of the system and are systemically important financial institutions.

7.4 Static Risk Contribution of Financial Sub-industries on Financial System

7.4.1 Data Selection

In order to quantify the static risk contribution of financial sub-industries to the whole financial system, the financial system is divided into banking industry, securities industry, and insurance industry. Meanwhile, the real estate industry is also included into the scope of quantitative analysis, since it has a close relationship with China's financial system. CSI 800 Financial Index is selected from a series of primary industries of CSI Index to represent the financial system performance in the stock market. CSI 800 Bank Index, CSI 800 Capital Goods Index, CSI 800 Insurance Index, and CSI 800 Real Estate Index represent the stock market performance in the banking, securities, insurance, and real estate industries, respectively. Data is collected from WIND Database, over the period from Jan. 2008 till March 2018. The reasons for choosing this index series are as follows:

(1) The CSI 800 Index Series consists of CSI Small Cap 500 Index and CSI 300 Index, which covers a wide range, can comprehensively reflect the overall situation of the financial system and sub-sectors. According to the institutions' behaviors, such as being listed or delisted in the index, suspension, resumption of trading, and business adjustment, CSI 800 Index includes and excludes institutions in real time, and revises the index to ensure the consistency of the index in time and the accuracy of the division of the business.

(2) The CSI 800 Index is divided into a primary industry and a secondary industry, which ensures the consistency of the sub-industry and the financial system in terms of coverage, weight setting, and correction methods so that the quantile regression and calculation of the conditional value at risk are feasible in terms of data selection.

7.4.2 Data Processing and Descriptive Statistics

Descriptive Statistics and Stationary Test

According to the descriptive statistics and the time series of daily return rate in table 7.4, the standard deviations of the return of the banking industry and the financial system are small, and their fluctuation ranges are small. The standard deviations and fluctuation ranges of the securities industry, the insurance industry, and the real estate industry are large. The means and medians of each time series of each industry are similar, approximately equal to zero. During the period from 2008 to 2009 and 2015 to 2016, the fluctuations in the return series of the insurance, banking, real estate, and financial systems expanded significantly, while the characteristics of the periodical fluctuations of the securities industry were not significant. Figures 7.3 – 7.6 and Figure 7.7 in the Appendix show the time series plot of banking, security, insurance, real estate, and financial system, respectively.

Table 7.4 Descriptive statistics of daily returns of the financial system and sub-industries

Sector/System	Mean	SD	Median	Min	Max	Skewness	Kurtosis
Banking	-0.006,4	1.938,7	-0.035,9	-10.501,9	9.556,7	-0.073,0	4.589,4
Securities	-0.025,6	2.642,2	-0.034,9	-10.349,7	9.528,3	-0.186,9	2.580,5
Insurance	-0.000,3	2.349,0	-0.012,8	-10.537,4	9.543,5	-0.046,0	2.881,3
Real Estate	0.003,9	2.238,0	0.029,1	-10.153,0	9.537,4	-0.470,2	2.512,8
Financial System	-0.008,5	1.968,1	0.009,7	-9.831,0	9.538,2	-0.268,0	3.784,7
Data source: WIND Database.							

According to the results of the Jarque-Bera test, the p-values of all the return series are close to 0, which rejects the normality hypothesis. The Augmented Dickey Fuller(ADF) unit root test for the return series shows that the p-value is 0.01, and the hypothesis that the unit root exists is rejected at 5% significance level, so that all sequences are stationary series.

Static VaR Based on Historical Return Series

As shown in table 7.5, the financial system as a whole has the largest volume and the extreme risk value at the tail $VaR_{0.01}$ is the smallest. In the sub-industry, the tail value of the banking industry is the smallest and the overall fluctuation is the smallest, close to that of the financial system. The extreme risks of the tail of the securities industry and the real estate industry are relatively large. And for the securities industry, the high absolute values of $VaR_{0.95}$ and $VaR_{0.01}$ show that it best meets the characteristics of "high-yield, high-risk."

Table 7.5 Static VaR of sub-industry and financial system

Industry/System	$VaR_{0.05}$	$VaR_{0.1}$	$VaR_{0.95}$	$VaR_{0.95} - VaR_{0.05}$
Banking	-5.806,8	-2.936,6	3.061,5	5.998,1
Securities Industry	-8.651,4	-4.336,7	4.258,8	8.595,5
Insurance	-6.843,8	-3.756,8	3.751,4	7.508,2
Real Estate	-7.301,3	-3.692,4	3.492,4	7.184,8
Financial System	-5.806,1	-2.971,3	3.175,9	6.147,2

Data source: WIND Database.

Static ΔCoVaR

The static ΔCoVaR reflects the risk contribution of the institution i to the financial system over a period of time. According to eq. 7.5 and eq. 7.6, $CoVaR_q^{system|i}$ reflects the value at risk of the system on the condition of i institution, $\Delta CoVaR_q^{system|i}$ reflects the tail risk spillover of i to the system, and $\hat{\beta}_q^{system|i}$ is the tail risk correlation coefficient at the qth quantile. The i can be substituted by different sub-sectors, selecting $\tau = 0.05$, or 0.01, then tail risk correlation coefficient β can be estimated (see table 7.6), and then ΔCoVaR can be calculated (see figure 7.1). Based on t test, the p-values of all quantile regression equations are approximately equal to 0, and the correlation coefficients are significant.

Table 7.6 Tail risk correlation coefficient β of sub-industry and financial system at $\tau = 0.05$ and $\tau = 0.01$

Item	$\beta_{\tau=0.05}$	$\beta_{\tau=0.01}$
Bank → System	0.941,0(0.021,8)	0.909,5(0.054,6)
Securities → System	0.656,4(0.028,1)	0.686,7(0.074,3)
Insurance → System	0.734,5(0.025,4)	0.736,2(0.057,2)
Real Estate → System	0.761,1(0.031,8)	0.739,7(0.086,6)
System → Bank	0.901,6(0.020,9)	0.941,4(0.051,8)
System → Securities	1.217,6(0.038,7)	1.268,4(0.139,2)

Continued

Item	$\beta_{\tau=0.05}$	$\beta_{\tau=0.01}$
System → Insurance	1.023,4(0.029,3)	0.978,5(0.106,0)
System → Real Estate	0.972,1(0.037,6)	0.909,7(0.092,6)
Data source: WIND Database standard deviation shown in brackets.		

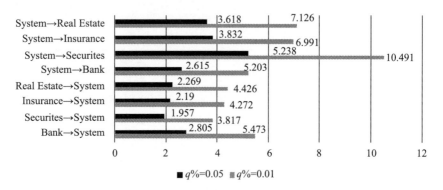

Figure 7.1 Static ΔCoVaR of the financial system

It can be seen from figure 7.1, the sub-industry contributes less to the marginal risk of the system, compared with the system's risk spillover to each sub-sector. ΔCoVaR of the financial system to banking is smaller, while, for the securities industry, ΔCoVaR value is quite large (especially at quantile 0.01). At quantile $\tau = 0.05$, the banking industry contributes the least to the system's risk, while the real estate industry contributes the most to the system's risk. And when the level of confidence decreases from 5% to 1%, which means that the risk shifts to a more extreme situation, the banking industry's contribution to the marginal risk of the system is significantly the highest.

7.5 Risk Spillover Effects Between Financial Sub-sectors

7.5.1 Static Risk Spillover Effects Between Financial Sub-sectors

Based on the Data in the above section and calculation of risk spillover, the risk spillover between financial sub-sectors, over the period from 2008 to 2018, can be obtained and compared directly. The results are shown in figure 7.2.

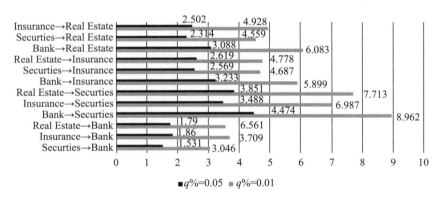

Figure 7.2 Static ΔCoVaR between industries

It can be seen that among the three industries, securities, insurance, and real estate industries, the highest risk of external spillover effects of the banking sector is on the securities industry. While according to the tail infection effects on banking, the primary source is from the insurance industry.

Among the external spillover effects of the securities industry, the risk value of insurance is the highest, while according to the tail risk contagion effect on the insurance, the primary source is from the banking industry. Among the external spillover effects of the insurance industry, the securities industry has the highest risk value; among the tail risk contagion effects on the insurance industry, the major source is from the banking industry. Among the external spillover effects of real estate, the securities industry has the highest risk value; the primary source of the tail infection effect on the real estate industry is from the banking industry. Regardless of the 5th or 1st quantile, the bank's ΔCoVaR to securities is the highest value, demonstrating a strong one-way tail risk spillover.

7.5.2 Dynamic Risk Spillover Effects Between Financial Sub-industries

Selection of State Variables

In order to achieve the joint distribution of X_i and X^j over time to get a dynamic ΔCoVaR, Adrian and Brunnermeier(2009) first introduced state variable to estimate VaR and CoVaR. State variables, M_{t-1}, denotes the lagged value of variables that represent the macroeconomic conditions. They should not be simply understood as systemic risk factors, but variables of conditional moving average and conditional variance.

The state variables selected by Adrian and Brunnermeier (2009) are: ①3-month short-term treasure bill; ②the changes of return curve slope, calculated as the difference between long-term bonds and short-term bonds; ③TED spread, calculated as the difference between the three-month London Interbank Offered Rate and the US 3-month Treasury Bill Rate; ④credit spread, calculated by the difference between Moody's Baa credit rating bond and 10-year Treasury bill rate; ⑤ market return, calculated by the week return S&P 500; ⑥excess weekly returns of the real estate industry to the financial industry; ⑦ market volatility, calculated by the 22-day rolling standard deviation of the CRSP return. Based on the previous domestic and foreign literature, the following state variables are selected and shown in table 7.7.

Table 7.7 Tail risk correlation coefficient β of sub-industry and financial system at $\tau = 0.05$ and $\tau = 0.01$

State variable	Calculation method
market return, MR	logarithmic daily return of CSI 300
market volatility, MV	20-day moving average of logarithmic daily return of CSI 300
term spread, TS	return of 10-year T-bill-return of 3-month T-bill
Ted spread, TED	China's 3-month T-bill-U. S. 's 3-month T-bill
credit spread, CS	return of A-level maturity return for short and medium term-AAA-level maturity return
yield change, YC	logarithmic return of 3-month -T-bill

The return of CSI 300 Index and volatility data are from the Resset database (www.resset.cn), China's government bonds rate and the short-term and medium-term corporate paper returns from the WIND database, and the US Treasury Bill return data from the official website of the Federal Reserve Bank of St. Louis.

Dynamic ΔCoVaR Among Financial Sub-industries

Based on eq. (7.9), the VaR quantile regression equation of an individual financial sub-industry is achievable. Adding the state variables, the following formula is established:

$$\text{VaR}_{q,t}^i = \hat{\alpha}_q^i + \hat{\gamma}_q^{1\,i}\text{MR}_{t-1} + \hat{\gamma}_q^{2\,i}\text{MV}_{t-1} + \hat{\gamma}_q^{3\,i}\text{TS}_{t-1} + \hat{\gamma}_q^{4\,i}\text{TED}_{t-1} + \hat{\gamma}_q^{5\,i}\text{CS}_{t-1} + \hat{\gamma}_q^{6\,i}\text{YC}_{t-1} \quad (7.12)$$

Substituting historical return series of financial industry i into left hand side of the above equation, and substituting historical data of lagged state variable into right hand side of the above equation, estimation of 7 coefficients can be achievable. The regression results show that most coefficients for banking and real estate industries are significant at 5% level, while seldom coefficients' estimates are significant at 1%. Insurance and securities industry have the adverse results.

In order to calculate the dynamic risk spillover effect of the financial sub-sector i on j at the 0.01 level, the tail risk correlation coefficient β in eq. (7.11) should be calculated first. Substituting the historical return series of financial industry i and j, and state variable series into $\mathrm{VaR}_{q,t}^{i}$, $\mathrm{CoVaR}_{q,t}^{j|i}$, and M_{t-1} in eq. (7.10), respectively, we can get the coefficient $\hat{\beta}_{q,t}^{j|i}$. Using the rate of return of the industry i at the 0.5 and 0.01 quantiles, we can get the fitted value calculated in eq. (7.12), and then substituting $\hat{\beta}_{q,t}^{j|i}$ into eq. (7.11) we can obtain $\Delta\mathrm{CoVaR}_{q,t}^{j|i}$.

Since the frequency of the daily data used originally is too high, the curve is densely fluctuating, and it is difficult to observe the overall trend, the data is converted into quarterly data, by getting the moving average of $\Delta\mathrm{CoVaR}_{q,t}^{j|i}$.

It can be seen from figures 7.8 – 7.15, the time trends of risk spillover effects received from each sub-industry and the contribution to other sub-sectors are roughly the same. The highest peak was between 2008 and 2010, after that from 2010 to 2014, the ΔCoVaR value fluctuated and reached a minimum after 2014. The second peak occurred between 2015 and 2016, along with three short-term surging downs and ups. It kept stable at a low level between 2016 and 2017, however, there were signs of a climb in 2018.

For the banking industry, before 2014, the risk contribution value of the insurance industry and the real estate industry were slightly higher than that of the securities industry. In the stock market crash of 2015, the risk contribution value of the securities industry rose to become the first source of risk among the industries. Regardless of the period in history, the risks of the banking industry are most likely to spill over into the securities industry, followed by insurance and real estate.

For the securities industry, before 2016, the risk contribution of the banking industry was much higher than that of the insurance industry and the real estate industry, especially in the two special periods of 2008 and 2015. While after 2016, the risk contribution value of the banking industry dropped significantly, which is lower than the insurance industry and the real estate industry. Overall, the risks of the securities industry are most likely to spill over into the insurance industry, followed by real estate and banks.

For the insurance industry, the risk contribution of the three industries to the insurance industry is not much different before 2016, but the risk contribution of the banking industry after 2016 is significantly reduced. Between 2010 and 2014, the insurance industry had the strongest risk spillover effect on the securities industry, and the spillover effect on the real estate industry was the strongest after 2014.

As for the real estate industry, the risk contribution of the banking sector is slightly higher than the securities and insurance sectors before 2016, while after 2016, it falls down to the lowest value. Throughout the whole observation period, the real estate industry always has the highest risk spillovers for the securities industry and the lowest risk spillovers for the banking industry.

7.6 Conclusion

The chapter focuses on the measurement of the systemic financial risk in China, based on the theoretical analysis and empirical research. The theoretical analysis includes the transmission mechanism and potential risk sources of systemic financial risks in China. The empirical research includes three parts: identifying systemically important financial institutions SIFIs, quantifying the financial sub-sectors' contribution to the financial system's tail risk, and risk spillover effects between financial industries. The empirical study applies the CoVaR idea and the quantile regression method, by using the weekly stock return data of 26 financial institutions and the CSI 800 series index, to establish models to measure the value of the tail risk contribution of the institution and the sub-industry such as static VaR, CoVaR and ΔCoVaR. Based on the results of empirical research, the following conclusions are drawn:

(1) Firstly, among the 26 financial institutions, most of the banks have lower left-tail risk value and lower right-tail high return, and the return

distribution is the most stable. Most securities institutions have large fluctuations in return. This reflects that China's banks have higher requirements for stable asset prices, stricter control, and securities institutions have obvious high-return and high-risk characteristics. Secondly, the institution's own tail risk is not necessarily positively related to its contribution to the marginal risk of the financial system. The empirical results of this chapter show that Bank of China, Industrial and Commercial Bank, China Construction Bank and Bank of Communications have the lowest tail risk value, but have the highest ΔCoVaR value for the financial system. They are typical SIFIs. The values of the tail risk of institutions such as Haide Limited, China Fortune Securities, Guoyuan Securities, and Changjiang Securities are very high, but their contribution values to the system are very low.

(2) Compared with the system's static marginal risk spillover effects on each sub-sector, the sub-industry contributes less to the system's static marginal risk. Among all sub-sectors, the risk correlation coefficient between banking and financial systems is the highest, followed by real estate, insurance and securities. At the level of 0.05, the banking industry contributes the least to the marginal risk of the system, and the real estate industry contributes the most to the marginal risk of the system. When the state of the financial system shifts to a more extreme level, all risk spillover effects are enhanced, and the banking industry's contribution to the marginal risk of the system significantly increases to the highest value. This shows that in the period of high risk, the banking industry helps to keep a stable financial system due to its low loss rate, and its destructive power to the financial system is not significant. When extreme risks occur, the bank's own losses significantly increase, and it has close contact with the financial system, causing the system ΔCoVaR significantly increasing. Whether at the level of 0.05 or 0.01, the ΔCoVaR values of the financial system to the banking sector are minimum, while that to the securities industry are very large, reflecting

the banking sector has a strong anti-systemic risk infection capability. The securities industry is significantly affected by the overall market and is more vulnerable to the financial crisis.

(3) According to the dynamic risk spillover effect graph between sub-sectors, the risk spillover effect received by each sub-industry and the risk contribution to other sub-sectors are consistent in time. Between 2008 and 2010, each ΔCoVaR reached its peak, fell down with fluctuations from 2010 to 2014 and reached a minimum after 2014. The second peak occurred between 2015 and 2016, accompanied by three rapid declines in the short term. And it was stable at a low level between 2016 and 2017, while there were signs of a climb in 2018. The risks of the banking industry and the real estate industry are the most likely to spill over into the securities.

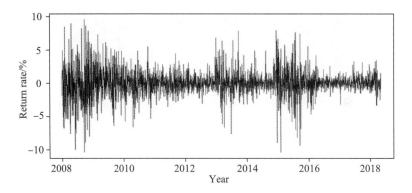

Figure 7.3　Time-series plots of the banking industry

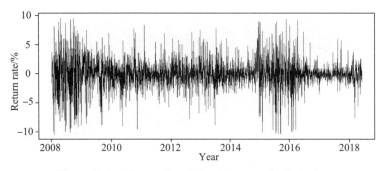

Figure 7.4　Time-series plots of the security industry

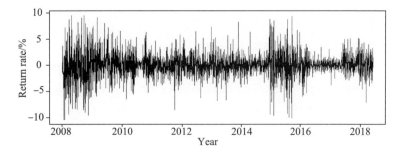

Figure 7.5　Time-series plots of the insurance industry

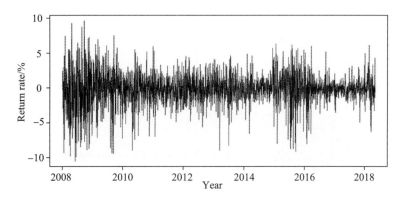

Figure 7.6　Time-series plots of the real estate industry

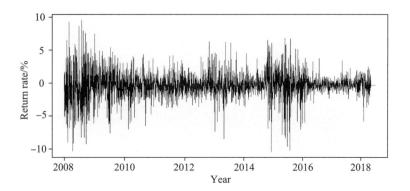

Figure 7.7　Time-series plots of the financial system

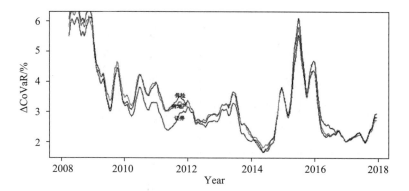

Figure 7.8 Other industries' spillover effects on the banking industry

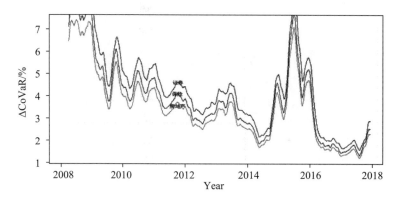

Figure 7.9 Banking industry's spillover effects on the other financial industries

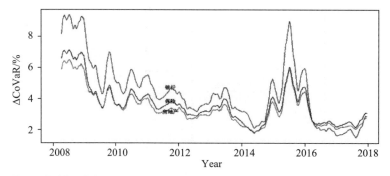

Figure 7.10 Other industries' spillover effects on the securities industry

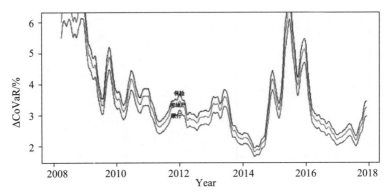

Figure 7.11 Securities industry's spillover effects on the other financial industries

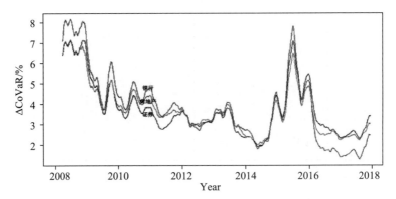

Figure 7.12 Other industries' spillover effects on the insurance industry

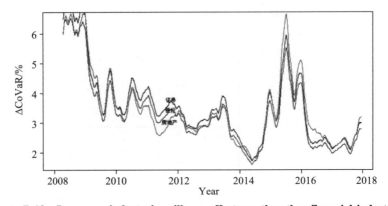

Figure 7.13 Insurance industry's spillover effects on the other financial industries

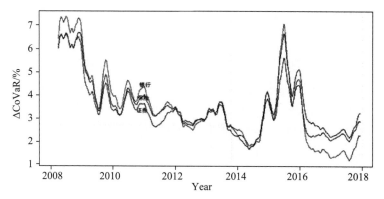

Figure 7.14 Other industries' spillover effects on the real estate industry

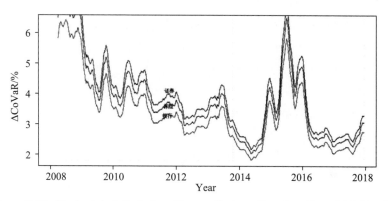

Figure 7.15 Real estate industry's spillover effects on the other financial industries

References

[1] Adrian, Tobias, and Markus K. Brunnermeier. 2009. CoVar: a method for macroprudential regulation. Federal Reserve Bank of New York Staff Report:348.

[2] Bernardi, Mauro, Antonello Maruotti, and Lea Petrella. 2013. Multivariate Markov-Switching models and tail risk interdependence. arXiv preprint arXiv:1312 −6407.

[3] Girardi, Giulio, and Ergün A. Tolga. 2013. Systemic risk measurement: multivariate GARCH estimation of CoVaR. *Journal of Banking & Finance*, 37(8):3169 −3180.

[4] Koenker, Roger, and Gilbert Bassett Jr. 1978. Regression quantiles. *Econometrica*: *Journal of the Econometric Society*:33 – 50.

[5] Mainik G. ,and E. Schaanning. 2012. On dependence consistency of CoVaR and some other systemic risk measures. Risk Lab, Department of Mathematics,ETH Zurich.

[6] Mainik, Georg, and Eric Schaanning. 2014. On dependence consistency of CoVaR and some other systemic risk measures. *Statistics & Risk Modeling*,31(1):49 – 77.

[7] 白雪梅,石大龙. 中国金融体系的系统性风险度量[J]. 国际金融研究,2014(6):75 –85.

[8] 陈建青,王擎,许韶辉. 金融行业间的系统性金融风险溢出效应研究[J]. 数量经济技术经济研究,2015,32(9):89 –100.

[9] 高国华,潘英丽. 银行系统性风险度量——基于动态 CoVaR 方法的分析[J]. 上海交通大学学报,2011,45(12):1753 –1759.

[10] 解其昌. 稳健非参数 VaR 建模及风险量化研究[J]. 中国管理科学,2015,23(8):29 –38.

[11] 李丛文,闫世军. 我国影子银行对商业银行的风险溢出效应——基于 GARCH—Copula-CoVaR 模型的分析[J]. 国际金融研究,2015(10):64 –75.

[12] 李建军,乔博,胡凤云. 中国影子银行形成机理与宏观效应[J]. 宏观经济研究,2015,11:22 –29.

[13] 李建军,薛莹. 中国影子银行部门系统性风险的形成,影响与应对[J]. 数量经济技术经济研究,2014,31(8):117 –130.

[14] 马君潞,范小云,曹元涛. 中国银行间市场双边传染的风险估测及其系统性特征分析[J]. 经济研究,2007,(1):68 –78,142.

[15] 毛菁,罗猛. 银行业与证券业间风险外溢效应研究——基于 CoVaR 模型的分析[J]. 新金融,2011(5):27 –31.

[16] 裘翔. 期限错配与商业银行利差[J]. 金融研究,2015(5):83 –100.

[17] 沈悦,戴士伟,罗希. 中国金融业系统性风险溢出效应测度——基于 GARCH—Copula—CoVaR 模型的研究[J]. 当代经济科

学,2014,36(6):30-38.

[18] 汪莉,吴杏,陈诗一. 政府担保异质性,竞争性扭曲与我国商业银行风险激励[J]. 财贸经济,2016,37(9):21-35.

[19] 谢福座. 基于 GARCH—Copula—CoVaR 模型的风险溢出测度研究[J]. 金融发展研究,2010(12):12-16.

Chapter 8
Markov Regime Switching in Quantile Autoregression Stock Market Return Model

Some researchers found the regime-switching characteristics in the stock return models. Most of previous studies used mean-based method or variation, which focused on the issue at the mean of the return only. But can the performance of the center represent the impact at tails of the distribution? This chapter applies Markov-switch quantile autoregression model to analyze the S&P return from Jan. 1980 to Feb. 2018. The empirical findings identify the presence of regime-switching and present the estimates of location for different regimes monotonically increase from left tail to right tail.

8.1 Introduction to Markov-switching Model

Hamilton (1989) introduced the Markov-switching model in time series analysis and found that the growth rate of U.S. GNP switches between the positively growing regime and negatively depressing regime. Since this influential paper, regime-switching methods have been successfully and widely applied in macroeconomic and financial fields. For example, Markov-switching model has been found to be a good tool of analyzing monetary policy, since it can depict structure changes and allow for periodic shifts (see Owyang and Ramey, 2004; Davig and Leeper, 2007; and Hutchison et al, 2013). In an assets pricing model, the beta coefficient, which measures the influences of the market return on the asset's return, may be time-varying, so regime-switching model is preferable to constant CAPM model (see Huang, 2000; Chen and Huang, 2007; Baillie and Cho, 2016, etc).

The fluctuations and crashes of the stock market have always been a major concern of researchers, investors, and policymakers. The returns of the stock market are frequently influenced by changes of policies and unexpected shocks, and then present structural changes, so as to make it hard to be described by using constant coefficients model. Some findings in the literature pointed out the characteristics of regime-switching in stock market (see Hamilton and Lin, 1996; Schaller and Norden, 1997; Turner et al, 1989, etc). Schwert (1989) identified a two-regime-switching process between a high and a low volatility in stock return model. Turner et al. (1989) also analyzed the fluctuation of the stock market, considering that the market switches between two states. Hamilton and Susmel (1994) explored a specification of stock prices by using a Markov-switching ARCH (SWARCH) process to show the persistence of low, moderate, and high volatility regimes for stock prices. Schaller and Norden (1997) demonstrated switching in mean and variances of stockreturns, and found the evidence that the difference between the mean returns in two regimes is surprisingly big. Gao and Chen (2007) described Chinese stock market returns as a mean and variance switching autoregressive model with three regimes.

The usual and traditional way to analyze the fluctuations of the stock market is based on the first two moments of returns distribution. However, the whole distribution is also our concern. Since the pathbreaking work of Koenker and Bassett (1978), Quantile regression model has been widely applied in economic and financial areas. The advantages of Quantile regression are that it is more efficient when the error term is not normally distributed, and it will be more robust if outliers exist in the data. By allowing for the possibility of Markov-switching regimes in quantile models, researchers have developed a Markov-switching quantile regression model recently. Ye et al. (2016) proposed the maximum likelihood estimation (MLE) for Markov-switching quantile regression model and assessed the quantile effects of stock returns. Liu (2016) extended the quantile autoregression models in Koenker and Xiao (2006) to allow for regime-switching in estimated coefficients of quantile regression model, and estimated the financial risk of S&P 500 index returns with regime changes. Liu and Luger (2017) proposed a Gibbs sampling approach for Markov-switching quantile autoregressive model (MSQAR model). This chapter investigates whether the MSQAR model is a useful tool for describing the behavior of fluctuating stock returns more generally.

8.2 Markov-switching Quantile Autoregressive Model for Stock Market Returns

In general, the stock return is considered as an autoregressive process with order k, M-state Markov-switching mean and variance. The linear QAR (p) model can be expressed as:

$$y_t = \mu(\tau) + \sum_{j=1}^{p} \varphi_j(\tau)(y_{t-j} - \mu(\tau)) + \delta \varepsilon_t, \qquad (8.1)$$

where y_t and $\mu(\tau)$ denote stock market return at period t and the location of return at the τth quantile, respectively. The error term $\{\varepsilon_t\}$ follows the asymmetric Laplace distribution with probability density function:

$$f(\varepsilon_t) = \tau(1-\tau)\exp(-\rho_\tau(\varepsilon_t)), \qquad (8.2)$$

where $\rho_\tau(u) = u(\tau - \mathbb{I}[u<0])$ is the asymmetric absolute deviation loss function. Following Schller and Norden (1997), Gao and Chen (2007), and Liu and Luger (2017), this section considers the quantile autoregression (QAR) model with possible regime-switching to analyze the stock market return beyond the first two moments. The corresponding regime-switching MSQAR (K,p) model for model (1) can be

written as:
$$y_t = \mu(\tau, S_t) + \sum_{j=1}^{p} \varphi_j(\tau)(y_{t-j} - \mu(\tau, S_{t-j})) + \delta \varepsilon_t, \quad (8.3)$$

or,
$$y_t = \sum_{i=1}^{K} \mu_i(\tau) \mathbb{I}[S_t = i] + \sum_{j=1}^{p} \varphi_j(\tau)(y_{t-j} - \mu(\tau, S_{t-j})) + \delta \varepsilon_t, \quad (8.4)$$

where S_t is a latent variable taking values in the set $\{1, 2, \cdots, K\}$. Given the past of y_t itself and the current state S_t, $\mu(\tau, S_t)$ is the location of the τth conditional quantile of y_t. The one-step transition probability matrix is
$$\Pr[S_t = j \mid S_{t-1} = i] = p_{ij}, i, j = 1, 2, \cdots, K, \quad (8.5)$$
$$\sum_{j=1}^{M} p_{ij} = 1, \quad \text{for all } i = 1, 2, \cdots, K. \quad (8.6)$$

The τth conditional quantile function can be expressed as
$$Q_{y_t}(\tau \mid y_{t-p:t-1}, s_{t-p:t}) = \mu(\tau, S_t) + \sum_{j=1}^{p} \varphi_j(\tau)(y_{t-j} - \mu(\tau, S_{t-j})), \quad (8.7)$$

where $y_{t-p:t-1}$ and $s_{t-p:t}$ denote the observations $y_{t-p}, y_{t-p+1}, \cdots, y_{t-1}$, and regimes $S_{t-p}, S_{t-p+1}, \cdots, S_t$, respectively.

8.3 Data Description and Empirical Results

This section investigates U.S Standard & Poor's 500 index monthly returns, y_t, from Jan. 1980 to Feb. 2018. Figure 8.1 shows the time series plot of market returns, y_t. It is obvious to observe three financial crises, which happened in 1988, 1998, and 2008, respectively.

Following the methods of MSQAR model with Gibbs Sampling by Liu and Luger (2017), we investigate the impact of the whole conditional distribution allowing for regime-switching. Two (a bull and a bear, i.e. $K=2$) and three (a bull, a steady, and a bear, i.e. $K=3$) markets for US

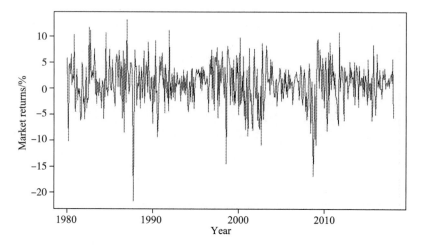

Figure 8.1   Time series plot of market returns

stock fluctuations are considered in this chapter. ①This chapter considers the MSQAR(K,p) model with lag length p = 1,2,3,4 and the number of regimes K = 1,2,3 at quantile levels τ = 0.1,0.2,⋯,0.9. Table 8.1 shows the log marginal likelihood of MSQAR(K,p) for each model at each quantile level proposed in Liu and Luger (2017) and QAR(p) in Koenker and Xiao (2006), and the last column shows the average log marginal likelihood across the values of τ. From table 8.1, we can find that the average log marginal likelihood of −1,325.3 maximizes in the case of K = 3, and p = 3, which provides the best MSQAR specification. Similarly, Gao and Chen (2007) also considered 3 regimes of stock market, which stand for a bull, a steady, and a bear market, respectively.

---

① If there is no regime-switching, i.e. K = 1, the MSQAR(K,p) model reduces to QAR(p) model, which was studied in Koenker and Xiao (2006).

Table 8.1 Log marginal likelihoods for MSQAR (K, p) at different quantiles

MSQAR (K, p)	0.1	0.2	0.3	0.4	0.5	0.6	0.7	0.8	0.9	average
MSQAR (2, 1)	-1,402.5	-1,484.6	-1,335.6	-1,314.1	-1,302.5	-1,306.8	-1,314.0	-1,334.1	-1,364.3	-1,350.9
MSQAR (2, 2)	-1,411.3	-1,365.0	-1,338.0	-1,316.0	-1,293.2	-1,302.8	-1,317.8	-1,336.7	-1,343.3	-1,336.0
MSQAR (2, 3)	-1,861.1	-1,478.9	-1,329.6	-1,303.8	-1,291.6	-1,295.8	-1,299.7	-1,388.1	-1,916.5	-1,462.8
MSQAR (2, 4)	-1,424.9	-1,364.6	-1,325.9	-1,303.8	-1,289.6	-1,288.3	-1,299.4	-1,322.5	-1,365.8	-1,331.6
MSQAR (3, 1)	-1,489.1	-1,422.1	-1,379.4	-1,348.2	-1,330.8	-1,329.8	-1,344.5	-1,368.2	-1,690.6	-1,411.4
MSQAR (3, 2)	-1,405.2	-1,353.1	-1,328.1	-1,308.8	-1,297.0	-1,298.2	-1,304.3	-1,317.1	-1,331.6	-1,327.0
MSQAR (3, 3)	-1,403.1	-1,352.9	-1,324.4	-1,310.0	-1,293.7	-1,296.5	-1,296.6	-1,314.7	-1,336.0	-1,325.3
MSQAR (3, 4)	-1,865.6	-1,796.7	-1,725.0	-1,716.6	-1,867.4	-1,891.6	-1,653.2	-1,576.9	-1,431.2	-1,724.9
QAR (p)	0.1	0.2	0.3	0.4	0.5	0.6	0.7	0.8	0.9	average
QAR (1)	-1,758.7	-1,472.5	-1,363.2	-1,318.6	-1,300.1	-1,299.7	-1,316.6	-1,376.2	-1,602.0	-1,423.1
QAR (2)	-1,576.4	-1,391.8	-1,341.3	-1,314.3	-1,298.0	-1,304.7	-1,358.1	-1,471.1	-1,768.2	-1,408.0
QAR (3)	-2,438.6	-2,385.3	-2,343.8	-2,296.7	-2,277.1	-2,297.3	-2,360.1	-2,519.3	-2,830.1	-2,416.5
QAR (4)	-1,431.2	-1,391.3	-1,350.9	-1,308.3	-1,290.1	-1,307.3	-1,379.5	-1,526.3	-1,848.8	-1,426.0

Table 8.2 shows the posterior inference results for MSQAR(3,3) at each quantile level, $\tau = 0.1, 0.2, \cdots, 0.9$, along with numerical standard errors (NSE). From lower quantiles to higher quantiles, the estimates of μ_1 monotonically increase from $-7.288, 9$ to $3.390, 6$, the estimates of μ_2 increase from $-4.737, 4$ to $5.917, 8$, and the estimate of μ_3 increases from $-2.431, 6$ to $8.223, 7$. We can see that the estimated values of μ_1, μ_2, μ_3 are significant at most quantiles and well separated, which indicates the presence of regime-switching. Although the estimates of location increase from lower tails to higher tails, the gaps from lower tails to higher tails are quite stable and have not changed a lot.

The estimates of φ_1 and φ_3 are positive at lower quantiles, and they turn to negative from the 50th to the 90th quantile. The estimates of φ_1 present significance at the 20th, 30th, and 70th to 90th quantile, however, the estimates of φ_3 show no significance at all quantile levels. The estimates of φ_2 are negative across all quantiles, but significant at the 80th quantile only. Compared to the cases that lag length is 2 or 3, the return of S&P 500 is more influenced by the return in the last month, i.e. lag length is 1, especially at lower and higher quantiles. At lower quantiles, $\tau = 0.1$, 0.2, the return positively and significantly impacts the return next month, which implies that in the period of bear market, negative stock index return in previous month is inclined to negative return in the next month. While at higher quantiles, $\tau = 0.7, 0.8, 0.9$, the return in the previous period negatively and significantly impacts the return next month, which verifies that the bull market is hard to sustain for a long period.

From the estimated value of transition probability, we can see that the estimates of p_{11} are smaller than 0.5 from the 20th quantile to the 40th quantile, which means when the stock market is in regime 1, the bear regime, there will be more than half of probability to switch to regime 2 and 3, the steady regime and bull regime. Consequently, the instability of regime 1 shows up for lower stock returns. Regime 2 is stable at middle

Chapter 8 Markov regime switching in quantile autoregression stock market return model

Table 8.2 Estimation results of MSQAR (3, 3) model

Item	μ_1	μ_2	μ_3	δ	φ_1	φ_2	φ_3	p_{11}	p_{21}	p_{31}	p_{12}	p_{22}	p_{32}
0.1	−7.288,9	−4.737,4	−2.431,6	0.589,0	0.055,3	−0.041,6	0.023,6	0.515,7	0.212,7	0.131,9	0.013,8	0.162,4	0.049,0
NSE	0.194,8	0.199,1	0.207,6	0.030,6	0.052,6	0.043,9	0.030,7	0.123,3	0.366,9	0.052,8	0.041,0	0.310,6	0.058,9
0.2	−4.995,1	−2.561,4	−0.361,2	0.959,1	0.136,8	−0.026,8	0.043,1	0.427,8	0.035,4	0.380,7	0.328,6	0.066,2	0.450,6
NSE	0.211,5	0.189,5	0.181,7	0.063,5	0.043,9	0.042,2	0.046,9	0.166,7	0.097,9	0.150,7	0.251,4	0.181,9	0.192,8
0.3	−3.131,3	−1.001,7	0.975,6	1.209,3	0.100,7	−0.018,8	0.028,5	0.380,1	0.336,5	0.359,2	0.059,1	0.128,0	0.356,1
NSE	0.213,2	0.212,5	0.170,6	0.073,8	0.049,6	0.042,4	0.036,0	0.144,0	0.309,6	0.264,3	0.141,5	0.268,3	0.389,5
0.4	−1.846,0	0.244,4	1.962,3	1.363,2	0.131,7	−0.062,4	0.017,8	0.122,9	0.578,3	0.488,6	0.096,7	0.104,4	0.433,4
NSE	0.184,5	0.191,5	0.192,5	0.076,8	0.091,4	0.053,1	0.043,2	0.210,7	0.402,7	0.235,1	0.147,0	0.252,2	0.275,4
0.5	−1.081,1	1.128,1	3.190,5	1.429,4	−0.064,1	−0.048,2	−0.029,0	0.671,4	0.016,2	0.366,3	0.088,1	0.952,4	0.092,3
NSE	0.188,7	0.146,0	0.208,7	0.081,0	0.078,6	0.049,3	0.039,5	0.241,3	0.020,6	0.302,6	0.242,1	0.074,5	0.134,9
0.6	−0.095,8	1.812,8	4.108,9	1.374,6	−0.068,0	−0.046,6	−0.021,1	0.528,2	0.019,1	0.319,6	0.056,1	0.970,9	0.079,7
NSE	0.211,5	0.161,9	0.189,9	0.084,5	0.064,9	0.049,7	0.038,0	0.329,1	0.025,9	0.254,1	0.119,3	0.025,7	0.103,2
0.7	1.248,6	3.244,4	5.155,1	1.202,3	−0.110,1	−0.083,1	−0.050,0	0.559,0	0.668,3	0.111,8	0.399,4	0.217,4	0.259,2
NSE	0.179,1	0.186,5	0.197,7	0.066,6	0.043,2	0.048,0	0.036,4	0.279,0	0.340,5	0.154,6	0.281,0	0.333,3	0.314,6
0.8	2.170,3	4.385,8	6.358,2	0.908,4	−0.137,2	−0.090,9	−0.069,8	0.828,9	0.163,9	0.789,4	0.008,8	0.688,7	0.091,6
NSE	0.166,7	0.211,0	0.216,4	0.052,2	0.038,6	0.038,7	0.039,6	0.066,0	0.287,2	0.177,1	0.013,4	0.381,5	0.147,7
0.9	3.390,6	5.917,8	8.223,7	0.510,2	−0.114,9	−0.043,1	−0.046,2	0.849,4	0.136,8	0.823,2	0.011,0	0.725,9	0.136,0
NSE	0.148,2	0.196,8	0.191,2	0.026,5	0.035,5	0.044,7	0.033,4	0.051,5	0.278,6	0.130,5	0.023,5	0.302,0	0.130,6

and higher quantiles, since the estimates of p_{22} are quite higher, especially at the 50th and the 60th quantile, the estimates of p_{22} are greater than 0.9. Regime 3 is the least stable among the three regimes, the higher estimate of p_{33} appears at the 10th quantile, which is 0.8191 ($1 - p_{31} - p_{32}$).

Figure 8.2 shows the posterior regime classification at the median (with a log marginal likelihood of $-1,293.7$). We can see the regime—switching from regime 2 or 3 to regime 1, bear regime, in the period of financial crises like 1998 and 2008. It can be also found that similar regime-switchings happened again several years after crises, which implies that the financial crises influence stock returns even after the bear regime—switching back to a steady or bull regime.

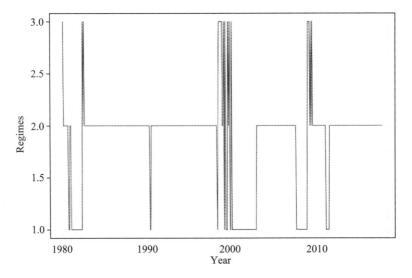

Figure 8.2 Posterior regime classification at $\tau = 0.5$

8.4 Conclusion

This chapter examines the regime-switching issue of U.S. stock market return in this article. Our investigation is based on employing a newly developed econometric technique, "Markov-switching quantile autoregression with Gibbs sampling." The distinct advantage of this method is that it allows researchers to investigate the regime-switching issue of stock return beyond the first two moments, which is not possible using traditional mean-based methods. Using this method, the regime-switchings of the location estimates are identified at all quantiles. The application of the MSQAR method provides rich description regarding the regime-switching issue of stock returns.

References

[1] Baillie R. T. and Cho D. 2016. Assessing Euro crises from a time varying international CAPM approach. *Journal of Empirical Finance*, 39:197 –208.

[2] Chen S. – W. and Huang N. – C. 2007. Estimates of the ICAPM with regime-switching betas: evidence from four pacific rim economies. *Applied Financial Economics*, 17:313 –327.

[3] Davig T. and Leeper E. M. 2007. Generalizing the Taylor principle. *American Economic Review*, 97:607 –635.

[4] Hamilton J. D. 1989. A new approach to the economic analysis of nonstationary time series and the business cycle. *Econometrica: Journal of the Econometric Society*:357 –384.

[5] Hamilton J. D. and Lin G. 1996. Stock market volatility and the business cycle. *Journal of Applied Econometrics*:573 –593.

[6] Hamilton J. D. and Susmel R. 1994. Autoregressive conditional heteroskedasticity and changes in regime. *Journal of Econometrics*, 64:307 –333.

[7] Huang H. – C. 2000. Tests of regime-switching CAPM. *Applied Financial Economics*, 10:573 –578.

[8] Hutchison M. M., Sengupta R. and Singh N. 2013. Dove or Hawk? Characterizing monetary policy regime-switches in India. *Emerging*

Markets Review, 16: 183 – 202.

[9] Koenker R. and Bassett G. 1978. Regression quantiles. *Econometrica*, 46: 33 – 50.

[10] Koenker R. and Xiao Z. 2006. Quantile autoregression. *Journal of the American Statistical Association*, 101: 980 – 990.

[11] Liu X. 2016. Markov switching quantile autoregression. *Statistica Neerlandica*, 70: 356 – 395.

[12] Liu X. and Luger R. 2017. Markov-switching quantile autoregression: a Gibbs sampling approach. *Studies in Nonlinear Dynamics & Econometrics*.

[13] Owyang M. T. and Ramey G. 2004. Regime-switching and monetary policy measurement. *Journal of Monetary Economics*, 51: 1577 – 1597.

[14] Schaller H. and Norden S. V. 1997. Regime-switching in stock market returns. *Applied Financial Economics*, 7: 177 – 191.

[15] Schwert G. W. 1989. Why does stock market volatility change over time? *The Journal of Finance*, 44: 1115 – 1153.

[16] Turner C. M., Startz R., and Nelson C. R. 1989. A Markov model of heteroskedasticity, risk, and learning in the stock market. *Journal of Financial Economics*, 25: 3 – 22.

[17] Ye W., Zhu Y., Wu Y. and Miao B. 2016. Markov regime-switching quantile regression models and financial contagion detection. *Insurance: Mathematics and Economics*, 67: 21 – 26.

[18] Gao J. and Chen X. 2007. Markov-switching model and its application to the stock market of China. *Chinese Journal of Management Science*, 15: 20 – 25 (in Chinese).